THE LESSONS OF WAR

THE
LESSONS
OF WAR

The Experiences of
Seven Future Leaders
in the First World War

WILLIAM VAN DER KLOOT

The
History
Press

First published by The History Press Limited in 2008

The Mill, Brimscombe Port, Stroud, Gloucestershire, GL5 2QG
www.thehistorypress.co.uk

Copyright © William Van der Kloot, 2008

The right of William Van der Kloot to be identified as the Author of this Work has been
asserted in accordance with the Copyrights, Designs & Patents Act 1988.

British Library Cataloguing in Publication Data:
A catalogue record for this book is available from the British Library

ISBN 978 1 84588 634 9

Typesetting and origination by The History Press
Printed and bound in Great Britain

Contents

I

Sarajevo to the opening battles

Adolf Hitler
28 June 1914

Toward the end of the afternoon, Hitler was painting a watercolour in his room on the third floor of his lodging house in Munich, at Schleissheimer Strasse 34. A twenty-five-year-old who specialized in views of notable buildings, his sales brought him enough to live modestly, with time free for arguing politics in coffee houses and for reading books from the State Library. His landlady, Frau Popp, recalled that a hubbub in the street brought her lodger downstairs, where she told him that the Austrian Archduke and his wife had been murdered in Sarajevo. Hitler's own recollection was that Peppi Popp, the thirteen-year-old son of the family, brought the news to his room, but the boy knew no details—just the headline. Hitler was jubilant—he detested the Archduke, a German who had degraded himself by marrying a Czech and who wanted to share power among the nationalities of the Austro-Hungarian Empire—it was divine justice.

Harold Macmillan
28 June 1914

Macmillan, a youth of twenty, elegant in white tie and tails, was attending a London ball. The stairs in the magnificent residence were decorated with carnations and spirited waltzes were provided by Mr Cassani's string band. At first he did not dance; the floor was too crowded for anyone so clumsy. He was tall, willowy and languid—a popular configuration at the time, with good features on an oval face; his upper eyelid was partially covered with a skin fold, suggesting Viking descent. As the evening went on, the older guests departed; the leeway on the floor overcame his shyness. Once started, he danced so vigorously that three times he changed into a spare clean collar. When he finally departed, he paid little attention to the headline shouted by a newsvendor: 'Austrian archduke and wife assassinated.' It was a remote affair in a distant, perpetually troubled quarter of the globe. He returned to his parents' house at 52 Cadogan Place. The next morning his mother Nellie grilled him about every detail of his evening; as usual they spoke in French. We do not know whether the murders were mentioned. Later that day he was back at Oxford in his rooms in Balliol College.

July 1914

The assassin was a Bosnian Serb, Gabreil Princip, one of a group of six young terrorists—aged from sixteen to twenty—provided with weapons and assisted in slipping across the border by a secret Serbian organization, *Union or Death*—commonly called the Black Hand. The Austro-Hungarians had occupied Bosnia-Herzegovina in 1878, to 'preserve order' as the Ottoman grip loosened. At the same time Serbia became an independent country. The Serbians wanted Bosnia-Herzegovina but were too weak to seize it. Shortly after the royal couple arrived for their well-publicized visit to Sarajevo a terrorist bomb bounced off the boot of their car. Hours later, by sheer chance, Princip was able to kill: the procession made a wrong turn and stopped to shift into reverse immediately in front of him. He had not meant to hit the wife, but in training had fired only a few practice rounds. One of the youths talked, so the police rounded up all of their helpers in Bosnia and they told them the names of their contacts in Serbia. The terrorists were tried in October. The assassins were too young to be executed. Princip was given twenty years and died of tuberculosis coupled with starvation in 1918; some of the older supporters were executed.

The eighty-four-year-old Emperor Franz Joseph wanted the Serbs to learn a strict lesson: they must renounce terrorism as a weapon in international politics. The Austrian Foreign Minister, Leopold, Count Berchtold, met with the Council of Ministers to recommend war. Tisza, the Hungarian Prime Minister, did not want more quarrelsome Slavs in their empire, so he delayed a decision by insisting that for war they must have unequivocal support from their German allies. Therefore, Berchtold wrote to Kaiser Wilhelm II—an intelligent, experienced ruler who was also a fool (to prove my point, in his autobiography Wilhelm tells us that the war was plotted in 1909 in a secret covenant between the British, French and Americans, organized by the Freemasons). Wilhelm was handed the letter by the Austro-Hungarian ambassador. In years past the Kaiser had refused to back adventurism in the Balkans; but now it was different. The Archduke and the Kaiser were friends; only a few weeks before the Kaiser had vacationed at their Bohemian castle. He promised the ambassador that he would support whatever the Austro-Hungarians decided to do. Next the Kaiser met with the Imperial Chancellor, von Bethmann-Hollweg, who was surprised by the 'blank cheque' given to their ally, but did not have the spine to invalidate it, even though under the constitution—written by Bismarck for Bismarck—it was his responsibility. He knew that if Austria-Hungary attacked Serbia it was likely to trigger an avalanche—thanks to the network of treaties negotiated to preserve a balance of power. If the Russians came to the aid of their Slavic clients then Germany was pledged to fight alongside the Austro-Hungarians. That would bring in the French. As the Kaiser pointed out when he had restrained a somewhat similar adventure proposed by the Austro-Hungarians two years before, "Paris will undoubtedly be supported by London. Thus Germany will have to embark on a life-and-death struggle with three great powers. We hazard all, and may lose all." It was a reasonable, statesmanlike analysis, which held with equal force in 1914. After the meeting, the Kaiser coolly resumed his summer vacation, yachting up to Norway.

Elated by the blank cheque, Berchtold proposed to invade immediately, but Tisza still held back. They agreed to issue an ultimatum, which Berchtold planned to make unthinkable for the Serbs to accept. They also agreed that if it came to war, they would let it be known that they would take no Serb territory. As they prepared the ultimatum in secret, Serbia faded from the headlines and from the public mind. The July weather was glorious throughout Europe and most people enjoyed it thoroughly.

Hitler combed the newspapers for scraps of news. Macmillan gave it little thought. The European army commanders were consulted by their political masters. All were ready to fight, and most regarded 1914 as a favourable time to do so. The public regained interest when the Austrian-Hungarian ultimatum was handed to the Serbians at 1800 on 23 July. The timing was set carefully. The President of France, Henri Poincaré, was on a state visit to St Petersburg. Poincaré promised staunch support, in effect giving the Russians their own blank cheque. The ultimatum was delivered after Poincaré left for home—so there was no chance for the French to cool the Russians down.

The ultimatum required the Serbian Government to renounce publicly all hostile acts, including propaganda, against the Austro-Hungarian Empire, and to punish all those who had engaged in such activities. They must dissolve the Black Hand and similar societies, arrest the officer who had provided the bombs and pistols and dismiss the customs officials who had smuggled weapons and assassins into Bosnia. To assure that these objectives were met, clause six permitted Austro-Hungarian agents to enter Serbia to look for accessories to the crime. The Serbians were given forty-eight hours to accept the ultimatum.

The Serbians agreed to every particular except clause six, which they claimed violated the Serbian constitution—presumably they hoped for a compromise that would shield the highest level of their government. When Wilhelm II read the Serbian response he observed that every cause for war was removed—but he had already signed the cheque. The Austro-Hungarian ambassador unhesitatingly declared that the response was unsatisfactory and severed diplomatic relations.

On 25 July the Serbians mobilized, Austria-Hungary partially mobilized, and the Russians announced war preparations for European Russia. Franz Joseph still hoped to stop short of war. On 27 July he was told that the Serbians were shelling the Austrian shore of the Danube. He signed the declaration of war the next day—no one told him that the shellfire report was an hysterical error. His declaration freed the Italians from their treaty obligation to come to their aid if they were attacked. The Germans warned the Russians that if they mobilized, they would mobilize also. The Kaiser appealed directly to his cousin the Tsar, writing as usual in English, begging him not to let events escalate. On 29 July the Tsar signed a partial mobilization order and the British sent a formal telegram to their armed forces, warning of imminent war.

Charles de Gaulle
29 July to 4 August 1914

On that day Lieutenant Charles de Gaulle was on leave in Paris, staying with his parents. He joined the large, enthusiastic crowd assembled at the *Gare d'Est* to welcome the returning President Poincaré. De Gaulle was not hard to spot in the crowd, towering well above them; he was 193 centimetres tall. His height was accentuated by a bird-like profile—a conspicuous curving nose and slightly receding chin; one of his army nicknames was 'Big Asparagus.' As soon as the official party appeared, the civilians bared their heads, the soldiers saluted, and all sang the *Marseillaise*. The de Gaulle family—mother and father, three sons and a married daughter—were for war; recovering the lost provinces of Alsace and Lorraine and revenging the humiliation of 1870 were worth any sacrifice.

On 30 July, the French ordered partial mobilization and the Tsar ordered full mobilization, so the red placard was posted throughout Russia to tell the largely illiterate reservists to report to their mobilization assembly points. German agents in Russian Poland stripped placards from the walls and sent them to Berlin, as positive proof of Russian mobilization. The next day, Austria-Hungary fully mobilized.

On 1 August, Charles de Gaulle was again back on the streets, mingling with the immense crowds along the boulevards watching the funeral cortège of the socialist leader Jean Jaurès, murdered by a young nationalist simply because he was a pacifist. The de Gaulles were not inclined towards pacifism or socialism, but they respected Jaurès for defending Captain Dreyfus—they, too, had been ardent Dreyfusards. The authorities feared violence, but the crowds were silent and respectful. The streets were hot and sultry; the leaves of the chestnuts were coated with dust. At 1645 the French government ordered mobilization, and soon the posters, topped by crossed tricolours, were everywhere. At 1700 the Germans ordered mobilization. Under their constitution they must be at war before they could mobilize, so they declared war on Russia. President Poincaré proclaimed a *Union sacrée*, a united France prevailing over class and politics. The Paris police requisitioned the buses to transport those on the list 'to be arrested at the outbreak of war' to prison, so travellers had to walk to the stations or be taken by car. The city was quiet; there were no demonstrations or cheering crowds. Prudent people, recalling the siege of 1870, were busy storing food.

Charles returned to his regiment, the 33rd Infantry at Arras, not far from his childhood home in Lille. He commanded the 1st platoon in the 11th company. He had served his mandatory year in the ranks in the 33rd before entering the military academy at Saint-Cyr. Thanks to his distinctive appearance and his appalling clumsiness he had been a figure of fun. His comrades laughed at his inability to perform such routine tasks as properly stowing gear in his field pack. The ragging did not get him down; he maintained a high opinion of himself, which he did not keep secret. When he was promoted to corporal, his commanding officer was asked whether it would not have been appropriate to make him a sergeant instead. "Why do you think I should make a sergeant of a young fellow who would not feel he had made his due unless he were made le Connétable (the title given to the supreme commander of the armies under the monarchy)." This gave de Gaulle another nickname—throughout his army career many of his mates knew him as le Connétable.

He graduated thirteenth in his class from Saint-Cyr, which permitted him to select his posting. Many of the best students chose colonial regiments for action and advancement; de Gaulle returned to the 33rd. In later life he wrote that a major reason for his choice was that he was so impressed with their new Colonel, Henri Pétain: "My first Colonel showed me the meaning of the gift and art of command." Note, however, that this was written after the war, when Pétain was the commander of the French army and de Gaulle was a member of his staff. To be sure, de Gaulle and Pétain had much in common. Pétain told everyone that the French colonial wars in North Africa, Indo-China and Madagascar were damaging diversions from the army's true business—the Germans. He never applied for colonial service, which hobbled his career. When de Gaulle rejoined the regiment it was taken for granted that Pétain would soon be gone; he had already purchased a retirement home.

Though not esteemed by his superiors, Pétain was popular in Arras. In 1913 he was fifty-seven years old. His fringe of remaining hair was white, his bushy moustache salt and pepper, but the skin on his pallid face was taut and his figure lithe. His light blue eyes were striking. On first acquaintance he was as cold as his icy appearance—though his manners were impeccable. Those who came closer uncovered his wry, irreverent, ironic sense of humour. Deeper still there was fire beneath the ice. A bachelor, he was extremely fond of feminine company: "I love two things above all, sex and the infantry." Some said that at Arras, Pétain and de Gaulle were attracted to the same ladies and competed in their lists of love. In later life de Gaulle never dismissed such talk. Pétain left the 33rd at the end of 1913 to command a brigade, so that the army could retire him as a general. De Gaulle thought that Pétain "had the presence of a deep reserve, intensified by a deliberate coldness of manner, quick sarcasm, and a pride which protected his aloofness"—the perfect role model.

De Gaulle's journey back to the 33rd was uncomfortable. The trains were jammed and schedules and routes disrupted—his trip took eight hours. Three days later the reservists reported to barracks; de Gaulle found both these men and the local people calm and resolute. The secret army estimate was that 13 per cent of the reservists would fail to report, but since almost all of the socialist politicians strongly supported the war only 1.5 per cent of them did not report. Three thousand deserters resurfaced, begging for the chance to serve.

On 2 August, President Poincaré instituted martial law by declaring the entire country in a 'state of siege.' The next day, Germany declared war on France and sent Belgium an ultimatum demanding passage for German troops, promising to leave when the war was over and to pay for any damages done. The Belgians refused. They thought that their army would be able to fend off whatever force that the Germans, fighting on two fronts, would be able to bring against them. The German move against Belgium got the British government off the hook. France, Russia and Britain were not linked by treaty, but they had an understanding of "sympathy and determination to protect mutual interests." The foreign secretary, Sir Edward Grey, had secretly authorized joint Anglo-French staff talks. They planned for a British Expeditionary Force (BEF), which would enter the line on the French left flank. The small BEF meant less to the French than the naval understanding: the British fleet would protect the Channel coast of France so that the French fleet could secure the Mediterranean, where they felt free to base almost their entire fleet. In the last days of July the anxious French pressed Grey to reconfirm this undertaking. Grey reminded them that the talks had been advisory and did not commit either side. A fair-minded man, he saw that the French had been backed into a trap. When he finally revealed what he had done to the cabinet some of his colleagues threatened to resign. They were brought back on board because in 1830 the British had signed a treaty pledging them to maintain the neutrality of Belgium. When the Germans invaded, Grey went before the Commons to invoke the treaty; the British declared war on 4 August.

Germany and Austria-Hungary now faced a coalition that outnumbered them in troops by a ratio of three to two, and which in the years just passed had spent twice as much on their militaries. The Germans must wage war on two fronts and if the Italians joined the Allies, so would the Austro-Hungarians. De Gaulle was confident the French would prevail.

Gustav Mannerheim
29 July to 5 August 1914

Mannerheim went for his dinner to the *Cercle de Chasse* clubhouse in Warsaw. The others were in white tie, but Mannerheim wore his uniform, decorated with the aiguillettes and monogrammed epaulets of a *Généréral à la Suite* of the Tsar and the insignia of a major general—in Warsaw he commanded the Brigade of Cavalry of the Guard. He towered above the crowd—he was as tall as de Gaulle—as fit-appearing a forty-seven-year-old man as you can imagine, though a trained eye might have noticed stiffness in some of his movements. The politics of the club was epitomized by their president, a Polish prince who once had been dragged in irons to Siberia to serve twenty years in prison. Nonetheless, the Russian general was a valued member of the club. His qualifications included his birth—he was a baron—and his passion for and skills with horses: rider, trainer, breeder, polo player and show jumper. But his crucial attribute was nationality—he was a Finn.

The Grand Duchies of Finland and Warsaw were both autonomous states within the Russian Empire, ruled personally by the Tsar. The Poles, tied together by language, religion and culture, had been split between the Tsar, Prussia and Austria in the late eighteenth century. Most Poles craved reunification and independence, and naturally assumed that Finns wanted the same. But Finland was different. It was almost evenly divided between Finnish and Swedish speakers. The Mannerheims spoke Swedish; Gustav's Russian was still flavoured with a Swedish accent, which many ladies found delightful. The revolution of 1905 had triumphed in Finland; the Tsar's governor was stripped of dictatorial powers and a parliament was elected by universal suffrage—women as well as men—to make the laws. Gustav's older brother, Carl, was allowed to return from exile in Sweden. Now the Mannerheims worried mostly about the armed workers' militia, the Red Guards, which had been formed in 1905 and was training for a class war.

The club also esteemed Mannerheim because he was a renowned explorer. In 1906 the Russian General Staff sent him into Central Asia; he could travel with a Finnish passport, which might make the Chinese less suspicious. Mannerheim was given two years salary in advance, travelling expenses to Peking and return, and funds for equipment. He raised more money for science in Finland, where his grandfather had been a notable entomologist. He started from Turkmenistan, stopping with each tribe along the way, studying customs, learning languages, and mapping the route and the major towns. He collected crafts and archaeological relics and took hundreds of spectacular photographs. He met the Dalai Lama, who had fled Tibet to keep out of the hands of the British. The Dalai Lama handed to him the traditional white silk greeting scarf, which he was to convey to the Tsar. In return, Mannerheim presented His Holiness with a Browning pistol—perhaps not a perfect gift for a Buddhist, but it was near the end of his trip and his supply of gifts had run low. He returned from Peking in 1908. The Tsar received him for a personal report and he was made welcome in the finest houses. According to his comrade and biographer, Paul Rodzianko, every lady in Moscow seemed to develop an insatiable curiosity about Central Asia, which could only be assuaged by private instruction from the handsome explorer. He subsequently published a book describing his adventures.

In the club dining room, Mannerheim was at the president's right. The group was buzzing with the latest rumour: a compromise had been reached—there would be no war. A servant passed Mannerheim a note ordering him to "present yourself at Brigade Headquarters at 12 midnight;" he made his excuses and slipped out of the room. He telephoned his officers, instructing them to report to barracks. A few minutes after midnight, he received a telegram: "Mobilization ordered to begin at midnight. Open sealed mobilization orders." When Mannerheim fetched the orders from his safe he read that his 1st Squadron of Uhlans was to entrain at 0200. He passed the order along but also telephoned his superior to warn him that it was impossible to get them off on schedule. At 0200 the commander of the 1st Squadron called to report that they were about to leave on the train. Shrewdly he had assumed that mobilization was coming and had his men ready. Mannerheim was credited at the highest levels for so handily carrying out an almost impossible order.

Mannerheim's household staff was accustomed to his being away; only a few weeks before he had been off in Germany buying horses and taking the cure for his rheumatism. He had been married for twenty-two years to a rich Russian lady, but his wife and their two daughters lived in the south of France. As he left his house he may have given his treasured Russian sofa an affectionate pat. He always showed it to visitors assuring them "that the most beautiful women in Russia had sat on it." They questioned whether he used the correct verb.

The brigade moved by train 170 kilometres southeast to the city of Lubin. They detrained in pouring rain and marched 35 kilometres south to a major road junction, 30 kilometres north of the border with the Austro-Hungarian province of Galicia. There Mannerheim learned that it was a partial mobilization; full mobilization came the next day—the Tsar had been dithering. His cavalry brigade was to protect the railhead where troops coming from Russia would detrain.

Adolf Hitler
2 to 3 August 1914

London was flooded with cheering crowds. Prime Minister H.H. Asquith, in his daily letter to "His Darling," an attractive twenty-seven-year-old lady named Venetia Stanley, recalled a predecessor's caustic remark: "Now they are ringing their bells; in a few weeks they will be wringing their hands." The streets of Vienna were filled with elated citizens, anxious to display their devotion to this great cause. The huge celebration in Munich is preserved in a notable, frequently reproduced photograph. Men fill every foot of the Odeonsplatz, but out of the mass, a careful hand has circled the features of Adolf Hitler, dressed in dark suit, high collar and tie, his flowing moustache carefully brushed to the sides. He waves his hat, eyes bulging with excitement, bellowing exultantly. The photograph was taken by a man who years later became Hitler's court photographer, and he made the print on which Hitler personally circled himself.

The cheering Hitler burned with an unprecedented desire—he wanted to join the army. A native of Austria, when he reached the age for military service he did not register for induction. Months later he was warned that the police in Linz, where he had lived before moving to Vienna, were looking for him. On 20 April 1913, his twenty-fourth birthday, he received his share of his father's estate, which enabled him to move to Munich. Leaving Austria to avoid military service was a crime punishable with imprisonment. On Sunday 18 January 1914, a Munich police officer arrived at his lodging with a summons requiring Adolf Hitler to present himself to the Austrian authorities. To insure his compliance he was arrested; he petitioned the Austrian consulate for a delay. He appeared on 5 February in Salzburg, where the examining physician found him too frail for military service. When he returned to Munich he was relieved that the Popps still welcomed him as a lodger, despite his brush with the law.

On 3 August, he shuffled for hours in the long line snaking toward the Munich recruiting office, only to learn that as an alien he must petition King Ludwig III for permission to serve in the Royal Bavarian Army. After an anxious time his petition was approved and he was instructed to remain at his lodgings until called to duty.

Harold Macmillan
August and September 1914

Macmillan was stricken with appendicitis and had emergency surgery. When he left hospital he was sent home to recuperate under his mother's strict eye. He was anguished as, one by one, his friends enlisted—they all were sure that the war would be over by Christmas and did not want to miss it. Rudyard Kipling caught the nation's temper:

> For all we have and are,
> For all our children's fate,
> Stand up and take the war.
> The Hun is at the gate!

Herbert Hoover
4 August to 8 August 1914

When the war erupted, 125,000 desperate American tourists were stranded in Western Europe—desperate to get home. Banks refused to honour their letters of credit, panicked hotels refused to accept American currency or travellers' cheques. Many of those on the

Continent travelled to England to book passage but once there could not pay for food or shelter, let alone book transatlantic voyages. On Monday 3 August, 2,000 desperate globe-trotters were at the American embassy in London. Their troubles were magnified when the British Government extended the Bank Holiday—which was that Monday—for three additional days.

One of the tourists, Fred I. Kent, a prominent banker, and a few friends, formed the American Citizen's Committee. Kent managed to slip through shut doors to borrow $20,000 from London banks on the collateral of a gold shipment that was then in the mid-Atlantic. The Committee set to work in the lobby of the Savoy Hotel. Stranded tourists queued before tables manned by committee members, negotiating for muchneeded funds. Other frantic tourists turned to the American Consulate for assistance. In the early afternoon of 4 August an American mining engineer walked from his office to the consulate. There is a difference of opinion over whether he came on his own initiative or was asked in. Hoover had little sympathy for the commercial travellers pounding on the Consul's desk, but was drawn to the quiet, polite, anxious teachers, folks who had saved for years for the privilege of a trip to Europe. They were like some of the "teachers of my own childhood." He telephoned for the £100 in cash he kept at home and for all of the cash held in reserve at his office. Assisted by workers from his firm, Hoover changed money at the usual rate and loaned 10 shillings to those who gave their word of honour that they had no cash on hand. That afternoon they helped about 300 Americans.

When the office closed for the day, the Consul telephoned to report to the American Ambassador, Walter Hines Page. Page asked Hoover to come to see him at once; they were acquainted from formal dinners at the Embassy. Hoover, then just a few days short of his fortieth birthday, was one of the most successful and renowned mining engineers in the world. At the Embassy Page told Hoover that the Citizen's Committee had called a mass meeting at the Savoy Hotel for that evening, and asked Hoover to attend. More than 1,000 anxious people jammed the meeting; there were many rambling speeches. At the end of the profitless proceedings, Hoover suggested to the organizers that he might enlist some resident Americans to help. They jumped at his offer. Hoover telephoned American engineers living in London, asking them to meet him at the Savoy the following morning. The hotel provided a few reception rooms, tables and chairs without charge. There were many American engineers in Britain, because some American universities provided first-rate instruction in engineering, while the major British universities still took the subject lightly.

By serendipity, Hoover's wife, Lou, had stopped by the Savoy during the day. She was dismayed by the number of women, many with children, travelling unaccompanied and now stranded. She volunteered to start a group to assist them and immediately set to work, calming the distraught and telephoning friends for help. When her husband ran into her, they joined forces. In public they could make decisions confidentially by conversing in Chinese; Bert, as she called him, only had about 100 words but that usually sufficed. That evening the Hoovers telephoned to enlist Americans living in London. Some of their acquaintances and many newspaper reporters thought that the Hoovers were driven by strong religious beliefs, knowing that his mother was a Quaker and deducing from their habitually sober dress that they followed in her footsteps. They might not have noticed that he smoked ten to twenty Havana cigars a day and that both drank alcohol; cocktails were served at all of his business lunches. As an adult he never attended meetinghouse and entered a church only for ceremonial occasions. They were compassionate and both loved to overcome obstacles—they were born 'pushers and doers.'

The American Resident's Committee for the Assistance of American Travellers met early the following morning. With Hoover in the chair the business was done promptly. He was elected chairman, even though the Hoovers' primary residence was a cottage on the campus of Stanford University, where they had been students. However, they had been based in London and still leased a charming place in Kensington, the Red House. They had come to London in March 1914, planning to return to the States in August for their boy's schooling. Hoover was preparing to quit the mining business and, with one eye on future public service, was negotiating to buy a newspaper in the US. He had all of the money they needed. The Hoover's sense of values was spelled out in the instructions Lou wrote to the man who would become the boy's guardian if both parents died: "… not to let them get a money measure for all the affairs of life."

The Resident's Committee went into immediate action at the Savoy. During the day they were joined by volunteers from American businesses in London and by capable recruits from among the travellers—by day's end they had almost 500 volunteers.

Charles de Gaulle
4 August to 30 August 1914

On 4 August de Gaulle updated his will and put his other papers in order. The next morning he shut down his little apartment, saying goodbye to his furniture, his familiar little treasures, and his books. The regiment formed up in the barrack square and then paraded out of Arras, de Gaulle riding a mare, colours flying, band playing and spectators cheering—they had to be restrained by the police from giving the soldiers an affectionate mobbing. The first day they marched for fourteen hours, heading west. It was an ordeal. Their uniforms were not meant for warm weather, and it was the hottest summer for many years. Sweat saturated their heavy wool red trousers and their long, thick, blue capotes flapped open, weighing down their shoulders. The column moved in fits and starts. The carts interspersed between the marchers slowed when they climbed a hill, and rushed as they hurtled down, and the marchers had to keep pace. But the carts were welcome because they carried the men's knapsacks and other gear. Coated with white road dust the soldiers looked like ghosts. By the end of the second day, they had marched 70 kilometres. They halted for dinner and a good rest. The reservists from sedentary occupations were in a frightful state and all of them were breaking in new boots—most had bloody feet. They had scarcely sat down when they were ordered to reform and to go for another 10 kilometres. Some of the carts had gone off, so now half of their gear was hauled on their backs. They arrived at their new destination at 1800 and then lingered for four hours before they were fed. The men slept in barns and sheds, the officers in homes. They were 6.5 kilometres south of the Belgian border; the next day they shifted a few kilometres to the west. They were the advance guard of a French army marching to the frontier. Mass was celebrated, and de Gaulle's heart was stirred by the quiet devotion of the celebrants. After the service they marched for another four hours. Along the way they heard that the Germans had seized Liège, where the principal railway lines cross the River Meuse.

The next day they rested and cheered the news that the French had occupied Mulhouse, one of the cities lost by the Franco-German war; in the evening de Gaulle strolled about to take in the local sights. During the night the sentries opened fire twice—startled by wildlife. The next day, in the fierce August heat, they marched on to Fumay on the Meuse, almost at the border, where they heard cannon fire in the distance. They rested again the next day; morale was excellent and they all knew that they were part of a large army moving precisely to plan. They then received their first mail; he had a letter from his parents posted five days previously.

They started again at 0300 on 13 August, marching north to cross the border. After dawn they were shadowed by a German aeroplane. The aviator knew just where to find them because a French cavalry officer had been captured with a map showing their route. The flyer reported that the French column stretched along the road for 18 kilometres. When they crossed the border, de Gaulle was not surprised by the transition; after the Jesuits were prohibited from teaching in France, he had studied at one of their colleges in Belgium. But many of the men were astounded—they were used to seedy, dishevelled, stinking French villages, with towering piles of ordure in each courtyard and masses of swarming flies; here were tidy towns in which you could smell the late summer flowers. They were greeted enthusiastically as liberators and were offered water, wine and beer. Next day de Gaulle's 11th company was the point of the column, spearheading the entire army; he was kept busy overseeing the scouts. That evening they billeted in a village whose residents freely shared their food and drink. De Gaulle went to his priest to confess, and when he left he felt the peace of God.

They were routed out of their billets at 0200; again, de Gaulle's platoon had the point. Keeping formation during any night march was demanding, but it was much harder scouting on the point. After 30 kilometres, another platoon took the lead. After daybreak they had to force miserable refugees off the road; they were heart-wrenching with their desolate faces and pathetic heaps of treasured belongings. When they stopped for lunch, de Gaulle ate in a café that he rated mediocre. As they were eating, a French bicyclist sped into the village with an order for the regiment to push on to Dinant on the Meuse; the Germans were approaching from the other side and the French must get there first to seize the bridges. The soldiers who had been served last had to leave their soup uneaten.

The French war planners expected the Germans to wheel through eastern Belgium and then swing south along the east bank of the Meuse. They did not believe the enemy could muster enough men to move across to the west bank, never anticipating that the Germans would bring their reserve corps of older men to the front immediately. The 33rd arrived in Dinant after another night march. It was a town with 8,000 inhabitants, on both sides of the river, with a sturdy bridge connecting its two parts. De Gaulle's 11th Company was on the left bank, near the railway station and the Hotel des Postes; across the bridge was the grand square with the town hall and the largest church, sheltering under a steep cliff of exposed limestone crowned with a ruined fortress. Most of the 33rd Regiment crossed the river to climb up to the heights while the 11th Company—the rear guard—waited on the left bank. Spent men slept on the street, and the servants borrowed armchairs for their officers. Two eggs were purchased for each man. At 0600 the first German shells burst in the city. "What was my impression? Why not say it? For two seconds of physical response—tightness in the throat." Then, "finally I am going to see them." His men laughed as he hurried them into cover in a ditch beside the railway line. De Gaulle returned to the square to lounge on a bench—sheer bravado. French wounded trickled back across the bridge; the Germans had reached the high ground first and held the abandoned citadel. Their riflemen shot at the French in the valley below. It was a long shot, so they did little damage. The scene became surreal when two well-dressed young ladies strolled into the square and asked de Gaulle whether it was safe for them to cross the bridge; regretfully, he told them no. More wounded walked or were carried back over the bridge.

On the right bank, the French bugles blew the retreat. A German machine gunner now had the bridge in his sights, so the retreating French sprinted across in small groups—but the fire was too daunting for the stretcher-bearers to risk bringing their burdens across. There was no response by French artillery because the infantry had not waited for them to come up. The 11th Company officers were called together and ordered to advance with the bayonet to prevent the enemy from crossing the bridge. To reach his men in their ditch de Gaulle had to run over an exposed level crossing—a tasty target, an awkward asparagus; his legs shook as he ran. He assembled his platoon and ordered other men sheltering in the ditch to join them; his servant brushed the dust from his black coat. The French officers wore distinctive uniforms so their men could easily pick them out—but so could enemy sharpshooters. He pulled on his white gloves and drew his sword. He ordered "*A la baïonnette*;" they rasped abrasively as they were rammed over the rifle barrels. The bugles blew the charge. De Gaulle leapt from the ditch, repeatedly yelling "*En avant*," waving his sword, racing in front of his men toward the bridge. He felt himself "split in two, the one running like an automaton and the other anxiously watching him." He had almost crossed the 20 metres of open space leading to the bridge when "something struck my knee, like a whip-lash." Falling to the ground, a moment later he was pinned there by the dead body of his sergeant. He heard the muffled thuds of bullets hitting dead and living bodies. He pulled himself free; his right leg would not work properly—he had to drag himself about. His sword was tied by a lanyard to his wrist, so it clattered behind him on the pavement. He shouted for his men to shelter in the buildings. Those wounded who could not move cried pathetically for help. French artillery finally opened fire.

A group of officers watched from an elevation on the left bank. All were French except for a British liaison officer, Lieutenant Edward Spears. First they saw the French wounded dribbling back across the bridge, followed by the retreating troops; then the Germans bombarded the zone around the French side of the bridge. Twice the French attempted counter-attacks. As we have seen, they failed, leaving the ground strewn with bodies. The Germans sent across a small detachment of Saxon Jägers, who deployed to defend their bridgehead with their rifles. About noon, two regiments of the French 2nd Division dashed toward the bridge. After a few volleys, the Jägers broke and fled back across the river. Spears considered the French lucky that there were so few Jägers and that they had not brought a machine gun with them. Whenever Spears hinted to his companions that he had not been struck by the sophistication of French tactics or operations, the invariable answer was that they operated by "*Le Système D*—": "D" for *Dèbrouille-toi*—muddling through. Spears acknowledged that *Le Système* often worked, but nonetheless considered it a method that should be reserved for the use of Frenchmen in France. Years later, General Spears had ample opportunity to discuss Dinant with de Gaulle; Spears was the liaison officer who brought General de Gaulle to London in 1940.

After dark, local peasants loaded the wounded into carts. De Gaulle was fully conscious, with little pain, but suffered because he knew they had been beaten. The wounded were taken to a village schoolhouse where teachers administered first aid and fed de Gaulle two swallow eggs. When he woke the next morning his right leg was paralyzed and without sensation—a bullet had tunnelled through the leg. He investigated the entrance and exit wounds, but could not make out what mischief the bullet had done in between. It was just the sort of wound expected from a modern high-velocity bullet; it streaked though skin and muscle and out again, leaving a clean, precise wound. A musket ball tumbling on its way would have made a hash of it. His bone was not shattered because bone splinters had not enlarged the exit hole. The wounded in the school were dejected; the unscathed men outside chattered gaily. He was examined by a corpsman and then by the chief physician of the corps, who ordered him to be evacuated by ambulance.

His first stop was Charleroi, where his married sister, Marie-Agnés lived; she was amazed to be invited to visit her wounded brother. For the rest of the war she lived in occupied Belgium. He was then moved back to Arras, where the doctor told him that the bullet had damaged his sciatic nerve, which accounted for his loss of sensation and inability to move his leg. He was evacuated to the Saint-Joseph hospital in Paris where they operated to clean up the wound; the nerve must recover by itself.

Gustav Mannerheim
August 1914

Austria-Hungary declared war on Russia on 6 August and, a week later, their army crossed the border and marched north to seize the railhead. Mannerheim was ordered to move his brigade to a designated defensive position to be held "at any cost." Mannerheim feared that the enemy might get there first, so he moved his brigade south in battle formation. His regiment of Hussars followed one road; his regiment of Uhlans used two others. Mannerheim, his staff, the scouts, the pioneer section and his artillery battery took a central road, bridging between the two regiments. He ordered his regiments to gallop until enemy fire obliged them to dismount and then to refuse to be moved from where they stood. Soon his brigade was engaged along a front of 9 kilometres. His six-gun horse artillery battery fired support for the cavalry on either side, but soon four of his guns were hit and out of action. Mannerheim shifted his two remaining guns to a more sheltered position. Lines of Austrian cavalrymen, on foot, repeatedly attacked his dismounted troopers, who repelled them with assistance from their four machine guns. Mannerheim reported to division head-quarters his position, the strength of the enemy attacks and his losses.

The response from headquarters showed how much had improved since they fought the Japanese so ineptly in Manchuria. A fresh battery came cantering up the road, assigned to his command. The gunners found him on a hilltop overlooking the battlefield, casually strolling back and forth smoking a cigar. By his height and uniform, he could be recognized from quite a distance; his courage had a splendid effect on his men in the firing line.

Later in the day, he was reinforced by an Uhlan regiment and by two squadrons of Cossacks from the frontier guard. Toward evening an infantry regiment arrived. He ordered them to take over the line in the centre of his position; their rifles would be more effective than cavalrymen's carbines and they would have more men firing because one in three was not needed to hold horses. The Austrians continued to attack, but with decreasing energy. Though his field glasses, Mannerheim watched as their lines became jumbled and uncertain. Toward evening his cavalry attacked on the flanks; the enemy bolted, leaving behind their dead and about 200 prisoners. His brigade had manoeuvred and fought well. After only a few months under his command—some of it fancy-dress soldiering as guards at the Tsar's Polish hunting lodge—in battle they had done everything he asked. He also gave division good marks for sending reinforcements promptly and placing them under his command; and he must have been pleased that in his first battle as a general, he had not only done well with his brigade, but had ended by successfully directing a formation closer in size to a division. It was a far more gratifying action than his only encounter with Japanese cavalry in Manchuria, where he had been outnumbered and could only distinguish himself by slipping off with light losses. His self-appraisal was endorsed when he was awarded the Sword of St George—a notable decoration. He wrote that his casualties were heavy, but gives no numbers. This is how he always wrote about war, in the style of Caesar, as moves across a map, with blood and humanity in the wings; although he does mention, with regret, the death of a promising young aide-de-camp.

Adolf Hitler
16 August to 17 October 1914

Hitler was finally instructed to report to Recruiting Depot VI in Munich. He passed his physical—standards were relaxed—and was issued a light blue Bavarian Army uniform and sent to the barracks, where he was assigned an iron cot holding bare boards on which a straw-filled mattress rested. In the latrine, twenty men sat side by side. For two weeks, he and the other recruits were initiated in a training detachment. Then he was transferred to the newly formed Bavarian Reserve Infantry Regiment 16. This regiment soon became generally known by the name of its first commander, so we shall call it the List Regiment. Hitler was #148 in the 1st Company. In 1914 a German infantry regiment had a complement of 3,394 men, 234 horses, 6 machine guns and 65 vehicles. The List was quartered in the barracks in Munich and did their training on its *Exerzierplatz*.

It must have been an electrifying jolt for Hitler to pass from unrestrained life to military discipline. Any soldier with longer service could demand instant obedience. Like recruits everywhere, he was harassed by NCOs screaming filthy invective about his ancestry and moral character. The List NCOs had been recalled from the second stage in their careers: after serving nine years with the colours, they had become policemen, postmen, or minor civil servants. They taught the recruits the exhausting goose step and the elements of close-order drill; for practical training they crawled across a muddy field while cradling their rifles. Then they were allowed a few minutes to spruce themselves up before a close inspection; any with a trace of un-brushed mud on their tunic repeated the exercise. When they were given a few hours at liberty in the evening Hitler would visit the Popps, who had agreed to store his goods for the duration. Herr Popp, a tailor by trade, would send Peppi out for Löwenbrau. He knew that Hitler did not care for beer, but he had to demonstrate his pride in his former tenant in some fashion.

On 8 October the List Regiment took part in its first military pageant. They marched to the courtyard of the Turkish Barracks where, under masses of blue Bavarian flags, with the band playing and spectators cheering, they swore their allegiance to their sixty-nine-year-old king, who then reviewed them. Hitler and two other Austrians had formally renounced their allegiance to the Austrian Emperor. They did not wear leather spike helmets, designed to deflect sabre blows, because there had not been time to manufacture helmets with the number 16 in the decorative metalwork on the front—instead they wore black caps of waxed canvas. Each infantryman had a shining leather belt from which was suspended a canvas bread bag, a water bottle, an entrenching tool and a bayonet. Tied to the bayonet haft was a coloured woollen knot and strap, the *Troddel*—the colour indicated the wearer's company. They carried ninety rounds of rifle ammunition in clips which were stored in pouches on their belts. The brass buttons on the fronts of their tunics flashed in the sunshine. Bavarians were distinguished by a thin blue and white chequered tape sewn around the field grey tunic collar; their shoulder straps displayed their regimental number. Their leather marching boots gleamed. A waterproof groundsheet was wrapped around the overcoat which was rolled and folded into an inverted U-shape around the knapsack (the following year their tunics were replaced by a design with a flap to cover blackened buttons. The leather belts were also darkened, and as boots wore out, they were replaced by ankle-height shoes worn with puttees).

When the review was over, they started on the road west. They marched for three days carrying full pack, now and again pausing for vigorous combat manoeuvres. The men were tortured by knapsack straps cutting into their shoulders and by feet blistered by stiff new leather boots. At night they camped in the open; they slept little because the nights were chilly. When they came down into the pretty valley of the River Lech, they marched through a camp filled with French prisoners. They gave the Frenchmen as smart a display as they could muster. It was the first time Hitler had knowingly seen a Frenchman. Each day the march was longer—on the third day they covered 42 kilometres. They treasured a night spent near the village of Graben, where the friendly inhabitants gloriously supplemented their rations. Their destination was a town near Augsburg, where they continued training. They learned of great victories: German armies were sweeping through Belgium to close in on Paris while others were encircling Russian armies, taking hundreds of thousand of prisoners. Everywhere there were pictures of Hindenburg—the great hero of Tannenberg, where the Germans had routed and surrounded a Russian army invading East Prussia, taking tens of thousands of prisoners.

On Saturday 17 October, Hitler participated in his second military pageant. They solemnly received their colours: six new banners for the Brigade. Hitler's 1st Company were at the fore as the colour guard. There were speeches, prayers, music, and singing beneath the waving, massed banners. Hitler was probably surprised at how these military pageants stirred his ardour and by the powerful emotions distorting his comrade's faces. He had long been enchanted with the spectacles of church and opera, but had neglected this genre of performance art. In his later political career, martial spectacles were one of his most effective tools.

Benito Mussolini
18 October to 15 November 1914

The Italians were deeply divided over what to do about the war: they could stay neutral, side with their allies the Austrians, or join the Allies. Which would help to complete the reunification of Italy? The Austro-Hungarians might be willing to turn over some of the lands many Italians thought their natural right, like the Trentino, the mountainous region north of Venice; nature had made an ideal natural border at the Brenner Pass. Many Italians also coveted the lovely cities along the Dalmatian coast, like Trieste, as well as other former Venetian island possessions in the eastern Mediterranean. All the lands they yearned for were currently owned by Austrians or the Turks. On the other hand, the socialists were not interested in expansion and they regarded war as a symptom of the blight of capitalism, offering working men nothing but death, mutilation and penury. In the election of 1913 the socialists had polled almost a million votes and won fifty-two seats in Parliament.

Socialist solidarity was shattered on 18 October when their leading newspaper, *Avanti!* published an editorial calling for war on the side of the Allies. It was written by the editor, Benito Mussolini:

> We have the privilege of living at the most tragic hour in world history. Do we—as men and as socialists—want to be inert spectators in this huge drama? Or do we want to be in some way and in some sense, the protagonists?

The words were the measure of the man: wilful; confident in his ability to lead; ready to throw the dice; sure that he would end up on top. The editorial transmuted him from relative obscurity into a national figure. It also meant his job, not a comfortable prospect for a thirty-one-year-old with a family, but he had prepared by first secretly negotiating with powerful pro-Allied figures, who promised to fund a new newspaper. After the editorial appeared, he travelled to Switzerland to meet agents of the French Secret Service, who, along with the Belgians, provided additional subsidies. The new journal was *Il Popolo d'Italia* (The People of Italy). Its first issue appeared on 15 November 1914.

Mustafa Kemal
August to November 1914

Lieutenant Colonel Mustafa Kemal, of the Ottoman Army, was stationed in Sofia, Bulgaria. At birth, a Turkish boy was given one name, which his father whispered into his ear—hence Mustafa. His second name Kemal—perfect—had been given by a teacher to honour his ability in maths. Now he had the challenge of serving as the military attaché to all of the Balkan countries; the Ottomans had just fought them in two wars.

There is another war to consider before we get to the Balkan wars. In 1912, Kemal was in the Ottoman province of Cyrenaica (now part of Libya), fighting Italian invaders. He had slipped in via Egypt, an Ottoman province, that was 'protected' by the British, and he commanded eight Ottoman officers and 160 men, with an artillery battery, two captured machine guns, and 8,000 Arab tribesmen. All of the Ottoman forces there were commanded by Major Ismail Enver, who, as we shall see, was one of the great bugbears in Kemal's life. They kept the Italians pinned into the towns along the coast. The Italians countered with naval power, bombarding Beirut, the forts at the entrance to the Dardanelles, and occupying Rhodes and some of the Dodecanese Islands.

The Russians were another galling sore in the Ottoman's side. They intended to have Constantinople and the straits, and were moving toward them step by step. They organized Serbia, Bulgaria, Greece and Montenegro into a Balkan League, to liberate Macedonia from Ottoman rule. The League attacked the Ottoman Empire in 1912. The desperate Ottomans made peace with the Italians, ceding the provinces in northern Africa but regaining Rhodes. The League took Macedonia and the Greeks entered Salonika (now Thessaloniki). The Bulgarians raced them to the city and occupied the suburbs. A bitter blow for Kemal; he had been born and reared there. His mother and sister fled, and his father had died years before. The Bulgarians besieged Adrianople (now Edirne), the largest Ottoman city in Thrace. When Kemal returned from Africa, he found his mother and sister huddled in a mass of refugees in the wintry, open courtyard of a Constantinople mosque. He was assigned as the staff officer for operations of an army corps on the Gallipoli Peninsula, where there was no fighting. The Ottomans sued for peace, but when the terms were delivered to the Sublime Porte, a rebel group, the 'Young Turks,' broke into the palace, killed the Minister of War, seized control of the government, and hanged their principal political opponents. They were led by a triumvirate: Enver, Talât and Djemal. Kemal was also a Young Turk, officially a part of the Committee for Unification and Progress (CUP), and had been active in underground politics for years, but he deplored the violence of the coup. Moreover, he deplored the leading roles taken by Enver and Djemal, army officers—Kemal wanted the army to keep out of politics. The new rulers did no better with the war than their predecessors; in May 1913 they had signed a peace treaty, negotiated in London, giving up all that their enemies occupied—including Adrianople, which the Bulgarians had taken.

Then the victors fell out among themselves. To enlarge their share of the spoils, the Bulgarians attacked the Serbs and Greeks, starting the Second Balkan War. The Ottomans took advantage of the quarrel to retake Adrianople. The Bulgarians were beaten and after a few months another peace was negotiated. The Greeks and Serbs divided Macedonia.

As military attaché in Sofia, Kemal had few difficulties with his former enemies. He was thirty-three years old, well-mannered, well-educated in the Sultan's military schools, spoke excellent French and adequate German, and was widely read in Western literature. Though of medium height, he stood out in a crowd with his erect posture, graceful slim figure, strikingly handsome blonde good looks and piercing blue eyes. He was so good-looking that even fellow officers often believed his boast that the girls in the brothels did not ask him for money. He drank alcohol with relish, danced well, and graced any society with his easy manners. Soon he was welcomed in the best circles in Sofia, often sporting a homburg rather than a fez; he threw himself into Western life. Before Sofia, his only time in the West had been a short visit to Paris, where the French had offended by acting as though he represented a light opera army. Kemal spent hours in the visitors' gallery of the Bulgarian Parliament, studying the debates so that he could advise the seventeen Turkish deputies on how to box above their weight. He also supervised the editorial policy of the two Turkish-language newspapers.

Kemal adored women and they reciprocated. He told fellow officers that the quality he prized most in a woman was availability, but in Sofia he courted a young lady of distinguished family and might have proposed were it not certain that her family would never let her marry a Moslem. None of this stopped him from writing loving letters in French to a lady in Constantinople, Corrine Lüthü, an officer's widow who had been born in Italy.

After the coup, Enver was awarded the title of Pasha, married an Ottoman princess and moved into a palace along the Bosporus. The triumvirate energetically set about remodelling the government; Enver, as minister of war, worked to regenerate the army, in close collaboration with the head of the German military mission, General Liman von Sanders—the Sanders was added when he was ennobled, it being the maiden name of his Scottish wife. The fifty-nine-year-old German was a general of cavalry in the Prussian Army and an Ottoman field marshal. Kemal always let German officers know that he appreciated instruction but resented his country being dominated by outsiders.

When the Great War broke out, Enver thought it would be short and feared that if the Ottomans dallied they might miss the spoils. He signed a secret treaty with the Germans, promising to enter the war after the Ottoman army was mobilized. Kemal wrote to his friends arguing that it would be a long war, that eventually the US would enter, and that, at least for the present, they should remain neutral. Ottoman public opinion was divided, though it was pushed toward the German camp by Winston

Churchill, the First Lord of the Admiralty. Even before Britain entered the war, he seized two newly built battleships floating in the river Tyne in Scotland. They had been paid for in part with money collected from Turkish schoolchildren; the two ships were now seaworthy and 500 Ottoman sailors were standing by to sail them to Constantinople, where the warships would begin to even the odds against the Greek fleet. The Ottomans were furious—it was piracy. When Churchill later wrote to apologize, they refused to accept his letter.

When Britain declared war, the German battle cruiser *Goeben* and light cruiser *Breslau* were in the Mediterranean, shadowed by British and French warships. The Germans slipped off, bombarded the port of Bone in Tunisia, wafted through the combined British and French fleets, and sailed through the Dardanelles to Constantinople. Belligerent warships could shelter in a neutral port for a few days only, so Allied ships waited for them off the entrance to the Dardanelles. The Germans gave the two vessels to the Ottomans as a personal gift from the Kaiser. The Turkish public cheered the German crews in their new fezzes.

The standoff between Ottoman doves and hawks persisted. Churchill withdrew the British admiral who was serving as the Ottoman naval adviser, maintaining:

> Nothing appeals to the Turkish Govt. but force; and they will continue to kick those who they think are unable or unwilling to use it against them.

In early September, at his urging, the British cabinet agreed that Turkish naval ships should not be permitted to leave the Dardanelles. In retaliation, the Turks shut the straits, thereby blocking sea traffic to Russia. At the end of October, the *Goeben* and *Breslau*, with their German crews but flying the Ottoman flag, sailed into the Black Sea. They sank Russian shipping in the harbour of Odessa, fired on the forts at Sevastopol and set oil depots afire. The Ottoman minister of marine maintained that he had not authorized the attack. The British ambassador in Constantinople urged patience, arguing that the raid was a wildcat operation and that the peace advocates still were likely to prevail.

The British foreign office warned that any Ottoman naval movements would be regarded as hostile. On Churchill's orders the British sank an Ottoman ship in Smyrna harbour and a British flotilla bombarded the town of Akaba on the Red Sea. On 3 November, a British fleet accompanied by two French battleships bombarded the forts at the entrance to the Dardanelles from a range of 13 kilometres. They hit the magazine of one fort, destroying almost all of its heavy guns. The next day the cabinet voted to give the Ottoman government a twelve-hour ultimatum: they must eject the Germans. There was no reply. The British, French and Russians declared war.

Kemal tried to persuade the Bulgarians to join with the Ottomans, promising them all that they had lost in the Second Balkan War, and, especially when he was drinking well at a dinner, much more. He also tried to buy arms from them. The fanciful Enver offered him command of three regiments that were to march through Persia to attack British India, but Kemal declined.

Herbert Hoover
10 August to 30 October 1914

The American Citizen's Committee did not waste a minute. They leased ships to take the tourists home. Members—identified by lapel pins displaying the Stars and Stripes—met disoriented travellers at the London stations, advising them to go to the Savoy Hotel, where they would be greeted by a shrewd front man who swiftly judged their character and needs and gave them a coloured card. A white card gained the holder admission to an office where cheques or other financial documents were exchanged for cash, which came from an account in a London bank personally guaranteed by Hoover and nine others for up to $1 million. Red card holders were asked to sign cablegrams to relatives in the States asking them to deposit funds in the Committee's account in an American bank. Blue card holders were destitute; they were provided with funds from donations to the Committee. Lou's group helped with accommodation and clothing and amused the children with excursions in London and into the countryside.

The US Congress appropriated $2,500,000 for the relief of the American travellers on 5 August. The next afternoon the cruiser *Tennessee* left New York harbour with the gold packed in oaken casks. When the *Tennessee* arrived in England ten days later she disgorged an assistant secretary of war, twenty-four army officers and an assortment of clerks along with the gold. The assistant secretary met with Ambassador Page and Hoover. Realizing that Hoover was both a "persistent fellow" and an able one, they agreed that the Residents' Committee would distribute the funds in England and do most of the work.

By mid-month Hoover was able to spare some hours for his business. His rise to head of what was probably the most successful mining engineering partnership in the world reads like unadulterated Horatio Alger. Orphaned in Iowa when he was only nine years old, he was taken in by an uncle in Oregon; from childhood, he worked and studied at top pace. His biographer, George Nash, attributes some of his characteristics to this difficult early life—his taciturnity, shyness, lack of small talk and avoidance of eye contact. A smart young fellow, he was a member of the first class to enter the new Leland Stanford University; it was tuition-free so he made his way on a small inheritance, part-time work during term and summer jobs. He graduated in 1895 with a degree in geology and started work in mining. Two years later he was hired by a leading British mining company who sent him to the Western Australian gold mines. They were in difficult, waterless and almost trackless desert. Hoover travelled about on Afghan camels, which he recalled "did not fulfil all of the anticipations of romantic literature." He inspected mines, evaluating their potential as a geologist and their value with a sharp financial eye. His company purchased those he found promising; the purchases did well.

In 1899, he became the Chief Engineer of the Chinese Engineering and Mining Company, with a salary of £20,000 (about £4 million today) plus expenses. He believed that this was the highest salary earned by any man his age in the world. On the strength of these riches he married Lou and the newly-weds immediately sailed for China. He was welcomed by superstitious mineworkers who thought that he could detect gold because he had green eyes, but he focused on coal and concrete, which were more profitable. He travelled far and wide, meeting such interesting folk as a living Buddha who was riding his bicycle around the courtyard of a Tibetan monastery. Hoover evaluated the potential of each operation and planned how to develop those that were viable. In 1901 the majority interest in the company was bought by Belgian interests. A Belgian director, Emile Francqui, took over. He was a hard-driving capitalist whose previous post had been in the Congo. He was soon at loggerheads with Hoover. After a nasty scene, with harsh words on both sides, Hoover resigned.

He returned to his old firm in London, spending most of his time in the field, problem-solving and evaluating new finds. Lou and their two boys often travelled with him, the babies in a basket. Some of his most interesting and profitable work was in the wild frontier region of Burma, at a mine that had been worked close to the surface by the Chinese for several hundred years. Hoover's examination convinced him that far deeper, below the water line, the pickings would be rich (he made a fortune when he sold his stake in 1918). In 1908 he established a consulting engineering company, recruiting young colleagues by personally guaranteeing them a minimum annual income and much more if things went well. They troubleshot ailing projects from offices in New York, San Francisco, London, St Petersburg and Paris. They also bought promising mining claims, formed corporations to hold the property and then sold the stock.

For recreation, Hoover wrote a successful textbook, *Principles of Mining*. He and Lou worked for five years translating from the Latin the first great textbook of mining and industrial chemistry, Agricola's *De Re Metallica* of 1556. Lou's Latin was excellent, but Agricola had invented words for all of the substances and techniques unknown to the Romans—it was detective work to ferret out just what his new words meant. A beautiful edition was published in 1912, the year that Hoover was elected as a trustee of Stanford. For bedtime reading he preferred detective stories.

During the first six weeks of the war the Citizen's Committee assisted 120,000 troubled Americans, including more than 30,000 teachers, and loaned $1,500,000, of which only $300 was not repaid. Lou and the boys, then eleven and seven years old, sailed for America; school had started. Father was to stay on for a few more weeks at the Red House, which had become a dormitory for volunteers. Hoover's business was a mess. Large projects in Russia and Burma were unfinished, but construction was stalled. Zinc mined in Australia could not be shipped to German manufacturers because of the blockade. Hoover needed cyanide because at the mines it is used for extracting metals from the ore. In late September he arranged to buy a supply from the Germans, to be shipped out of Rotterdam. The blockade prevented shipment so he was forced to renege and buy his cyanide from the British at a higher cost.

II

First Ypres to trench warfare

Adolf Hitler
21 October to 1 November 1914

Three days after receiving their colours, the List learned that they would move to the front, where they expected to be given rear echelon duties while they completed training. He wrote to Frau Popp, stating that he hoped to get to England. They left on 21 October aboard three trains. As the battalions marched to the trains they sang, "*In der Heimat, in der Heimat, da gibst ein Wiedersehen.*" When they stopped at the station in Augsburg, Red Cross ladies came aboard with drinks and treats. Then:

> For the first time in my life I saw the Rhine, as we journeyed westward to stand guard before that historic German river against its traditional and grasping enemy. As the first soft rays of the morning sun broke through the light mist and disclosed to us the *Niederwald* Statue, with one accord the whole troop train broke into the strains of *Die Wacht am Rhein*. I then felt as if my heart could not contain its spirit.

While their trains chugged westward the soldiers of the reserve army sat and talked. Hitler was a washout at the lad talk: he despised casual chit-chat about sex, but he shone when the talk became serious, even though he was in a group of good talkers. He used vivid language, with flashing blue eyes, a high-pitched emotional voice and expressive gestures. Twenty per cent of the reserve army came directly from the classroom. Most of the rest had already completed excellent schooling—surely they were the best-educated divisions that had ever gone to war. Their thoughts are preserved in their letters home, and in Hitler's case, in *Mein Kampf.*

There was much talk of honour—their own, their nation's, their regiment's. As Hitler later wrote:

> Despite all views to the contrary, this honour does actually exist, or it will have to exist; for a nation without honour will sooner or later loose its freedom and independence.

Another favourite topic was German superiority in science, education, art, music and philosophy. They were inspired by Hegel's teaching that their *Kultur* flowered in direct historical line from the ancient Greeks—now their envious foes were determined to destroy it. They had no compunctions about bloodletting. Ministers and priests assured them that war was part of God's plan. Others based their readiness on Plato:

> … when a man dies gloriously in war shall we not say, in the first place, that he is of the golden race?

The modern-minded cited Nietzsche:

> … the present-day European requires not merely war but the greatest and most terrible of wars—thus a temporary relapse into barbarism …

Such fuddle-headed, irrational, pulse-accelerating rhetoric was heard throughout the Europe of 1914.

The talk also overflowed with bad biology. Charles Darwin's multifaceted ideas on how organisms evolve had been debased by popularisers like Herbert Spencer who vividly portrayed a nature "red in tooth and claw." The "survival of the fittest" and the "struggle for existence" were accepted as a new gospel, usually without thought about how accurately they portrayed life in nineteenth-century European societies. The real mischief came when the jungle was spiced with a credo vigorously promoted by a school of physical anthropologists who maintained that races were discrete units—your unit could be precisely determined by the ratio between the length and breadth of your fleshless skull—too bad that while living you could not be certain of your race. Hence, the war was for the survival of the fittest race. Scientific twaddle, for sure, but twaddle that has underpinned atrocity, enslavement and murder. The volunteers were prepared to die for honour and the survival of their race. Again, Nietzsche:

> So live your life of obedience and of war! What matter about long life! What warrior wisheth to be spared!

When Hitler talked about his past, he surely told the story later printed in *Mein Kampf*, but the written version was shaped by the reactions of his fellow soldiers. He had a talent for keeping his finger on his audience's pulse and adjusting his pace, emphasis and content to hold their attention. The story he told of his early life is a masterpiece of selective editing, turning a shabby tale of self-destruction into a dogged and ultimately successful battle to overcome the bad deal life had given him.

His father had been a customs official; Adolf's mother was his third wife. Father was determined that son would become a civil servant; son was determined to become an artist. They fought bitterly. Mother was submissive, retiring and loving. Hitler didn't tell his audience that their family physician, Dr Edward Bloch—a Jew who was driven into exile in the 1930s—said that he had never seen a stronger attachment than that between Adolf and his mother. All his life, he kept a picture of her nearby. At twelve he was taken to his first opera, *Lohengrin*. From then on he passionately admired Richard Wagner and all of his works. His father died in 1903, appropriately enough at the *Gasthaus Wiesinger* over his glass of wine. But the son was still not free; his mother insisted that he was obliged to do as father said, so he persuaded her that he was too ill for further schooling—his formal education ended at sixteen. The family moved to a comfortable apartment in Linz, where for the next two years Adolf was ministered to by his mother, his Aunt Johanna and his sister Paula. He was given a grand piano, but gave up lessons after three months. He slept late, spent the afternoons lounging, painting, reading and writing poetry. He grew a wispy moustache; in the evening he would put on his black cloak and broad-brimmed hat, take his cane with its ivory handle, and step out to the theatre or the opera. In 1906 his mother treated him to a two-week trip to Vienna; the next year he persuaded her to let him move to Vienna to enter the Academy of Fine Arts. Aunt Johanna helped by loaning him 924 Kronen—about a year's salary for a newly qualified teacher.

The cloud over those easygoing days was his mother's illness. She had breast cancer, and when the doctor told Adolf and Paula that there was little hope, he saw the tears spurt into Adolf's eyes. She was in dreadful pain. In September 1907 he went to Vienna to apply for admission to the Academy, which required him to submit a folio of his work. It was good enough to enable him to take the two three-hour examinations, in which applicants were required to draw assigned subjects—he was "quietly confident of success." When he received a letter of rejection it was like a thunderbolt from heaven, though the competition was steep: only twenty-eight of the 146 applicants were admitted. Hitler called on the Rector of the Academy to discuss the reasons for his failure. The Rector said that he could not draw humans adequately for the Academy but that he drew buildings well, so he had the makings of an architect. He should attend the Technical Building School, where admission required a certificate from a Middle School, which he must obtain first.

He returned home, telling no one he had failed. His mother died in December 1907; she was forty-seven. According to Dr Bloch he had never seen anyone "so prostrate with grief as Adolf Hitler." He returned to Vienna. In his narrative he then fell like Satan from heaven. He claimed that the family money had all gone for mother's treatment and funeral, so he was penniless when he entered the period of his life that "hardened me and enabled me to be as tough as I now am." He spent five years, first as a casual labourer and then as a "painter of little trifles." All time outside of work was spent reading and studying. His only recreation was an occasional visit to the opera, giving up food to pay for the ticket. He managed to climb out of this hell by the artistic talents that the Academy had spurned.

This is profoundly misleading. He fell step-by-step into the nether regions, trod down by his own devils. He returned to Vienna with the money from his aunt and a modest orphan's pension; his father's legacy was in a trust he would not receive until he was twenty-four. He shared a room with a childhood companion from Linz who was studying music. Hitler loafed, not lifting a finger to make up his deficiencies so that he could study architecture. When the friend returned from a summer vacation he found that Hitler had vacated their room, leaving no forwarding address. He had moved to a poorer part of the city, registering with the police as a student. He continued his feckless way until his pockets were empty. It was then that he began the hardening period that he so loved to brag about his own "struggle for existence in Vienna."

Day by day, his clothing became shabbier, his stench stronger, his grooming poorer. His moustache straggled over his stubble. He had to learn how to sleep on the street when he could not afford a doss, and how to obtain a daily bowl of soup from the nuns at the convent in the *Gumpendorferstrasse*. On the pavements people would move to the side when he approached; when he entered a shop the clerks became shifty-eyed and anxious. To maintain self-esteem, he focused his contempt and hate on all those he looked down on: Jews, Czechs, Poles, Serbs—everyone but Germans. Some work could usually be had, but was easily lost. He claimed that he often worked on construction sites, where the other men tried to persuade him to join their union. The unionists were social democrats who believed in the solidarity of the working class, regardless of ethnic origin. Of course the idea of entering into any such association disgusted Hitler to his core; he rejected their overtures haughtily. When things got slow they were glad to see him off the job. Incidentally, historians are not convinced that he ever worked in construction or had problems with the unions.

After many months he obtained a place in a newly established charity for the homeless, where he could sleep in the dormitory at night, wash and have his clothes disinfected. There he met another itinerant, Reinhold Hanish, who persuaded him to write home for funds for his studies. It was probably Aunt Johanna who sent him fifty Kroner. He bought a used overcoat from the government pawn shop, paints, paper and drawing pencils and they both moved on to the Men's House, a newly established charity in the northern part of the city. He set to work doing postcard-sized watercolours of the sights of Vienna, which Hanish peddled on the street or to framers. He would usually do a painting each day and usually they sold for five Kroner, which the partners split. The partnership ended when Hitler did a large watercolour that sold for fifty Kroner; Hitler accused Hanish of cheating him of his share and called the police. Hanish spent a few days in jail, but Hitler never got his money. He continued in the Men's House for two more years, either selling his work himself or using another resident as intermediary. We have already seen that the legacy from his father enabled him to dodge military service by moving to Munich, which in *Mein Kampf* he claims he undertook to breathe the pure air of Germany.

The trains carried the List Regiment through the damaged railway station in Liège and through the ruins of Louvain. They were warned that they might be sniped at and lights were forbidden. During the last stage of the journey the train crept along for fear that saboteurs might have extracted some of the rail spikes. They stared wide-eyed as they passed blown bridges and smashed railway cars and equipment; minds filled with newspaper stories of how their wounded comrades' eyes were gouged out by bloodthirsty Belgian matrons. Their enemies read of Germans cutting off the hands of young male Belgians so they would never be able to use a rifle. The German timetable for passing through Belgium was slowed more by sabotage of railway traffic than by fortresses. Keeping the railways working was crucial to the German plans; they suppressed hostile acts by retaliating harshly against accused civilians. The List crossed the frontier and arrived at Lille after midnight and marched past soot-blackened tenements along filthy streets. The French had declared Lille an open city and withdrawn, so it had not been bombarded. They were billeted in the courtyard of the Bourse. It was freezing on the cobblestones, so few slept, but Hitler, surrounded by his 'lot,' must have felt it was a step up from when he froze in solitude on the streets of Vienna. He was getting along splendidly with his comrades; they called him 'Adi.'

The List was in Lille because the great German wheel through Belgium and western France had failed. They had assigned too many men to their left wing, along the French-German frontier, and, frightened by the Russian advance into East Prussia, Chief of Staff Count Helmut von Moltke transferred men to the Eastern Front, where they arrived too late to fight in the great victory at Tannenberg. The French, commanded by Joseph Joffre, halted their frantic, suicidal attacks along the German frontier and moved men west by train from the frontier to meet the wheel. The reinforced garrison of Fortress Paris sallied to hit the German flank, while other French units and the BEF thrust at the Germans along the Marne. Moltke's headquarters were in Luxembourg, almost 400 kilometres from the crucial point on his front. He sent his intelligence officer, Lieutenant Colonel Hentsch, a novice in combat, to evaluate the situation, with the power, if needed, to issue orders to the army commanders in Moltke's name. Hentsch ordered a retreat to a defensive line along the River Aisne. Therefore, in the battle of the Marne, the allies advanced against a retreating German rearguard. On the Aisne, the Allied attacks on the trenches the Germans had dug on the heights were bloodily repulsed. Moltke was replaced, at first secretly, by the Prussian War Minister, Erich von Falkenhayn. He chose to shift front to smash through the French and British flank in Flanders. In a desperate gamble, he threw raw units of the Reserve Army into the attack (Hindenburg completed training the Reserve Army units allotted to the Eastern Front before deploying them in combat).

The next morning the List heard gunfire from the direction of Armentières—"The roar of cannon seemed to be endless"—and were told that they were going to the front. They cheered lustily. They would fight the English, which added to their pleasure, because they despised the mercenaries who made up the British ranks, regarding them—as Wellington had—as drunken scum; beasts who had herded Boer women and children to die in concentration camps. A citizens' army would teach them a lesson. There surely were many recitations of the new poem that had enthralled Germans, *The Hymn of Hate*:

> An oath for our sons and their sons to take.
>
> Come, hear the word, repeat the word,
>
> Throughout the Fatherland make it heard.
>
> We will never forego our hate,
>
> We have all but a single hate,
>
> We love as one,
>
> we hate as one,
>
> We have one foe, and one alone—England!

Hitler shared the sentiment, but may not have enthused over the poem because it was written by Ernst Lissauer, one of the Viennese Jews he so hated.

The List was assigned to Army Group Fabeck, which was to seize the Messines Ridge and then to drive the British back to the coast. Opposed to them were the British 7th Division, three cavalry divisions and two reduced battalions of Indian infantry. According to the British Official History the odds were six Germans to one Briton.

As the clock ticked on the Bavarians' exuberance faded—they remained in Lille. The following day they drilled and then were permitted to sightsee. "Gigantic columns" of troops marched past gawking bystanders, giving way when necessary to trams and racing staff cars; the cafés fringing the main square were jammed with German soldiers. Many well-dressed civilians strolled about. That evening in their billets, "… we all sang, many of us for the last time." The alarm sounded at 0200, the List Regiment fell in and marched off. It was a starlit, cool autumn night; they marched for six hours, rested for two and then marched on for twelve more, covering 40 kilometres. An hour after they stopped the cookers came up and they were fed; cookers freed the men from carrying pots and pans. They were exhausted but sleep was hard to come by. Four paces from Hitler was the stinking corpse of a long-dead horse; just behind him a howitzer battery fired two shells every fifteen minutes, heaving the ground and lighting up the bivouac like the flash of an arc lamp. As the night went on the fire along the front built in intensity; hearsay had it that the English were attacking. They lay pressed against one another for warmth, staring at the starry sky and talking in whispers. At dawn, they hauled the foul horse carcass to a nearby crater, shoved it in and covered it with a scattering of dirt. At 1015, they marched on.

That evening Hitler and some others were billeted in a wretched farmhouse; Hitler was on guard. At 0100 bugles blew the alarm. They were issued additional ammunition and coffee and breakfast. When they formed up they cheered their major, Count Zeck, who rode by to tell them that they were to attack the English. The major led the 1st Company down the road running from Menin to Ypres, a straight cobble-stoned avenue with a row of linden trees on either side. As each company marched past they were blessed by their chaplain, Father Norbert, a distinctive stout figure in a brown robe girdled with a rope and with a soft military cap crowning his round, good-natured, bearded face. The countryside had a gentle roll. At 0700 on 29 October, the 1st Company was led off the road and marched through a wood. They reached a clearing where four 77mm field guns were dug in; they were ordered into a line of foxholes behind the guns. It was a foggy morning and the gun smoke mingled with the mist. The sharp, vicious crack of the guns crashed against their eardrums. They crouched into the holes as enemy shrapnel ripped over their heads; the bullets hit the edge of the woods just behind them, slicing down trees "like wisps of straw." Hitler thought it more curious than dangerous. Out of the fog a group of khaki-clad figures came toward them, carrying a machine gun. There was a momentary alarm, but they were British prisoners shepherded by a proud escort.

The Bavarians were ordered out of their foxholes and formed into a line that started forward at the run, officers in front and NCOs behind to prevent straggling. They trotted through a short strip of woods and then ran across a field toward a small farm. Bullets whistled by. As Hitler recalled it:

Shrapnel exploded in our midst and spluttered in the damp ground. But before the smoke of the explosion disappeared a wild 'Hurrah' was shouted from two hundred throats, in response to this first greeting of Death. Then began the whistling of bullets and the booming of cannons, the shouting and singing of the combatants. With eyes straining feverishly, we pressed forward, quicker and quicker, until we finally came to close-quarter fighting, there beyond the beet-fields and the meadows. Soon the strains of a song reached us from afar. Nearer and nearer, from company to company, it came. And while Death began to make havoc in our ranks we passed the song on to those beside us: *Deutschland, Deutschland über Alles, über Alles in der Welt.*

British survivors of the attacks by the Reserve Army confirm that the attackers often sang; part of it was patriotic furore, but there was more to it than that. Many units were dressed in out-of-date uniforms or headgear, like the black caps worn by the List, so they sang to let other German formations know which side they were on (the List was issued regulation spike helmets in early November). The odd headgear persuaded some of the British that they donned their student caps before their suicidal charges. The singing by the untrained volunteers as they were cut down became part of the German mindset about the horrors of 1914, usually called the 'slaughter of the innocents.'

The 1st Company crossed the field and sheltered behind the farm buildings, panting, for perhaps ten minutes. Then they started running forward again. The NCO just in front of Hitler was hit; they broke line to dash past the dying man. Ahead was a drainage ditch,

kept unblocked by generations of Flemish farmers, which ran across the field toward the
enemy line. Their captain threw himself into the ditch, waving for them to follow; they
crawled down the ditch in Indian file. It was so shallow that now and again a man was hit
in the back, if he could not move on he was shoved out of the ditch and then they heard
bullets smack into his body. At the end of the ditch there was another open field, also
under heavy fire. Each man came out of the ditch and dashed forward for 20 metres into a
small pond that gave them some cover while they got their breath and reorganized. Their
captain had fallen, so now they were commanded by a vice-sergeant, "a magnificent hulk
of a man." He led the sodden men out of the pond across 100 metres of field into a small
patch of wood; those who made it safely crowded around their leader. Hitler thought they
were very few. The NCO ordered them to crawl to the edge of the wood, which was under
heavy fire:

> The shells burst in the wood … and threw up showers of stone, earth and sand, tore up the
> heaviest trees by their roots and smothered everything in a horrible greeny-yellow stinking
> vapour.

They lay at the woods' edge until Major Zeck came forward, ordered them up and led
them off across more fields. Hitler "leapt and ran as best I could across ditches, negotiated
wire entanglements and hedges." Then they heard a shout: "all of you in here." Ahead
there was a long trench; Hitler ran forward and jumped in. His landing was cushioned
by a body on the trench floor—a dead or dying Englishman. The trench had been taken
by Württembergers. They pointed out English trenches to their left and right; fierce fire
pinned the Germans into their own trench.

At 1000, German guns came into action, their high explosive shells ploughed into the
English trenches: "They poured out like ants from an ant heap." The Germans chased after
them, some threw down their rifles and raised their arms—the others were shot. The Germans
continued onward. When they neared an orchard a few English came out to engage them,
but they were shot down by a "blistering fire." As they advanced through the orchard they
flushed out the English sheltering there; most surrendered, the others were killed. When they
came to the boundary of the orchard the first Germans who ventured into the open were hit.
The English seemed to be firing from a group of farm buildings off to their left.

They crouched behind trunks in the orchard until their "madcap" major arrived,
puffing on a cheroot as calmly as though he were strolling the streets of Munich. The
1st Company now had no officers, only a handful of NCOs. The major and his adjutant
examined the lay of the ground. The major told them that they had too few men to
advance successfully and ordered Hitler and several others back to bring up stragglers;
Hitler returned with some Württembergers. The major was lying on the ground with his
chest split wide open; they gawked at his collapsed lungs and still heart. Other bodies

lay about helter-skelter. They beseeched the adjutant to lead them forward. Four times they left the edge of the wood, only to be driven back. Before the fifth attempt, they pummelled the farm buildings with rifle bullets until the enemy fire fell off. By this time all of Hitler's 'lot' had fallen. At 1400 they made their fifth try. As he ran forward, a bullet tore off the right sleeve of Hitler's tunic, but he was unhurt. They took the farm buildings. At 1700 they started to dig a trench for the night.

On their first day in action, 29 October, the List Regiment had 349 officers and men killed, almost one man in ten. Colonel List was among those killed, hence their name. They saw how hideously men die in battle—images the survivors would never forget. They continued to attack for three more days, and according to their regimental history they "got the better of the English", but this judgment is debatable. Their attack the next day was pressed hard, but in the words of the German History, "did not have the success expected." The enemy suffered more from the German artillery than from the infantry. After four days fighting in Belecelare, Polygon Wood and Gheluvelt, the remnants of the List Regiment were taken out of the line and marched back to Werwick for three days' rest. According to Hitler, regimental strength was down from 3,600 men to 611; only three officers remained, none in the 1st company. Four of the companies were disbanded. Hitler wrote that he "… survived by a near miracle. Even our step was no longer what it had been." The rank and file of the List Regiment had not been trained to fight effectively, but they knew how to "die like old soldiers."

Hitler had done well—he had been clear-headed and brave—and so he was made a regimental staff runner: "it's slightly less dirty work but all the more dangerous." A regiment had eight to ten runners; in action, they carried only a pistol and a dispatch case on their belt. The dispatches were marked with one to three crosses to indicate priority. Three cross messages were sent by two runners, hoping that one would get through. Three of the eight runners were killed on Hitler's first day with them, during which they attacked twice to turn the left flank of the London Scottish on the Messines Ridge. The London Scottish advanced in kilts with pipes swirling; the Germans advanced singing and with bands playing and then shouted "harrah" as they tried to drive their attack home. According to Hitler this time it was "hard going" and a determined counter-attack forced them back. They did not take the ridge. Before the second attack, Hitler and a comrade accompanied their new regimental commander, Lieutenant Colonel Englehardt, on a reconnaissance. A machine gun opened up on them. The two soldiers jumped in front to shield their leader with their bodies and then pushed him into a ditch. The next day Englehardt called together the four company commanders to discuss recommendations for decorations. To preserve confidentiality Hitler and the other runners were sent out of the headquarters dugout; they settled down a little ways off, lazing on the ground. Five minutes later a British shell smashed into the dugout, killing or wounding the entire staff: "It was the worst moment of my life. All of us worshiped Lieutenant Colonel Englehardt."

Hitler and his comrades pulled Englehardt out of the smoking ruins and applied the field dressings that saved his life. Englehardt was evacuated and the paperwork for Hitler's decoration went no further. On 1 November Hitler was promoted to lance-corporal. Falkenhayn's toss of the dice had failed bloodily. He decided to put his army in the west on the defensive; they picked their ground, and dug in.

Harold Macmillan
October and December 1914

When Macmillan was finally liberated from his sick room, he joined a volunteer formation known as the Artist's Rifles. They drilled in mufti with broomsticks for weapons, in the open spaces of the Inns of Court. The instructors were men who had acquired some training along the way and like their students were eager for more committed employment. One of them was Clement Atlee, a future prime minister. After a few weeks of this, Macmillan, perhaps through family influence, was given an appointment to appear before an officer selection board. The interviewers relied largely on a list of acceptable public schools. He had been at Eton—no need even to consult the list. The physical examination should have been more of a hurdle, but was so jammed with applicants that no one noted that he was lost without thick spectacles. He was commissioned as a second lieutenant in the King's Royal Rifle Corps, in one of the new battalions being raised by Secretary of War Kitchener, whose face was immortalized in one of the most effective recruiting posters of all times, with his cross-eye repositioned to stare straight at the onlooker. Officers were required to equip themselves. The newspapers were filled with advertisements; Burberry would clothe an officer in four days, at Moss Brothers uniforms could be obtained off the shelf. An infantry officer's sword cost £5, and decent binoculars £7/10/0. These items added up because Macmillan's annual salary was £136. By late autumn 1914 he was lodged at a seedy

?   hotel in Southend-on-sea, a dingy resort town on the North Sea, and was sprouting an officer's moustache, which shrouded his sensitive mouth for the rest of his life.

He did not enjoy the seaside. The young officers fumbled to find their way. They spent evenings poring over the drill book and moving matchsticks, trying to figure out how to 'form platoon from the right' and similar gyrations, manoeuvres devised to get seventeenth-century musketeers into a firing line. The military manuals they studied had only a few striking insights, for example: "Officers of Field Rank on entering balloons are not expected to wear spurs." During the days they tried to get their troops, usually in driving rain, to duplicate the movements of the matchsticks. Musketry instruction was given in a small public hall—pure theory, they had no rifles. The troops wore hotchpotches of civvies and newly issued parts of uniforms. Their colonel was a Boer War veteran, with white hair and moustache, ruddy cheeks, and aquiline nose, looking the image of the retired officer in a cartoon. He was kind, but seemed to have no idea of what to do with his inept officers and eager but clueless troops. Two sergeants torn out of retirement were equally vague—they satisfied themselves with profane shouting.

As Macmillan studied *Infantry Training 1914* surely his eye was caught by an item in the section of General Remarks for Platoon Commanders:

> (h) Being blood-thirsty, and for ever thinking how to kill the enemy, and to help his men to do so.

Unlike his hunting fellow officers, Macmillan had never gone out of his way to kill anything. Nonetheless, he must make himself into a first-class officer; his family would stomach nothing less. But how to do so from jumbles in the rain? He had always worked toward clear objectives, first set by his mother, who was devoted "but somewhat alarming and even forbidding," and then by his tutors and schoolmasters. Somehow he always felt "that, on the whole, the world was something alarming, and people of all ages were more likely to be troublesome than agreeable." This apprehension certainly applied to the men he was supposed to lead; most were older and came from a world he had never penetrated. He envied those novice officers who were accustomed to order about men from the lower classes, taking obedience and respect as their due. Most of the men from the lower orders that Macmillan had dealt with were school servants, 'scouts,' who were more NCOs than underlings. He had grown up in a house of women—his mother and her staff of nannies, maids and cooks. His father was so busy publishing that he was remote from his youngest son, a late addition—he was forty-one when Harold was born; his mother was thirty-eight. His two brothers were older, they were never his playmates. The intimate moment in the week was Sunday evening, when his father sat in his big armchair and read poetry to the family. He also questioned his physical equipment for soldiering. At age five he had been sent once a week to a neighbourhood gymnasium and dancing academy, where he discovered that he loathed performing in public, and on top of that did many of the exercises poorly; one manoeuvre performed with Indian clubs he found to be "particularly distressing and in which I showed an extreme lack of agility." It would take every bit of his moral fibre to bring himself up to snuff.

Gustav Mannerheim
September to December 1914

The Austro-Hungarians started the war by concentrating much of their Army against Serbia, which they expected to whip easily. The Serbian Army had been schooled in the Balkan wars, and the men were defending their homes. The Austro-Hungarian attack was bloodily repulsed, so they had to leave the Serbs for later, and transferred troops to Galicia to reinforce their abortive push against the Russians. Consequently, their second drive toward the Russian railhead was stronger and they pushed to within 30 kilometres. Mannerheim was allotted two additional regiments and a mounted battery and was ordered to turn the enemy's left flank. To get at the flank, he led his men across a river, where he found that he was about to be outflanked, so he pulled back and destroyed the bridges. Reinforced by an additional cavalry regiment, he shifted further west, forded the river, and established a bridgehead. The 91st Russian infantry regiment was brought across to the bridgehead. He led his command south, marching along miserable forest tracks through boggy thickets. At last he emerged into the open on top of a ridge. What he saw below was like the battlefield in a painting, with long lines of enemy infantry advancing northward; he was behind their flank. When his guns opened fire, the Austrians panicked, retreating headlong. The 91st Russian infantry took more than 1,000 prisoners. The next day a report jettisoned by a crashing enemy aviator revealed that they had routed most of an Austrian corps.

Operations against the Austro-Hungarian right had not gone nearly so well; there the Russians had been pushed back so far that their railway line was cut—but by this time the Russians had brought hundreds of thousands of troops into Poland. They counter-attacked at the beginning of September. In three weeks they had pushed the Austro-Hungarians out of the Duchy of Warsaw, across the border into Galicia, and along part of the front had pushed them entirely off the Polish plain into the foothills of the Carpathian Mountains. They threatened Krakow, the capital of Austro-Hungarian Poland, and invested the great fortress at Przemysl, with its garrison of 120,000 men. It was a handsome victory, which helped to sweeten the bitterness of Tannenberg. Some Austro-Hungarian divisions lost two-thirds of their effectives—one corps lost 80 per cent. Even higher per centages of professional officers were gone, irretrievably weakening their army. Overall the Austro-Hungarians lost 400,000 men—100,000 as prisoners—and 300 guns. Not that the Russians got off lightly: they had 250,000 fewer men and 100 fewer guns. They also lost a substantial per centage of their junior officers and NCOs. Mannerheim's brigade continued to distinguish itself, and he was accordingly rated one of the most effective young generals in the Russian Army.

Herbert Hoover
15 October through December 1914

Hoover was wrapping up the Citizen's Committee and had booked his passage home. It was then that an American mining engineer named Shaler came to him for advice. He started by filling Hoover in on the situation in Belgium. It had the highest population density in the world—almost the entire country had been taken by the Germans, hundreds of villages were destroyed and more than 1 million refugees were on the roads. The food situation was grim; little of the 1914 harvest had been gathered and food stocks had been requisitioned by the contending armies. In peace time they imported more than three quarters of the grain for their bread; now, with the British blockade, the Belgians faced starvation. To compound the problem, with factories closed and the entire country disrupted, many workers earned no money. It was much the same in the occupied regions of Northern France.

As the crisis developed, the Mayor of Brussels asked the German governor-general of Belgium to help. Happily he was a wise and humane old field marshal, Colmar von der Goltz, who in his free time wrote well-regarded histories. They agreed that food must be brought in from abroad, but saw the obvious sticking point. The field marshal obtained a public promise from his government that imported food would not be requisitioned, and they notified the warring and neutral governments of this pledge. The Mayor then turned to Belgium's richest citizen, Ernest Solvay, who formed a committee to try to find food for Brussels. He enlisted American bankers in Brussels then acquired the patronage of the American and the Spanish ambassadors. They sent Shaler, carrying $100,000, to London, where he easily bought grain. He then applied to the British Board of Trade for permission to export it. Permission was refused on the grounds that the Germans would seize the food—regardless of their pledge—and that the Germans were obligated to feed the people in the territories they occupied. Shaler came to Hoover for advice on how to break the logjam.

Hoover suggested that a permit might be given if the American ambassador in Britain acted as the consignor of the goods and shipped them to the American ambassador in Brussels. He took Shaler to thrash out the matter with Ambassador Page. Page could do nothing without approval from Washington; Hoover drafted a cable to the Secretary of State. After some back and forth the British Foreign Office agreed to the shipment—but it would be the last. Hoover told a visiting friend, the general manager of the Associated Press, that the American people should know about the plight of Belgium and of those Frenchmen under German occupation. The AP reporters picked up on the story, the cables hummed and articles appeared. Hoover knew the power of publicity.

Before Hoover was to sail, Ambassador Page asked him to the embassy to meet representatives sent by the Belgian Committee to discuss long-range solutions. One of them Hoover knew all too well—Francqui, his old foe in China. Hoover steeled himself for a renewal of hostilities. Page told them that he had the approval of the Secretary of State to use his good offices, but he could make no commitments in the name of the US. They sat discussing all of the problems—purchase, payment, shipping and, above all, blockade. Hoover said little. Abruptly, Francqui turned to stare Hoover full in the face; Hoover braced himself. Francqui spoke directly to him:

We must have leaders to organize and conduct this matter. They must be men of wide administrative experience and knowledge of the world. They must be neutral and must be Americans.
They must have the confidence of the American Ambassadors. We in Belgium and Northern
France are faced with life and death for millions of our people. You alone have the setting for this
job. If you will undertake it, I will either serve under you or retire from any connection with it.

They worked alongside one another for the rest of the war—occasionally duelling for
control.

Hoover could quickly evaluate the magnitude of the task—science was a great help. In
the decades before the war the number of calories a person needed per day and the caloric
content of foods had been measured. With his slide rule and knowing the populations of
Belgium and of occupied France, he could calculate how many tons would be needed each
day. He would have to find the food, raise the money to buy it, move it past navies at sea and
armies on land, distribute it fairly and collect payment from the recipients, while making
sure that the Germans got none of it. He asked for a day to consider. When they met the
next day he agreed, but only if he were given "absolute command, one could not conduct a
job like that by a knitting bee." He would not accept salary. There must be a committee in
Belgium to see to the distribution and payment collection, which Francqui must lead—they
all agreed. When Hoover left the meeting he called his broker to buy immediately ten million
bushels of wheat futures on the Chicago exchange; he was sure that prices would skyrocket
when news of the relief effort got out. He cancelled his steamer passage. He called together
his co-leaders in the Resident's Committee and proposed that they establish a Commission
for Relief in Belgium (CRB). They would have to form a partnership—not a corporation—
so they would assume unlimited financial responsibility. One banker withdrew; "in a few
moments" the rest agreed. Later that day the Spanish ambassadors in London and Brussels
became honorary chairs of the CRB. On their letterhead they listed American, Spanish and
Dutch diplomats—Danish, Norwegian and Swedish diplomats declined, fearing German
retaliation. On the sage advice of one of the CRB, who correctly prophesized that sooner or
later "some swine" would accuse them of pocketing money, Hoover asked a leading British
auditing firm to keep books and to countersign every check. They agreed if only the bare
salaries of their men on the job would be paid from the CRB's funds. The audited accounts
were published in full after the war. By telegraph, Belgian Relief Committees were set up in
major cities around the world.

They needed American volunteers to oversee operations in Belgium. After the
newspapers announced the formation of the CRB a young American Rhodes Scholar
at Oxford walked into Hoover's office to ask how he might help. He was sent to recruit
fellow scholars and within days, fifteen of the brightest young Americans were on their
way to Brussels. Some of them became Hoover's life-long friends. Within a week of the
founding of the CRB a shipment of 20,000 tons of food purchased in the Netherlands

arrived in Belgium by canal. The Belgians estimated that 80,000 tons of food would be needed every month, which would cost $4 or $5 million. The Governors of each of the American States were cabled and asked to gather donations of food, which the CRB would transport to Belgium. American railways pledged to haul the food without cost, while the City of New York promised to pay for the piers where the ships would be loaded. Hoover choreographed a sustained series of newspaper and magazine reports about the starving Belgians and the Germans resolve to do nothing to feed them, reinforcing the unfolding image of the brutal Hun.

The first shipload of food left London on 30 October for Rotterdam, where it was transhipped to Brussels by canal. Sir Edward Grey permitted it to pass through the blockade. The first ship direct from the US arrived in Rotterdam on 16 November. It was greeted by cheering crowds and unloaded by 500 volunteer stevedores. In early November Hoover and some of the other CRB members asked Grey for £500,000 per month for the relief effort; Grey promised to consult the Cabinet, but nothing came of it. During these hectic days, Hoover was also busy fending off other groups who wanted their fingers in Belgian relief. He understood that to get the food to the needy the CRB must be in total charge; otherwise the governments would play one organization off against the other—they must have a monopoly.

Hoover travelled to Belgium at the end of November. It was a tedious, disagreeable journey. At British customs he stood in line for four hours before being strip-searched. He sailed on the packet for Rotterdam and from there drove through the southern Netherlands to the barbed wire fence marking the border, where he was searched roughly by a German soldier. Once in Belgium he found a country that seemed in "suspended animation," a country in which no one smiled or laughed. A new German governor-general wanted to terminate the programme. Restrained by his predecessor's commitments, he imposed large indemnities on Belgian communities and used the money to buy food from Belgian farmers for German use. In the big picture it was not a large amount of victuals, but British intelligence knew what was going on. The CRB had to negotiate a passage with the German Navy for each incoming food ship so that it would not be torpedoed. When the cargos arrived in the Dutch ports they were searched by German agents. The bright young CRB administrators had to negotiate with each local German authority, each with its own regulations. Some of the German officers they had to work with were obliging and constructive; others were mulish and suspicious—hoping to catch Americans spying. When Hoover returned to the Netherlands he borrowed some flour from the Dutch government to keep supplies coming in while they waited for more shipments from overseas.

Things were no easier in England. Churchill and Kitchener were determined to destroy the programme—it was aid to the enemy. They demanded that Grey prohibit it, but he would not. Therefore, the Admiralty filed legal papers charging that Hoover was a spy and was personally corrupt. After prolonged private hearings by a King's Bench judge, Hoover was exonerated and praised. But this was all merely a sideshow compared to the desperate state of the CRB finances. They were feeding more than nine million people (Hoover always rounded it up to ten million), at a cost of $12 million per month. The funds of the Belgian Government in exile at Le Havre were exhausted—they had contributed $13 million to get the programme started. To keep the food pipeline stocked Hoover personally borrowed $12 million, far more money than he had. It was not quite the gamble it sounded, because if the worst came and he could not raise the money, the food could be sold to the British at a relatively small loss. The only way food could be kept in the pipeline was for the Allied governments to pay for it.

He would cross that bridge when he had to. To meet the immediate urgent need he had to borrow or buy 10,000 tons of Canadian flour stored in England. He pulled every string to meet with Prime Minister Asquith. Through a friend Hoover obtained an appointment for fifteen minutes. Asquith was unlikely to have been impressed by this engineer, a man of medium height, slender build, small hands and a slightly brutal face. His hair, parted near the middle, always seemed to be in a state approaching disorder. He may even have jingled the coins in his pockets—one of his little vices—as they settled down in the office in Number 10. He gave the impression of being a prim office type, not an international adventurer. Only those who knew him intimately realized how edgy he was beneath his bland exterior. Asquith was a distinct contrast; he, in the apt words of his wife Margot, "looked Cromwellian."

Asquith began, using the voice that had made him the master of the courtrooms and then of the Commons and with his customary brilliant choice of phrase. He was forthright, the case was simple and he delivered his opinion at the outset. The Germans as the occupying power were obliged to feed the Belgians, it was a "monstrous idea" that the British should shoulder their enemy's burden. Then it was Hoover's turn. Characteristically he did not look at his listener's face. He spoke calmly, in his high-pitched voice, in his curious monotone, without vocal emphasis, using simple language. His logic was forceful and he did not mince words. The British food blockade had created the emergency. The British declared loudly that they fought for the independence of Belgium, would they starve the people they had undertaken to save? Furthermore, the British helped their own cause by feeding Belgians, who were still battling the Germans—refusing to run their railroads, dig their coal, or operate factories of military value. If forced to choose between working for the Germans and watching their families starve, could there be any doubt of the outcome? He ended by assuring Asquith that one of the CRB's obligations was to let the Americans and the rest of the neutral world know what was going on and who was responsible.

Asquith responded with some heat that he was not accustomed to being addressed in such a manner. This seems an unexpectedly strong reaction to Hoover's presentation as recounted in his *Memoirs*. Other sources say that Hoover concluded his presentation by passing over a copy of a letter that was in the hands of the CRB press representative in New York, outlining the British responsibility and a cablegram he was prepared to send authorizing the release of this letter. It was Asquith's choice. This accounts adequately for the prime minister's pique—but he also knew when the other side had a better case. So he agreed to set up a series of meetings which resulted in the British loaning the Canadian flour to the CRB, a tiny stopgap, but it would keep the Belgians eating through Christmas. Hoover also played the American public opinion card on the Germans, demanding that they contribute 5 million marks a month—they did not.

We have a wonderful record of Asquith's life during these months from his letters to Venetia Stanley, often two every day. These letters are wonderful reading, filled with state secrets, romance, an occasional poem and vivid sketches of his political interactions. Disappointingly, in his letter that evening he did not mention Hoover. However—quite out of the blue—he wrote about how years before a notoriously combative bishop responded to an inquiry from a friend about why he had not locked horns with one antagonist: "Sir, because I do not wrestle with chimney sweeps." Perhaps this is how Asquith accounted to himself for the drubbing he had taken from Hoover.

Lou Hoover returned to London, leaving the boys in school in California. Bert and Lou spent Christmas in Brussels, oiling the administrative arm of the CRB in Belgium.

Adolf Hitler
December 1914

On 1 December the List regiment's strength was twenty-one officers and officer-candidates and 1,431 others. They were withdrawn from the line and replacements built their strength up to thirty-one officers, 1,528 men, and 180 horses. Ten days later day Hitler was awarded the Iron Cross, Second Class, on the recommendation of Adjutant Eichelsdorfer. The ceremony again showed him how military ritual moved the human heart; he wrote to his friends that it was "the happiest day of his life," asking Herr Popp to preserve the Munich newspaper announcing his award. He wanted to "save it as a keepsake if the Lord should spare my life." He also wrote a letter describing his experiences and successes to a friend in Munich, Assessor Ernst Hepp, who had bought one of his paintings in a café. When he talked with the young artist he was struck by his ardour and knowledge, and recommended Hitler's paintings to his friends. Hepp invited his young friend to his country house and occasionally gave him tickets to concerts and operas. They were united by shared prejudices:

> I often think of Munich and each one of us has only one wish: that he might soon get a chance to even scores with that crew, to get at them no matter what the cost, and that those

of us who are lucky enough to return to the Fatherland will find it a purer place, less riddled with foreign influences, so that the daily sacrifices and sufferings of hundreds of thousands of us and the torrent of blood that keeps flowing here day after day against an international world of enemies will not only help to smash Germany's foes outside but that our inner internationalism, too, will collapse. This would be much more than any gain in territory. Austria will fare as I have always said she will. Once more my sincerest thanks and respectful regards to your dear mother and wife.

Yours most sincerely,
Adolf Hitler.

His correspondence tapered off after this. The List became the home he had not had for years. He was sociable and liked to sit over meals chatting about this and that; even as Führer, he preferred to eat informally with his secretaries and personal staff. In the List, he was a charter member of a tightly knit group of chums, but they were not his intimates—he never shared his innermost thoughts. A factor in his later success was that he concealed so much from his followers, who spun their own fanciful interpretations of his aims and motives; hence, many had little idea of his underlying amoral savagery. His comrades in the List were rather fond of 'Adi,' though some felt that he lived in his own world. They laughed at his occasional rants about politics—going on and on about how the Kaiser was hamstrung by Marxists and Jews—and at his inability to perform satisfactorily the simplest bit of cooking. He rarely bothered to stand by at mail call; he acknowledged the occasional food package with a postcard, writing that he was well fed and did not need more. He would never accept a morsel from his comrade's parcels; instead he spent most of his pay on jam, which he adored. As the years went by he also became notable as the only one in his lot who continued to attend church parade. His closest comrades were his fellow runners—Privates Schmidt, Wimmer and Tiefenboch. All three survived the war and became a master builder, a coal merchant and a tram-car company employee respectively. Hitler kept in touch with these old comrades for the rest of his life. They laughed at his eccentricity in despising dirty jokes and how he turned his back from off-colour banter, telling them he had no time for that sort of thing, and wagging a finger as though he were their mother. It was not that he did not like to laugh. In his prodigious memory was a large file of jokes that he happily recounted at appropriate moments. When one was greeted with especially gratifying guffaws he would top it by comically crossing his startling blue eyes. He also lectured his fellows now and then on the evils of tobacco and alcohol—he swapped his share of such rations for sweets.

The List Regiment left the trenches on 23 December, coming out in a light snowfall. They spent Christmas Eve in Messines, billeted appropriately in a battered monastery, where the service was in the cloister, conducted jointly by Father Nobert and a Lutheran minister. They were back in the trenches for Christmas Day. The scene was macabre; No

Man's Land was littered with frozen, rigid corpses, but there were Christmas trees on the German parapets and colourful signs wishing their opponents "Happy Christmas" erected along parts of the British line. Socialization began with an exchange of songs between the two trenches, then a few brave souls climbed up onto their parapets; soon they met halfway to shake hands. They talked with one another as best they could, sang one another's songs, shared holiday drinks, and in a few places played football. The Germans rolled beer barrels out between the trenches while the British produced army rum and wine and spirits acquired for the holidays. Those with cameras snapped away, and opponents admired one another's family photographs. The List men were surprised that the English infantry they were facing—the 1st Norfolks and the 2nd Manchesters—ranged in age from fifteen to forty. Privates in the List were in their twenties. They found these mercenaries good fellows and improvised gifts were exchanged. An Englishman played his mouth-organ and men danced. Tunic buttons were prized souvenirs—a spike helmet was far better, but costly.

Hitler was at regimental headquarters. Some of his comrades invited him to go with them to see the festivities; he could ride up on his messenger's bicycle. They were snubbed in his loftiest manner; it was quite inappropriate in wartime and those who fraternized lacked a sense of honour. The generals on both sides agreed with him one hundred per cent. Staff officers were dispatched to stop the conviviality and to make certain that the war would resume the next day. In following years, stringent precautions were taken to avoid any repeat. For the troops, it had been educational: the Germans learned that the mercenaries they were fighting were not sub-human barbarians—from then on they were 'Tommy.' The List Regiment had another reason to appreciate the holidays of 1914: from 22 to 29 December they did not have a single casualty.

Charles de Gaulle
October to December 1914

In early October de Gaulle was transferred to a barracks in Cognac to complete his physiotherapy. Cognac was far more elegant than most towns in south-west France; he knew because his family kept a summer home there. For company there were other wounded officers from the 33rd. He was measured for new uniforms: the French were replacing their red trousers and dark coats by a grey-blue that blended with the landscape, and they no longer marked officers so clearly as targets. It was one lesson learned, but it was well into the next year before they realized how desperately they needed howitzers firing high explosives for trench warfare. He and his comrades lunched at the *l'Hotel de Londres*—*très bien*.

In mid-October he returned to the 33rd, now on the line in Champagne, 37 kilometres due south of Reims. At headquarters, he had an agreeable interview with the divisional commander. Then he saw how warfare had changed in a year. That night he was led up into the trenches, stopping to freeze whenever the enemy launched a star shell. In his platoon's trench the next morning, he was woken by the roar of guns. He lunched with his colonel. He was temporarily commanding the 7th Company—because of the heavy casualties professional officers had to fill more responsible positions; they were replaced by new officers chosen from able NCOs and reservists in the ranks. The men covered their blue and red uniforms with blue-grey overalls while waiting for new uniforms. In some places their front line was only 50 metres from a German trench while at others the separation was so great that they did not know where the German line was. The French trenches were just shallow ditches—de Gaulle always had to double over—at best protected by only a strand or two of barbed wire. The Germans, committed for the present to the defence, were carefully dug and wired in. It was not all bad; on some days, officers had both champagne and sauternes with their meal and his mother had sent him an electric lamp, toothpicks, cigars and letter paper.

In mid-November, they were relieved for rest. The village they were billeted in was shelled by a German heavy howitzer; de Gaulle had a close call which he did not enjoy. The officers were billeted in a once lovely country residence, now crumbling away with the shelling. He wrote to his father that they had learned that the Germans had massed so many combatants on two fronts by using their older reserves. De Gaulle had still not seen an active enemy—they were hidden behind periscopes and slits in the iron shields built into their parapet; he did, however, see two prisoners from the 65th Regiment of Landwehr. He dealt with constant minor bothers, like soldiers G., H. and M., who left their shelter without proper equipment and were punished with four days confinement during the relief period. De Gaulle was bored much of the time.

He stirred things up by having a sap dug toward the German line; he was ordered to stop and reprimanded. Then he was allocated two trench mortars. A fellow officer cautioned him not to fire because the German artillery would retaliate. He let off a few shots nonetheless—with the predicted tit for tat. There was no more mortar firing and he claimed that his major did not speak to him for a week, but this may be an exaggeration because a few days later he was appointed regimental adjutant, a nice step-up. He was glad for the post, but sorry to leave his company. While he commanded them they had twenty-seven casualties, regarded as about par. In mid-December the 33rd Regiment moved to the Chalons-sur-Marne sector, an exceptionally miserable place. The roads were torn up by the military traffic, it rained almost daily and the men, animals and shells churned the earth into mud—the nasty, chalky mud of Champagne, which sticks like glue. On 16 December Adjutant de Gaulle reported 3,199 effectives in the companies of the 33rd Regiment, plus 101 men in their train. They had ninety-six horses. When they were out of the line the men were instructed in judging distance and throwing grenades. On Christmas Day there was much cannon fire.

III

Dardanelles to Neuve Chapelle

Adolf Hitler
January and February 1915

On New Year's Eve, the List Regiment was back in Messines for a four-day rest, where they also received replacements from Munich—three officers, seventeen NCOs and 400 men. While there, Hitler repainted the officers' dining room in a requisitioned villa with a shade of blue he had chosen to set off properly a romantic painting hung on the wall. As he painted, he had his first real conversation with Lieutenant Wiedemann, the only professional officer in the regiment (who, after 1933, served for four years as the Führer's adjutant, but then resigned over differences about foreign policy). Wiedemann found him a serious person who had been through quite a lot in life. Some of his comrades thought Adi a bit too solicitous about officers' comfort—conduct they described with more vivid language. They returned to the trenches with twenty-eight officers and 1,766 men. On their first day back, three were killed and many wounded, and the next night they had additional casualties from their own artillery firing short. From 7 to 10 January the British fired something like 8,000 shells at them. Their food was adequate but monotonous; when they were in the line, the hot meal came up at 0300—almost invariably a thick soup with tough meat and noodles suspended in it. They also received half a loaf of rye bread, a bit of sausage and a pat of margarine for sustenance during the day. In the trenches a man could expect to get about two hours of uninterrupted sleep a night.

Then Hitler had a great piece of luck: he came by a deserter from the English, a little white mongrel dog with a floppy, black left ear—he named his dog 'Foxl' (little fox). Foxl was a smart little fellow, soon comfortable with German, and Hitler spent long hours teaching him tricks, which both delighted in showing off—Hitler called him a "proper circus dog." He always slept next to his master, who now had someone to love.

During the winter, the sick rate increased. In the 1st Battalion eighty men were down with typhus. When they came out of the line they had their first issue of hand grenades and were taught how to throw them. Hitler wrote to the Popps about the difficult conditions they lived in; he sometimes could not "even wash for 14 days at a time" but vowed that "Here we shall hang on until Hindenburg has softened Russia up." They were visited by King Ludwig III on 5 February, another chance to taste the stirring emotions of a military ceremonial. They were now part of the Sixth Army, which was commanded by the Bavarian Crown Prince Rupprecht. The regiment occupied relatively comfortable rest quarters in the Gallant factory in Comines.

Hitler carried an artist's pad in his pack and did drawings and watercolours of buildings that appealed to him. To entertain the comrades he also drew humorous sketches and caricatures on pasteboard cards. He read a great deal and wrote the occasional poem:

> And with all the skill he could muster he did his best for the child
> Washed it, nursed it, to demonstrate that we are not really wild …

He carried a battered volume of Schopenhauer throughout the war. He liked to quote the philosopher's allegation that the "Jew was the great master of lies" and agreed with his ideas on the power of will. He could read French and English, not fluently, but well enough to translate parts of captured newspapers and in later life to enjoy films without subtitles. He read every German newspaper he could lay his hands on and briefed his comrades on the news. He was a bitter critic of the Kaiser and the entire Hohenzollern clan, advocating elected monarchs—as was the practice in Germany in the Middle Ages—and idolizing Frederick the Great.

Mustapha Kemal
January to June 1915

Kemal was so frustrated in Sofia that he was about to return home without orders, if necessary to enlist as a private soldier. Before he could do so, Enver's deputy telegraphed an offer to command the 19th Division. When he reported at the War Office in Constantinople, he was surprised to be taken to see Enver, who had been campaigning in the east. Enver was pale and strained; he told Kemal: "We were beaten, that's all." Against Liman's advice he had tried to cut off the Russian army in the Caucasus Mountains. After they were beaten, he left the starving remains of his army to extract themselves as best they might from the snows and storms. He returned to the capital to prepare for new adventures.

Enver and Kemal had a wary relationship. Kemal had started secret political activities while he was at the staff college, forming a small group with fellow students. At graduation, he was arrested, imprisoned, beaten and then released with the proviso that he be stationed far away from Constantinople—he was sent to Damascus, which he hated. Eventually his friends arranged a transfer home to Salonica, where his small group merged into the

CUP. Early in 1908 the CUP leaders were invited to Constantinople for discussions, along with hints of rewards. One of those invited, Major Enver, ignored the invitation and took to the hills as a guerrilla, where he was soon joined by others. The CUP issued an ultimatum to the Sultan, demanding that he restore the Constitution, which he had suspended in favour of rule by fiat, otherwise they would march on Constantinople and place his brother on the throne. The Sultan sent more troops to Salonica, but their officers turned coat and joined the CUP. The Sultan capitulated. The victorious CUP leaders appeared on the balcony of Salonica's best hotel, acclaimed by a huge, happy crowd. In the photographs of the leaders Kemal appears as a vague shadow in the last row. Enver is prominent in the front row—handsome, debonair, commanding. Kemal felt that Enver was determined to keep him down. The other members of the ruling triumvirate were Djemal, an army colonel, and Talât, a former post-office clerk. The success of the CUP changed the appearance of the officers, which is illustrated in photographs of Kemal. Hitherto they had favoured moustaches that swept up over the cheeks, like a boar's tusks; now they cropped their moustaches short and confined them to the upper lip.

Enver congratulated Kemal on becoming commander of the 19th Division. However, when Kemal went to the General Staff Office to find where his division was stationed they knew nothing about it—it was not on their rolls. Perhaps the Third Army Corps on Gallipoli was planning to form that formation; he should pay them a visit. Before leaving, he was introduced to Liman. Kemal was greeted courteously and then asked whether the Bulgarians thought that the Germans would win—"No"—"And what is your opinion?"—"I think that the Bulgarians are right." Kemal left without another word. Like Kemal, Liman had a high self-regard, was a bit of a hothead, and having once formed an opinion was the devil to budge. While the Ottoman government was dithering about entering the war, he considered challenging both the war and naval ministers to duels, and recommended that the German mission be withdrawn. Kemal went to Gallipoli, where he found that the 19th Division *did* exist, and he set to seeing to their training. Gallipoli was a military backwater; the action was in the south, where a small force sent by Enver was attacking the Suez Canal. They were easily defeated.

The Allies launched a naval attack on the Dardanelles on ~~18 March~~ 19 Feb. A force of obsolete battleships—reinforced with the brand-new dreadnaught *Queen Elizabeth,* who was there to calibrate her guns—lay well off the entrance, lobbing shells at the helpless forts, which mounted only old-fashioned, short-range nineteenth-century guns. At 1400, the fleet moved in to 6 kilometres. Some of the smaller forts returned fire, but the larger ones, shrouded in smoke and dust, were silent. As the winter sun began to set the fleet pulled back. They had fired 139 shells. For the next five days the weather was filthy. Liman protested to Enver because the troops on Gallipoli and on the Asiatic shore had different commanders; Enver placed the troops on both sides into a new Fifth Army and gave Liman command. The new army worked feverishly. Admiral Usedom, a German expert on coastal defence, assembled

500 German experts on communications, artillery and mines. Many slipped through Bulgaria as commercial travellers, aided by a bit of bribery. The minefield in the narrows near the entrance to the strait was enlarged. Howitzers were hidden in the valleys to fire on ships entering the straits. Barbed wire was requisitioned from the farmers and troops and labourers set to fortifying the feasible landing beaches on the Peninsula and on the Asiatic shore. A few machine guns and crews from the German warships were positioned. The Ottomans planned to evacuate the government from Constantinople into Anatolia.

When the weather cleared, minesweepers fought their way against the current up toward the field in the narrows. Several were hit by howitzer shells and all turned back. The next attempt was at night, but five Ottoman searchlights fixed the trawlers in their beams while the howitzers fired at them. The ships tried to shoot the lights out, but failed. One trawler hit a mine and sank; some of the others never put out their sweeps. The mines whose cables were cut by the sweepers were propelled by the current toward the British covering ships—there was a wild scene as they made about and fled the straits. The next night they tried again with no better success. The defenders enlarged the minefield.

On the nights of the 13 and 14 March, sweepers, supported by one of the old battleships, destroyers and other small vessels, entered the straits, opposed by fire from four forts and forty–sixty mobile guns, and illuminated by four searchlights. They swept some of the mines, but within days they were replaced by ersatz mines made from torpedo heads taken from the supply on the *Goeben*. Ten British and French battleships started up the channel at 1045 on 18 March, firing on five forts and three batteries. One by one the forts stopped firing. At 1354 one of the French battleships spouted black smoke, turned keel up, and in three minutes slipped beneath the waves. Fifteen minutes later a British battleship hit a mine and listed to starboard; her ship's company was taken off before she sank. Another British battleship struck a mine but managed to keep afloat. Yet another British battleship hit a mine at 1805, took on a steep list, was abandoned and sank in deep water. Twenty minutes later a French battleship was hit; she was run aground on an island, her bows mauled by gunfire. Five battleships were out of action. The Ottomans cheered and celebrated, the government decided to stay in Constantinople.

Kemal watched the naval action from the high ridge running the length of the peninsula, which gave a marvellous view of the straits. Liman anticipated that if the enemy landed they would do so at the narrow neck of land that connects peninsula to mainland—that is what he would do in their shoes. He concentrated his reserves there, toward the northern end of the peninsula. There were so many possible landing beaches that he could afford to place only light forces at each. He kept some troops on the Asiatic shore, even though a landing seemed unlikely because there were no roads. He had 34,500 troops, eight machine guns and 283 cannon.

To visualize the topography of the Gallipoli Peninsula, take a sheet of paper, crumple it between your hands and then spread it out again. You will have a network of ridges and depressions, running about senselessly. Start at a point and try to work out a good route to the second or third elevation away, and you will see that you are working in a maze. Most of the hilly ground was covered with low-lying scrub and brush, with only an occasional stunted tree. The heath, myrtle and the thyme that gently scented the air were not a problem; the bushes with thorns the length of two finger joints, which tore at clothing, had to be avoided. There were only a few small towns along the strait and a few isolated cottages and shelters for goat herders. The problem was water. During the winter rainy seasons the runoff surged through the gullies, cutting them deeper—but for the rest of the year there was little rain, so the streams were dry. Goats and their herders were sustained by scattered springs near the tops of the ridges. Most of the beaches are narrow and shadowed by nearby heights. The peninsula runs roughly south to north.

On 25 April 1915, the British came ashore at Cape Hellas, at the southern tip of the peninsula, while the French landed on the Asiatic shore as a diversion. The Australians and New Zealanders landed further north on the Aegean side of the peninsula, about 24 kilometres from the tip—their beach became famous as Anzac Cove. It was not exactly where they planned to land; their small boats were driven off course by the current. On day one, they landed 15,000 men along 3 kilometres of shoreline. An unconvincing demonstration was made during the night against the narrow neck that connects the peninsula to the mainland. One man swam to shore and fired rockets (in World War II he was a New Zealand field marshal).

The landing at Anzac was almost unopposed, and soon the men were swarming up the steep cliffs that enclose the beach, heading toward the crest of the highest ridge that is the spine of the peninsula. Once there they would look down on the narrows and the Ottoman forts and artillery positions. To get there they must climb over a series of smaller ridges. When the first wave reached the crest of the headland above the beach, they encountered the 27th Regiment, who were sheltering behind the crest from view of the fire-control officers on the British ships. When the two lines met there was a sharp fight. The outnumbered Turks gradually backtracked—the Anzacs pushed metre by metre toward the central ridge.

The 19th division was stationed near the neck of the peninsula, more than 4 kilometres away from Anzac Beach; they were alerted in the morning by the thunder of the bombardment. Kemal sent a cavalry squadron toward the sound of the explosions to scout. They reported that the enemy had landed and that a small force was heading inland. At 0630, he received a message from the commander of the division nearest to the landing, requesting a battalion to join in the defence. Kemal was sure that a battalion was too few; however, his orders were to stay in place until ordered to move by corps. This was no time to stick to the book. One of his regiments, the 57th, was formed up in ranks, ready to start on a training exercise. He ordered them and a battery of mountain guns to set off for the heights just inland from the beach; his other two regiments were to follow as soon as possible. He dictated a message to his corps commander reporting what he had done. He then mounted, and headed off with his aide-de-camp, orderly officer and chief medical officer, threading their way through the scrub and convoluted, rocky valleys toward the sound of the guns, followed by the 57th Regiment. When they reached the crest of the highest ridge on the peninsula Kemal looked toward the Aegean—there were scores of warships offshore, and small boats loaded with troops were heading in. The beach itself was hidden by the heights along the shoreline. He did not see any enemy infantry. When the 57th arrived, he ordered them to take a ten-minute rest in an undulation out of sight of the sea while he reconnoitred. He started to ride toward the beach, with his small group of officers and the commander of his battery of mountain guns, but the ground was so broken that they soon dismounted and went ahead on foot.

Ottoman troops came running toward him. He waved them down and shouted, "Why are you running away?"—"Sir, the enemy." They pointed back toward a crest nearer to the shore. Sure enough a skirmishing line was just emerging into view. They were already closer to him than he was to his own troops; all he had in hand were the fugitives. If the enemy took the crest, it would all be over. "You cannot run away from the enemy"—"We have no ammunition"—"If you haven't got any ammunition, you have your bayonets." He made them fix bayonets, formed them into an extended line and then ordered them to lie down, faces toward the enemy. The Australians saw them, thought they were about to fire and hit the dirt also. One of them remembered firing at a lone officer standing near a tree. The officers, with their cylindrical grey astrakhan hats—the kalpak—were easy to distinguish from the men, with their greyish-khaki cloth helmets with the ends of the fabric tailing down to shield their necks. Almost surely the Australian's target was Kemal—he missed. Kemal sent his orderly with orders for the 57th Regiment and the battery to join them.

The 57th came up at the double. The sixty men in the foremost Australian line were now outnumbered, but eight battalions were coming up in support. Because of the choppy ground, they could not form a line for the attack, so they came on as small groups. As each group came into view, Ottoman fire forced them to ground and into a fire-fight. When his mountain battery arrived, Kemal showed them the ridge where he wanted them and helped to manhandle the guns up the steep slope. They started to spatter shrapnel on the Australians, who had no cover other than swells in the ground. The naval guns could not reply, because they had no idea where their own men were. At 0932 Kemal sent a message to his corps commander telling him they had checked the enemy advance inland and that he was about to attack them; they were in regimental strength and about 600 metres away. Kemal ordered the 57th to advance. He was a master of his men's psychology:

> I don't order you to attack, I order you to die. In the time which passes before we die other troops and commanders can take our places.

He also sent a cavalry officer to the Ottoman regimental commander on his left, suggesting they also charge. He judged that the enemy was in a poor position because they were spread along a long front, and cut into small groups by the many small valleys. His quick-firing mountain battery was now hitting the beach, delaying the landings that were still underway. Kemal showed the way by running from point to point along his line, shouting orders and encouragement. The Ottomans attacked, and so did the Australians—they met midway in mindless tumult.

Kemal decided that the rest of his division should be placed further to the right when they came up, because new landings had been reported there. So he rode back to meet them on their march and to give the necessary instructions. Along the way he was hailed by the staff of the corps commander, so he detoured to meet with them. He told the corps commander of the news of the latest landing and summarized his own plans. They were approved. Kemal led his arriving regiment to their position, and ordered them forward toward the beaches. He urged his division, along with the regiment on their left, forward. After sunset the British destroyers came close inshore and turned on their searchlights, playing them over the top of the cliffs so the Anzacs could see anyone coming at them. Finally the Ottomans were too exhausted to continue. They had lost more than 2,000 men on the first day. In places the spring flowers—tulips, thyme, cornflowers and poppies—were splattered with scarlet. Kemal wrote about the 57th:

> a famous regiment this, because it was completely wiped out.

At the end of the day, when the rain began, Kemal's men held the crest of the main ridges on the peninsula. If the high-level planners in London—with their casual contempt for Turks—had seen them in action, they would have had cold shivers.

That evening, two of the senior commanders on Anzac proposed an immediate pullout. The British commander, Sir Ian Hamilton, ruled out re-embarkation, which would take at least two days, and directed them to dig in. This was easier to order than to do—their light tools were inadequate for rocky slopes. On the other side, the Ottomans had failed also—they had not driven the invaders into the sea.

During the night, Kemal "could not get any clear information from anywhere." Toward dawn, he rode the length of his front, to see how his survivors were faring. He selected a high point for his command post, and ordered a telephone exchange set up just beneath it; this became famous as the *Kemalyeri*. In the morning, the British attacked, using fresh troops that had been landed during the night. The Ottomans were outnumbered, so Kemal kept enough distance between attackers and defenders so that there was no possibility of a surprise bayonet attack:

... It was an important day, won thanks to the firmness and tenacity of our troops and the bravery and determination of our officers and commanders.

In retrospect, Kemal thought it the hardest day of the war.

The history books used by Turkish schoolchildren teach that Kemal's initiative, strategic insight and heroism on 19 April saved the Dardanelles and their country. This is close to the truth. An extraordinary man, with just the right mix of bravery, determination, insight and willingness to contravene authority could step up to make history. He did not do it alone. Liman acted promptly when the landings began; he was not fooled by the demonstration on the neck and skilfully shifted troops to where they were needed. Not worrying about scrambling units, he sent along those nearest and set up ad hoc command structures to control them. Early in the day, he learned that the enemy landings on the tip of the peninsula had not succeeded in getting more than toeholds. Some faced determined resistance from well-prepared positions; others landed easily at unprotected beaches, but their commanders lacked initiative and drive, so they sat until enemy troops sealed them along the coast, well short of dominating heights. His weak point was the unfortified beaches at Anzac. If the men landed there could fight up to the crest of the highest ridgeline, it would be the end—directed naval gunfire would do the rest.

Two days later Kemal was reinforced with two additional regiments, and he decided to attack at 0800. In some places the British began to withdraw rapidly as the Ottomans pressed toward them. By afternoon, along one part of the front the enemy had retreated to "the last rifle trenches, left their rifles and, almost as a body, came out in front of their trenches, and waving hats, white handkerchiefs and flags sought to give themselves up." Kemal and his staff watched from the Kemalyeri. But other enemy units stood firm on the heights above the beaches. When darkness fell, Kemal's field officers reported the men too tired to go on, so he ordered them to dig in along their new lines.

From the outset, Kemal was awed by his men: "Their strength is their unquenchable spirit. It is an astonishing thing to see." He took full advantage of them. He attacked, convinced that eventually he would achieve a decisive result; but their attacks were scattered, piecemeal and uncoordinated. Naval gunfire blasted his positions as the men assembled for an attack. As they attacked to the sound of their bugles and drums they chanted "Allah, Allah." Those who could read died with Koran in hand; those who could not recited the Martyr's Prayer. When the Anzacs attacked they sang *Australia will be there* and *Tipperary*. Kemal could not find weak points in the Anzac line; the attackers died, but he kept on attacking.

The British kept landing men. On 26 April, nine transports were putting men on the shore, and eight others were on the horizon. The swelling Anzac line was 200–300 metres from the Ottomans. Kemal asked for enough troops to drive them all into the sea before they became too strong to budge. He was given the numbers he asked for, but the ground was so tangled that his attacks were ineffective. Kemal's idea remained fixed:

> I am of the wholehearted opinion that we must finally drive the enemy opposing us into the sea if it means the death of us all. Our position compared to that of the enemy is not weak. The enemy's morale has been completely broken. He is ceaselessly digging to find himself a refuge.

Neither side would give way; they stood nose to nose. At the end of April, Enver Pasha sent four more divisions and forty-eight machine guns from the fleet—many with German crews—as reinforcements.

On 1 May at 0500, there was a brief barrage from the Ottoman mountain guns and then the infantry rose to advance. The opposing lines were too close for the naval guns to fire at No Man's Land without killing their own; instead, they plastered the Ottoman rear area. British rifles and machine guns kept the attackers at bay. Kemal watched from the *Kemalyeri*, certain that, if pushed hard enough, they would succeed. At 1600, he ordered a bayonet attack. Again the Ottoman infantry hauled themselves out of their trenches and started forward in short rushes. In a few places they managed to get into the enemy trenches, but in most places they took what cover they could get short of their objectives. Kemal brought up his reinforcements, convinced that after dark they could gain the 20–50 metres between the Ottoman firing line and the enemy trenches. They attacked again at midnight, but did not succeed anywhere. At dawn he ordered them to stop attacking and to start digging. He encouraged his exhausted men:

> All soldiers fighting here with me must realize that to carry out completely the honourable duty entrusted to us there must not be one step toward the rear. Let me remind you all that your desire to rest … may lead to our whole nation being so deprived until eternity.

By 4 May, there were about 14,000 Ottoman casualties on the Anzac front.

On the morning of 18 May, there was an eerie lull in the firing of the Ottoman howitzers and guns. British fliers reported troops massing behind the enemy lines. The storm broke at 1700, a massive bombardment; then, as the sun set, all was quiet again. The waves were heard crashing onto the beach. At 2335, the moon went down. Heavy rifle fire poured from the Ottoman trenches. The Anzacs braced themselves, but it fell quiet again. At 0305, the first attacking wave jumped out of their trenches and started forward. This time it was Liman's operation. He had brought up the 2nd Infantry Division and had moved the 3rd Division moved over from the Asiatic side, assembling 42,000 men against the 17,000 men on the bridgehead. The first wave was shot down in No Man's Land. A second wave jumped out of the Ottoman trenches—destroyed. After the first two waves, the Anzacs held their fire to give the enemy officers time to get their men out of the trench and in line to attack. Then they shot them down. The attacks continued until midday. By that time, 5,000 dead and wounded Ottomans were lying between the lines, while a similar number were back in the Ottoman trenches.

The commanders on both sides worried about the health hazards posed by the piles of corpses in No Man's Land. Hamilton authorized throwing notes into the Ottoman lines stating that a request for an armistice would be granted. An Australian colonel had a Red Cross flag broken out on their parapet, hoping to send litter-bearers out to bring in the wounded. In seconds, the flagstaff was shattered by a rifle bullet. An Ottoman officer came sprinting over, apologized, ran back to his line, and moments later Red Crescent flags appeared. A party of Ottoman officers, including Kemal, came forward under a white flag. They were blindfolded, goose-stepped over non-existent barbed wire entanglements, and brought to meet General Birdwood, the commander on Anzac. Speaking French, they agreed to a nine-hour truce on the following day.

The next day the enemies mingled in No Man's Land, chatting as best they could, while breathing though handkerchiefs soaked in creosote, and swapping unit patches and buttons as souvenirs. A British officer pointed out a Turk who was taking advantage of the armistice to repair his loophole; an Ottoman officer belted the offender with a cane. The day changed British attitudes profoundly. They had thought that they were there to fight cruel, fanatical, vile barbarians. Ideas had begun to change as they battled; mingling during the truce tipped the scale completely. From then on, to the British they were "Johnny Turk," a "true sportsman," brave, decent, cheerful chaps. It worked the other way as well. As they threw bombs at one another, they also fired off friendly jibes.

Benito Mussolini
January to May 1915

On 6 January, *Il Popolo* published a draft constitution for a group known as the *Fasci d'azione revolutionaria*. It was to be a "free association of subversives from all schools and political points of view," although the newspaper maintained a distinctly republican slant. Intervention, they argued, was the path toward social revolution. By mid-March, the paper still had only 1,600 subscribers. Mussolini tried to whip up interest with violent attacks on Parliament: "the shooting, I say <u>shooting</u> in the back of some dozen deputies." A political opponent was to get "five bullets in the stomach."

Mussolini allied himself with an organization of interventionists who called themselves *Fasci*, after the bundles of sticks carried in ancient Rome to illustrate the moral that a stick is easily broken while a bundle is not. Soon he was their leader. They demonstrated for war, organizing marches through the city centres of thousands of young men linked arm in arm. Mussolini would speak from his newspaper's front window. He was an effective orator, a square-jawed fellow with a clipped moustache and a receding hairline that left him with a widow's peak. In repose, he looked thoughtful and academic, but when he spoke, his face contorted, his eyes flashed and his jaw thrust forward. He had a loud metallic voice and he used repetition and short, punchy phrases to work his audience's emotions to the full. He seemed completely spontaneous, his passionate feelings bubbling out almost beyond control. In fact, every nuance and gesture was rehearsed carefully. At first, the marchers were middle-class youths and college students, but as the campaign progressed, they were joined by workers—all eager to shed their blood for greater Italy. At the time, Mussolini made much of the blood-chilling, vivid accounts, provided by the Allies, of German atrocities in Belgium (after the war, when he became aware of the exaggerations, he took the unusual step of apologizing in the Italian Senate for passing them on as truth). He spoke all over the country. When he overstepped the boundaries in a speech in Rome, he was arrested and sentenced to a few days in jail. After he was released he wounded an opponent in a duel with swords; it was only one of his duels in those years. He kept himself fit by practicing fencing, and also entertained himself with horse riding and driving a fast motor car, conserving some energy for his wife, two mistresses and an occasional fling.

As the *Fasci* carried on their fight in the streets, the Italian Government shopped secretly for the best deal. Parliament was sent home on recess so they would not interfere with the bargaining. The Germans were strongly for meeting almost all of the demands, but the Austro-Hungarians held firm—they would only hand over areas with substantial Italian populations. Relations between the two allies never recovered from this impasse. The Allies were far more open-handed—they could afford to be, giving away other's property. The Italians were promised the Trentino (the South Tyrol up to the Brenner Pass), Trieste (the formerly Venetian cities along the east coast of the Adriatic), Rhodes and the Dodecanese Islands, and Kenya. If Turkey was split up, they were to have a province. The British would loan at least £50m and they promised naval support in the Adriatic, with destroyers, cruisers and even a squadron of old battleships. The Russians would keep at least 500,000 men battering the Austro-Hungarians in Galicia. The terms were written into the secret Treaty of London, signed on 26 April. The public were not told that the Italians were to become sovereign over 600,000 Slavs, 230,000 Germans plus large numbers of Turks, Albanians and Africans, still to be counted.

While the deal remained secret, the struggle in the streets went on. On 11 April, hundreds of thousands, many of them socialists, defied a Government ban to demonstrate for peace in Rome, Milan, Ancona, Florence, Naples, Turin and smaller places. On 5 May, there was a great interventionist rally in Rome, featuring survivors from Garibaldi's Thousand. The principal speaker was the writer Gabriele D'Annunzio. The following week Mussolini addressed a huge rally in Milan, speaking from a window in the *Il Popolo* office. On 16 May there was a general strike, which the Army suppressed. The Italian Government declared war on Austria-Hungary on 24 May, 1915. The vote in the Chamber was 407 to 74; the Senate was almost unanimous. They did not declare war on Germany until August 1916.

Intervention was a triumph for Mussolini. Despite his success, expulsion from the Socialist Party surely must have been hard to swallow—he had been born a socialist. His father named him after Benito Juarez, the Mexican political leader who liberated his country from the French, and his two middle names celebrated Italian socialists. He was born in a hamlet about 70 kilometres to the southwest of Ravenna. His father worked as a smith, later as an innkeeper, but his mother, Rosa, was of a different stripe. She had a diploma to teach in an elementary school and was known locally for her piety. To the young boy Mussolini, "to displease her was my only fear." As he entered his teens, his mother sent him to a normal school for six years' training as a teacher. He finished the school but after teaching for one year, he "had the urge to escape." At nineteen, he went to Switzerland, with a medallion of a bust of Karl Marx as his talisman. He worked as a labourer and as a mason, sometimes sleeping rough. He had some help from home, and later probably exaggerated how often he worked in menial jobs. "Above all, I threw myself headforemost into politics." He studied, made speeches, wrote articles for socialist newspapers, was picked up by the police, spent a few days in various jails and was expelled from two Cantons. Part of the time, he had the company of his younger brother and best friend, Arnaldo, who had graduated from an agricultural college. Both studied to improve their French and German; Benito worked with a mistress on a translation from the German. Some years later the mistress, stung by his apostasy from socialism, wrote:

> He thought of himself as an 'intellectual,' a leader, and the contrast between this conception of himself and the humilities of his daily life had induced him to an exaggerated self-pity and sense of personal injustice.

In Switzerland in 1904 he published his first book, *L'uomo e la divinità*. The first sentence is: "God does not exist."

In April 1904, he was tried in absentia by an Italian court martial and sentenced to one year in prison for not reporting for military service. It seemed as though he must be an exile for life, so he considered emigrating to the US, but when the Italian Government issued an amnesty to deserters, he returned home. In 1905, he joined the 10th Bersaglieri regiment; his mother died that spring. He was deeply touched by a letter of condolence from his company commander, and in his reply he wrote that he hoped to perform "deeds worthy of the heroes who had cemented with their blood the unity of the motherland." After twenty-one months in the army, he became a village teacher and again wrote for the socialist cause. In the summer of 1908 he supported a strike of workers from a threshing-machine factory, leading a demonstration by 7,000 men. The troops shooed them all out

THE LESSONS OF WAR

of the town. A few days later the factory owner bicycled past Mussolini, who was carrying a walking stick—Mussolini called out, "I'll give you a good belting." He was convicted for threatening and sentenced to three months in prison, but was freed because he had been in jail for twelve days while awaiting trial.

This incident elicited a job as the editor of the socialist weekly newspaper, *L'Avvenire del Lavoratore*, which was published in Trent. Trent was the principal city of the Trentino, the region between the old Venetian northern border and the crest of the Alps that was still part of Austria-Hungary. Before long, Mussolini was sentenced to three days or thirty crowns for slandering the morals of a priest. Soon after, he was convicted of slandering three priests by charging them with sexual misconduct, and was later sentenced again for calling a priest "a dog with hydrophobia." The Austrian administration tired of him; in September 1909, he was taken to the frontier and handed over to the Italian police.

His next project was a novel, *Claudia Particella, the Cardinal's Mistress*. The heroine of this bodice-ripper is an ambitious courtesan who plies her wiles to rise in the hierarchy until she is poisoned by a rejected lover. He also wrote a more measured work on how a socialist viewed the Trentino, in which he rejected calls for Italy to go to war to take the disputed ground. A man of romantic disposition, he later chronicled in his autobiography (apparently largely written by brother Arnaldo) at least some of his love affairs, though surnames were abbreviated to the first letter. Now an attractive sixteen-year-old blonde, Rachele Guide, came to live with him. They did not wed because of their socialist principles, but they had a daughter together. He became editor of the socialist paper in Forli. Among his memorable phrases of the time is:

The national flag is for us a sieve to be filled with manure.

His father died in 1910; according to Benito the cause was syphilis and alcoholism, which he regarded as attributes of a real man, though for most of his life he scarcely touched alcohol himself.

As he read political theory, he became enchanted with the ideas of the French syndicalist Sorel, who argued that the mob must be led by the elite. The leaders were not to be elected; they would simply take over because they knew their place—Mussolini felt that this described himself perfectly. When Italy went to war to take Libya from the Turks, the socialists tried to fan opposition, but the fire would not burn. Mussolini was charged with inciting to violence. He told the court, "If you find me not guilty I will be pleased. If you find me guilty, I will be honoured." Honoured he was, the sentence was one year in prison; it was reduced on appeal, and in the end he served five and a half months. He was elected to the National Executive Committee of the Italian Socialist Party in 1912, and was also appointed editor of *Avanti!*—accepting only half the salary his predecessor required, he doubled its circulation in a year. He moved to Milan, leaving his wife and daughter in the village. He trumpeted the party's slogan: "Not one man, not one penny, for imperialist war." Two years later he discarded socialism for imperialist war. At the meeting where he was expelled from the Socialist party, they hissed him; he told them, "You hate me because you still love me."

Harold Macmillan
January to August 1915

Gradually Macmillan lost heart; while great victories were won in France—the Marne and Ypres—they were fumbling about at a dismal seashore. There was nothing for it; he called in the heavy weapons. He wrote to his mother, with her extensive social network. Shortly thereafter, he was summoned to London for an interview at the Guards Barracks in Buckingham Gate, just across from the Palace—"The smart saluting of the sentry and of the sergeant put me to shame." The lieutenant colonel who interviewed him was kindly and in March 1915 Macmillan was ordered to join the Reserve Battalion of the Grenadier Guards in London at Chelsea Barracks. He justified his special privilege because all "I sought was to get myself killed or wounded as soon as possible."

It was a brave new world. The men were in smart, sharply-creased uniforms; their brass glittered, their boots smashed the ground. He arrived in his Royal Rifle uniform—and was immediately given the address of a tailor who could provide properly and instructed that while he waited for correct attire he was to appear in "plain clothes"—bowler hat, blue suit and a stick. A kindly major instructed the small cadre of new officers in proper behaviour and regimental traditions. One of the regimental idiosyncrasies was that for them, the rank of lance corporal, with one chevron on the sleeve, simply did not exist, though some men wore the insignia. The rules of etiquette included never carrying a suitcase or a parcel, not reversing when waltzing and not smoking Virginia cigarettes—only Turkish. An officer must not let his fellows down; if he did so he was "called to cart," meaning that he was ostracized. Macmillan conformed to the letter. He stayed at the family home; in London Guards officers always lived on their own. In peacetime, officers were required to attend Orders at 1000—they could wear civilian dress. After a glass of port in the mess at noon, they were free for the rest of the day for sport, boating and lounging. In the summer it was a bit more arduous, since there were the ceremonial duties at the Palace and a few weeks of musketry and divisional exercises; but they had four weeks leave per year. In wartime, they had a somewhat longer day.

When the new officers were taken by the drill sergeant to a distant part of the square to learn the rudiments of their new profession, Macmillan assumed that his experience with matches gave him a distinct advantage—not so. The drill sergeant soon let him know, politely but firmly, that he could not right or left turn properly, let alone salute. Once these rudimentary defects were remedied the student officers took turns commanding the group. Now Macmillan found that he had been far too casual with the orders he had shouted to his trainee riflemen. Even such simple commands as "halt" or "forward" when given after marking time had to be given at a precise instant in the cadence, else all hell would break loose. Even the timing must be adjusted to the distance between the officer and the marching ranks. When these intricacies were mastered, the new officers moved on to the business of actually drilling troops, with an instructor close on hand to whisper advice and criticism. Before this big event, Macmillan—as always—had an attack of nerves, just like before an examination or a debate in the Oxford Union. He dealt with nerves by finding a place to be alone where he braced himself for what was to come. It worked. At the Union, the University newspaper reported his "brilliant maiden speech" and wrote:

> His phraseology was wonderful and except for a tendency to become inaudible at the end of his sentences his delivery was almost perfect.

Once comfortable on the drill field he delighted in giving orders to guardsmen, trained to execute them with the precision of a ballet corps. The simultaneous slaps of hands on rifles—real rifles—at the appropriate instants and the crash of boots when they came to a halt was a joy. If a man made a mistake, which was rare, an NCO would take on the chore of humiliating the offender with inventive obscenities and threats delivered at full volume. Years later, when he was prime minister, he delighted to watch from the back windows of Number 10, which overlook Horse Guards' Parade, the rehearsals before the Queen's Birthday celebration.

The men in the Grenadier Guards were regular soldiers who had learned how to treat a junior officer; there was none of the awkwardness about roles he suffered with the untutored recruits in the rifles. The Guards NCOs could make junior officers look as though they knew what they were doing. The Reserve Battalion was made up of new recruits, men transferred into the Guards and men returning from hospital. As needed they were sent as replacements to one of the three active battalions in France. In July 1915, the Grenadier Guards established a 4th Battalion to become part of a new Guards Division of elite shock troops. Macmillan was transferred to the new battalion, which trained at a camp a few miles up the Thames from Windsor, as a platoon leader. It was like a perpetual garden party, with a stream of friends and family out from London and entertainments of all types provided by the local landowners.

After a month, the 4th Battalion entrained to Southampton docks and marched up the gangplank onto the cross-channel steamer. The officers saw to their men and then headed to the saloon for their meal. They found tables fitted out with snowy linen, china plates, silver cutlery and crystal glasses. Each officer was led to his place by Charles, the *maître d'Hôtel* of the Ritz. The waiters had familiar faces—they were also from the Ritz.

They served an exquisite list of wines accompanied by a magnificent dinner, all courtesy of a company commander whose generosity matched his wealth. The officers were in splendid form when they disembarked at Le Havre; the battalion marched through the town to the depot accompanied by the cheers of the citizens. They proceeded to a village two kilometres southeast of St Omer. Macmillan and five other officers from his company were billeted comfortably in the home of a French *bourgeois*. Their first priority was to prepare the 4th Battalion for an inspection by their brigade commander—he was satisfied. The other Guards formations for the new division were in the vicinity, and after a month they all assembled for an inspection by the division commander, Lord Cavan:

> ... the time passed pleasantly enough, in fine weather, some training, a little bridge, and much chaff.

Charles de Gaulle
January to July 1915

In de Gaulle's 33rd Regiment, five officers and 300 men were sick on 9 January. On the same day their artillery fired a fierce six-minute bombardment of the intensity known as 'drumfire,' because you could not make out the individual explosions. Then an infantry company attacked, but the men who reached the enemy trenches were driven back by fire from the flanks. It was one of a series of local attacks along the front in Champagne. According to de Gaulle the attacks were made on poorly chosen ground where they skidded in the mud and stumbled through a fascine of French corpses. Coordination was poor because the telephone network was inadequate. By now infantrymen were bitterly aware of the long odds against advancing 10 metres into No Man's Land without injury or death. The French commander, General Joseph Joffre, the victor on the Marne, remained serene when an offensive was shattered, confident that they could make things better the next time. De Gaulle was mentioned in dispatches and promoted to temporary Captain, but typically, for the men of the time, does not tell us why he was honoured.

In February, the 33rd Regiment prepared to attack again, as soon as the ground dried a bit. De Gaulle showered the company officers with memoranda, directing them to instruct their men that losses were "... of small importance, as long as the result is achieved." They improved their trenches so that they would be better for jumping off, and their supply depots were well stocked. Adjutant de Gaulle wrote detailed attack instructions for each of the battalions and listed the material each man should carry, including 200 cartridges, an empty sandbag and an entrenching tool. Each company was issued a periscope. Saps were dug out into No Man's Land so that the attackers would have less distance to run forward above ground. Mines were dug beneath the German front line trench.

The French attack began on Shrove Tuesday along a 10 kilometre front, just to the right of the 33rd Regiment's position. Three corps attacked two German reserve divisions; they shelled the German front line trenches for two hours with 600 guns firing 200,000 shells. The shrapnel scarcely scarred the German trenches, but parts were blown away by exploding mines. The French infantry overran these blasted areas; in some places they penetrated 500–800 metres, but the men in these bulges were hit by heavy small arms' fire and shrapnel from their flanks. Elsewhere the first wave was pinned down on the open plain without shelter. Fresh troops were supposed to pass through them, but the second wave did not get to the front because there were too few communication trenches and they were too narrow—they were gridlocked. It took hours for reinforcements or supplies of ammunition, grenades and sand bags to reach the attack line, or for the wounded to be evacuated and for runners to bring messages through. The artillery observers in the French front line could not see how far their infantry had progressed, so all they could do was to fire blindly on the German rear. German counter-attacks recovered most trenches lost to the mine explosions and the Germans rushed up reserves on the first-rate railways running behind this part of the front—another French failure.

Undaunted, Joffre expanded his front of attack to the west, so the 33rd Regiment entered the battle. The attackers climbed out of their trench, started across No Man's Land and were driven back short of the German wire. After regrouping, they tried at another point a few hours later. As soon as German fliers or kite balloon observers saw the enemy trench filling with the next wave of attackers, their artillery plastered them—they had heavy losses even before facing the machine guns. The fighting continued long into the night and then swelled up again at dawn. In two days the regiment lost eighteen officers and 750 men. French prisoners told their captors that Joffre was confident that they would break the German line in two days, but as de Gaulle wrote, "it was a sad experience." A shell splinter ripped through de Gaulle's left hand. It was bandaged and he kept at work, but it became infected, red lines ran up his arm, his hand was paralyzed and he had a high fever. After suffering for several weeks, he was evacuated to the hospital at Le Mont-Dore, 26 kilometres southwest of Clermont-Ferrand in central France, where they saved his arm. As he recovered, he wrote a satirical piece deprecating the pluck of the French gunners.

Adolf Hitler
March to May 1915

The List Regiment came out of the line on the night of 8 March. The next morning, reveille was not sounded; they were permitted to sleep as late as they pleased. The regiment was assigned to army reserve and they looked forward to an easy time. By early afternoon, the gramophones were playing and most of the men were sitting about chatting, many with sewing kits out stitching rent clothing. At 1500 the buglers sounded the alarm.

Early that morning the French had attacked north of Arras, but most never reached the German front line. The only success was a carefully prepared attack by the corps commanded by General Pétain. Two of his divisions broke through the German lines. They advanced 4 kilometres on an 11-kilometres front; at some points they were over the crest of Vimy Ridge. Prince Rupprecht at his headquarters in Lille prepared to pull back his entire line. However, the attackers on either side of Pétain were stymied, so the Germans counter-attacked the open flanks. Pétain needed reinforcements, but his commander, General Ferdinand Foch, had only one brigade in reserve and it was too far back to intervene effectively.

The British attacked near Neuve Chapelle with their 7th and 8th Divisions and the Merrut Division of the Indian Army. Their objective was the Aubers Ridge—only 15 metres high—less than two kilometres behind the German front. The German trenches were in excellent condition because the Lille electrical grid powered pumps that kept them dry. They were building a second defensive position, 1 kilometre behind the first, but it was unfinished. The first British objective was the village of Neuve Chapelle. They unleashed a 35-minute barrage by 342 guns, which fired more shells than the total used in the Boer War. Then their infantry took the village and swept through four German trench lines. The attack failed only on the northern sector of the 4-kilometre length of front, where the artillery had not been brought up in time and the German wire remained intact. Prince Rupprecht had to rush in reserves to plug the broken line.

The List Regiment knew nothing of this, but by 1530 was loaded onto trains. Some speculated that they were heading for Russia, the jokers settled on Bohemia as a likely destination—neither seemed like a good guess because their artillery was travelling by road. When the trains pulled into Lille they could hear guns roaring in the west and the station overflowed with wounded. They detrained, had a short march through the city and then went into night quarters. The next morning they marched 28 kilometres toward the front, the gunfire becoming louder with each mile. The trees along the way already had green-grey buds. Their 1st and 3rd Battalions were assigned to support the 79th Prussian Infantry Brigade, which had been badly mauled in the attack. The 2nd Battalion was in reserve. The last part of the march was at night along miserable roads; at the tiny village of Halpegarbe each man received two empty sandbags. The last part of the march was in dead quiet and the two counter-attacking battalions were ordered to fix bayonets at 0530. They gave a "hurrah" and started forward across the open fields. They were far from the German firing line and were in plain view as they advanced so they were hit by murderous artillery and small-arms fire. They splashed through three creeks along their way. When they finally arrived at the front they were mixed among the troops remaining from the earlier encounters. The British attacked again the next day, but made no progress whatsoever.

We do not know anything about Hitler in this battle. The messengers went between headquarters in Halpegarbe, at the end of a telephone wire, and the front line, travelling across the open fields in full view of the British observers—a 4-kilometre round trip. It was a perilous journey; the previous day a German unit had failed to attack because all of the runners transmitting their orders had failed to get through. At least Hitler had acquired life-saving skills since his first battle, when he often could not tell whether German or British guns were firing. Now his ears were exquisitely tuned. From the report of an enemy gun, he could judge calibre and direction and, if required, throw himself into whatever shelter offered. As Remarque wrote:

> It is not conscious; it is far quicker, much more sure, less fallible than consciousness. One cannot explain it. A man is walking along without thought or heed;—suddenly he throws himself down on the ground and a storm of fragments flies harmlessly over him;—yet he cannot remember either to have heard the shell coming or to have thought of flinging himself down.

Hitler was not facing fire in the spirit he displayed on the Menin road—

> A feeling of horror replaced the romantic fighting spirit. Enthusiasm cooled down gradually and exuberant spirits were quelled by the fear of the ever-present Death. A time came when there arose within each one of us a conflict between the urge to self-preservation and the call of duty. And I had to go through that conflict too. As Death sought its prey everywhere and unrelentingly a nameless something rebelled within the weak body and tried to introduce itself under the name of common sense; but in reality it was Fear, which had taken on this cloak in order to impose itself on the individual.

And he worried about what would happen to Foxl if he were hit.

The following morning was dull and misty. Overnight the Germans had dug a continuous trench line linking up their new positions. The sector was shrouded in thick mist the following day also, when the List Regiment was ordered to stand by as reserve for a counter-attack. Again, orders had failed to reach the line—the attack was therefore carried out by the 21st Bavarian Reserve Infantry Regiment, which came up and passed through the List—a manoeuvre that led to a confused, uncoordinated assault. The German general commanding had not waited for artillery reinforcements, so the bombardment was weak; at first, the attackers pushed back the Sherwood Foresters, but were then driven back themselves. Next, some units of the List attacked the Garhwall Rifles and the Seaforth Highlanders. They were repulsed.

The List Regiment was relieved on the night of 13 March. They had lost four company commanders and 243 dead or seriously wounded other ranks. Their regimental doctor had 638 wounded pass through his aide station, 375 of them from the List. Total British casualties at Neuve Chapelle were given as 11,652. The List moved to Grande and Petit Moisnil, where they rested and reorganized. Three days later they took over a sector of the front near Fromelles, which is about 3 kilometres northeast of Aubers. Here the opponents were separated by a stream lined with willows, a "real no-mans-land." The ground was too marshy for trenches; the defences were a breastwork of sandbags that they had to make higher and thicker. Regimental combat headquarters was in a basement in the castle of Fromelles, which was up on the ridge; on a clear day, they could see Mount Kemmel, in Belgium, on the horizon. The staff was quartered in the house of a notary in Fournes. Until communication trenches were dug, dispatches to the front had to be carried down the slope of the hill in full view of the enemy—good practice for their machine gunners. The troops grumbled because their trenches were down in the sodden valley instead of up on the ridge; the little stream was not a serious obstacle. At first their opponents were the Indian Army, and the antagonists took business seriously. When the English replaced the Indians, there was good-natured shouting back and forth between the lines.

At the beginning of May, the English artillery became lively. On 9 May at 0500, the English started bombarding headquarters; at 0645, they escalated to drumfire. At 0700, two mines exploded under the German front destroying 60 metres of the line and sending men "flying into the air." The English infantry came onward repeatedly but could not reach the German front line. In two days of attacks, the List Regiment saw thirteen officers and acting officers killed, along with 566 other ranks. They captured two English officers and 140 men, three machine guns and 329 rifles.

IV

Suvla Bay to Loos

Mustapha Kemal
June to December 1915

The Turk's future was settled in secret, by an agreement between Sir Mark Sykes, for the British, and Georges Picot, for the French, signed in May 1915. Southern Anatolia and the Lebanon would be under direct French control, they would have influence over what is now northern Iraq and Syria—at that time, the northern Iraqi oilfield was unknown. The British would have influence over what is now Jordan and part of Southern Iraq, with its oilfields. The British would control Baghdad, the valleys of the Tigris and Euphrates down to the Persian Gulf, Kuwait and the Arabian shores along the Gulf. Palestine would be under joint control, including Russia. Northern Anatolia was left to the pleasure of the Russians, when they took over the straits. The Italians had been promised part of Anatolia also. The agreement became public knowledge when the Bolsheviks unearthed it in the Russian files and published it.

Kemal was promoted to colonel and awarded the title of Bey in June. Soon thereafter Enver Pasha came to visit the front. Kemal had persuaded his corps commander to permit his division to attack a position he considered the linchpin of the Anzac beachhead. Enver thought it would only waste lives, and he and Kemal went at it head-to-head, bitterly and sparing no words. Liman made peace between them and permitted the attack to go forward. It was a failure. Enver, of course, let it be known whose assessment had been correct—Kemal resigned. Once Enver returned to Constantinople, Liman persuaded Kemal to return to duty. Enver cancelled Kemal's promotion to acting corps commander.

As Kemal thought about the stalemate, he became convinced that the enemy would eventually stop trying to batter an exit through the trenches walling them into their beachheads and would slip around a flank. His depleted 19th Division was shifted to a quieter sector toward the right end of the Ottoman front that stretched along the ridge line dominating the Anzac beachhead. Part of their front faced the British, but further north the British line curved away to meet the sea. Kemal was also responsible for a long length of ridge, with poor fortifications and little artillery support, which did not face any enemy trenches. The high point on the ridge is Chunuk Bair—Kemal regarded it as the key to the peninsula. He did not have enough infantry to man all of his line; some of it, including Chunuk Bair, was covered only by cavalry patrols. He thought that the British would swing out of their left flank on Anzac to attack this weak point, so he made himself a nuisance, continually badgering about how few men he had, the inadequacies of the commanders of the units on his flanks and the gaps between the defender's units. He was especially anxious about his right flank, where the next unit in line was a ragtag assembly of police under the command of the German Major Willmer. The two commands were separated by the Sazlidere ravine. Kemal thought that the enemy would attack up the ravine and he insisted on a ruling about who was responsible for defending it. His corps commander came up to have a look for himself. They stood on the crest of Chunuk Bair. To their left was the Anzac bridgehead, which ended short of where the Sazlidere ravine met the sea. Extending off to the right was Willmer's territory, a broad plain known as Anafarta, graced with a large salt lake, dry at this time of the year, ending with a lovely beach edging the blue waters of Suvla Bay. The corps commander thought the country between the Anzac lines and the opening of the ravine too rough to attack over—"they can't do it"—and dismissed any idea that the enemy might land on the shore of the bay. "God willing, Sir, things will turn out as you expect," replied Kemal. That night he wrote to Corrine Lüthü, telling her how fortunate it was that his men were so brave and believing that, if killed in battle, they would immediately enter paradise, "… where the houris, God's most beautiful women, will come to receive them and remain permanently at their disposal. Supreme happiness!" He also asked for some French novels, which would have to stand in for her conversation, which he missed so much.

Kemal prepared as best he might with map exercises with his officers, working out counters to possible enemy moves. Liman had other worries. His friends in Constantinople warned that he was likely to be replaced by Field Marshal von der Goltz, who had been transferred from Brussels to become the senior German officer in the Ottoman Empire (von der Goltz died of spotted fever in Mesopotamia in 1916). Liman argued that it was a bad time for a change and he stayed. In August, the enemy did just what Kemal had predicted. They moved men from Helles to reinforce Anzac. As diversions there were strong attacks at Helles—calibrated so that no more than 4,000 men would be casualties— as well as along the line defending the Anzac bridgehead, striking at an Ottoman strong point known as Long Pine. During the preliminary artillery bombardment the Ottoman commander withdrew most of his men from the front trench. When the Anzacs leapt out and rushed across No Man's Land they reached the first Ottoman trench before the bulk of its defenders reoccupied it. The attackers took the first line; both sides lost thousands of men. Another diversionary assault was across a narrow part ridge called the Nek, so narrow that only 150 men could advance abreast, toward a well constructed Ottoman line. The attack was preceded by the heaviest bombardment yet achieved on the peninsula. The guns fell silent seven minutes before the infantry were allowed to leave their trenches, because watches had not been properly synchronized. When their watches showed the designated moment, the first wave of Australian Light Horsemen emerged on foot to be shot down in No Man's Land. One man from the second wave reached the Ottoman trench, waved a flag and disappeared. The third wave did no better; two-thirds of the attackers were killed or wounded. This massacre is the climax of Peter Weir's film *Gallipoli*.

British formations slipped out of the left flank of Anzac on the night of 6 August, marching northward along the sea. They readily pushed through the weakly defended enemy picket line. Next they were to swing inland to attack up the Sazlidere ravine. Kemal's division was not involved in the first fighting, but they were hit by naval gunfire. At 0330 Kemal issued an order:

> It is probable the enemy will attack our front in the morning. Owing to the close distance and in order to be able to repel it … it is essential that troops are awake and ready to use their weapons.

Meanwhile the advance up the Sazlidere ravine was losing cohesion. In the dark, exhausted, sick men—many with severe dysentery—stumbled here and there, led by officers guiding by map through a nightmarish tangle of ravines and spurs. By dawn on 7 August, only a few of the attackers were climbing toward the undefended peak of Chunuk Bair. They were in a race for the peak. After the attack at Lone Pine was smashed, two reserve regiments commanded by Colonel Kannengieser were sent to Chunuk Bair. He arrived at 0600 with the twenty men of his advance guard. The view astonished him. Off in the distance he saw scores of small craft landing men on the beaches of Suvla Bay—the enemy was making a new landing. Down in the ravine he saw a column of New Zealanders climbing toward them. The men in his guard were too terrified to fire, so Kannengieser took a rifle, lay on the ground and opened up. As his bullets whizzed by, the New Zealanders flattened and crawled into a hollow for shelter. They then took a break for breakfast. As they ate, the main body of Kannengieser's troops began to arrive on the crest; while positioning them he was shot in the chest. He was evacuated, as his main body came into position. In the middle of the morning the New Zealanders and two companies of Gurkhas attacked up the ravine—they were pinned down on the slope.

British artillery blasted the summit of Chunuk Bair, driving the Ottomans off. The Wellington Battalion of New Zealanders rose, advanced and, when their artillery stopped firing, took a toehold close to the crest. The Gurkhas on the left were also near to the top. However, the Ottomans beat them to the crest and pinned the attackers down with a fierce torrent of small arms fire. The Wellington's front line became so choked with bodies that the survivors had to scrape out new shelter further down the ridge. They had no reinforcements and no water. The final straw came at 1700 when a heavy barrage struck the pitiful ruts that served the British as trenches. Most likely the shells were fired by British Army howitzers who thought they were firing on Turks—but some blame the navy. As soon as darkness fell, the survivors who were able to walk retreated back down the slope.

Kannengieser had seen the first of 25,000 fresh troops that were landing on the beaches at Suvla Bay to roll up the Ottoman flank. The bay swarmed with ships—small boats shuttled back and forth bringing in men and supplies, while the warships fired at any likely target. The British used specialized armoured landing craft with front ramps, 'beetles,' developed for long-planned landings on the German Baltic coast. Most of the British who landed dillydallied along the shore. They had little opposition: Major Willmer had pulled his three gendarme battalions back to the Anafarta heights. When Kemal heard of the landing he sent a message to headquarters requesting that overall command be given to an officer who knew the area well—"for the safety of the nation." A regiment from the reserve was ordered up to defend part of the heights. Its commander called on Kemal to ask whose command he would be under. Kemal did not know, so he told him, "to advance at once … events will appoint a commander." As the Ottoman units shifted to new positions under fire, many of their officers were casualties—confusion spread.

Kemal was telephoned by Liman's chief of staff for his appraisal of their situation. Kemal reported that they would soon be pushed off the entire ridge. What was to be done? Kemal replied: "The only remedy is to put all of the available troops under my command"—"Won't that be too many?"—"It will be too few." That evening, Liman "… gave command of all the troops in the Anafarta section to Colonel Mustafa Kemal Bey"—the XVI Corps, 9th Infantry Division and Willmer's group. Now Kemal was commanding unfamiliar formations and defending unfamiliar ground, at the crisis of a great battle—and remained seemingly unfazed. He ordered his former division, the 19th, to attack the British next morning. Then he rode off north to the Anafarta ridge—it would be the critical area when the enemy army on the plain finally moved. It was his third night without sleep. With him was his doctor, who would set up medical facilities and try to control Kemal's malaria, and a cavalry officer replacing the aide de camp who had been killed during the day.

They came across a division commander and his staff; they were awake but too far from the front. Kemal issued orders for the next day and instructed them to move up. When they rode on they spotted a cluster of silent tents. They shouted—a night-gowned man appeared, and after some prodding, led them to a hut where Willmer was sleeping. He was given a bee in his ear. Kemal reached group headquarters at 0130, where he took command. He sent orders to all his units, directing them to report their exact position and to advance on the enemy at dawn. He then arranged for the bringing up of food and ammunition and for the establishment of medical services. As dawn neared, his small band rode to the top of the ridge from which they would have the best view of the impending battle. Offshore they saw the blazing lights of the hospital ships, with their brilliant red crosses.

The British at Suvla had wasted two days. Their sixty-one-year-old commander, Sir John Stopford, had never been in combat and for the past five years had served as Constable of the Tower of London. He had made a reputation as a military historian and led at Suvla because of his seniority in the service. Finally Sir Ian Hamilton came ashore and, with uncharacteristic determination, told his subordinates that they must immediately seize the high point of the ridge that bounded the plain—a hill known as Tekke Tepe. Kemal had the same objective in mind. The Ottomans won the race by thirty minutes. They swarmed over the crest and then down the slope, headed at the advancing British—"The Turks on us!" From his ship, Hamilton saw the enemy emerging over the crest and his own men turning tail. Kemal's men were not allowed to chase because they were outnumbered—they had driven their foes off by sheer audacity. Some were ordered to dig in on the crest, while two regiments were marched back to Chunuk Bair, where the British were finally making a strong push up the ravine. Kemal ordered hot soup for these men to drink along their way. He concluded that the enemy commanders were paralyzed by responsibility.

Kemal then rode back to confer with Liman, telling him that he planned to drive the Anzacs back that night. They disagreed over the best axis for this attack, but Liman concluded by saying:

> I don't want to influence you in your plans. I only wanted to tell you, purely as an observation, what came into my mind.

He was now learning how to deal with his prickly, talented subordinate. When Kemal issued orders for the attack, his staff warned that it was sure to fail. Most of the troops had already been repulsed twice and only one of the two additional regiments that had been ordered to reinforce them would have time to get into place. Kemal did not budge. He spent the night—his fourth without sleep and with his malarial fever rising—untangling the units that would attack.

One of his regiments was in the front trench, only 20 metres from the foe; two others were in the second trench, a further 30 metres back. They were to attack just before daylight. For surprise, he prohibited rifle and artillery fire. Kemal walked through the trenches, whispering instructions to his troops. He promised them victory if they attacked at just the proper moment, when the light was just right—"Let me go ahead first, when you see me raise my whip, then you will all leap forward." A line of officers in No Man's Land would relay the signal. As first light neared, he climbed out of the trench—so did his officers, spaced so they could just make out their neighbours in the starlight. Kemal stood judging the illumination. At the brink of dawn he raised his whip; the other officers followed his lead. With a great cry of "Allah, Allah," the men rushed across and leapt into the British trenches with bayonets extended. When light came, Hamilton could see his troops retreating down the hill. Hamilton reported:

> The Turks came on again and again, fighting magnificently, calling on the name of God. Our men stood to it, and maintained, by many a deed of daring, the old traditions of their race. There was no flinching. They died in their ranks where they stood.

The British units on the flanks of the attack fell back. The Ottomans had secured the ridge line.

Once the infantry pulled back, the British guns had a field day on the Ottoman survivors spread over the hillside facing the sea. Chunuk Bair was wrapped in fire and smoke, masses of earth were thrown into the air, burying those close to the explosions. A shrapnel bullet struck the watch in Kemal's breast pocket, so he escaped with only a skin wound. Later Liman was given the shattered watch as a souvenir; in return, Kemal received a gold chronometer engraved with the arms of the von Sanders. Hamilton, as ever, was philosophical:

> The Turks were well commanded: that I admit. Their generals knew they were done unless they could quickly knock us off of Chunuk Bair. So they have done it. Never mind; never say die.

The British kept attacking, but with less force and with no surprises. Kemal stayed near the front, so his men could see him sharing their dangers; to them he was a talisman of triumph and a maker of legend. They told how one day he was sitting in a trench. An enemy shell dropped into the trench, 60 metres away; the next was 40 metres off, the succeeding 20 metres. They waited for what seemed the inevitable; Kemal was pale, but unflinching—"I cannot set my men a bad example." He stood smoking; there was no fourth shell. A few days later he was facing a British attack on a poorly defended position. His reserves needed time to get there. He ordered the officer commanding a small cavalry contingent to charge headlong at the attackers. The cavalryman hesitated. "Do you understand what I said?"—"Yes, sir ... You ordered us to die." And they did. Meanwhile, the reserves arrived and the attackers were driven back.

The fighting continued until the last week in August and then the fronts fell relatively quiet; as Allan Moorhead later wrote, "a dull implacable ennui began to settle on the Allied Army." The Ottomans welcomed a pause. Everything changed when the Bulgarians joined the Central Powers in attacking Serbia on 5 October. It was a triumph for German and Austro-Hungarian diplomacy. Serbia collapsed and the fate of the Gallipoli adventure was sealed, because the rail line to Constantinople was opened—a battery of Austrian 240mm guns, one of German 150mm guns and a mortar battery, mountains of shells, 500 technicians and three general staff officers were on the way. Kemal set up quarters behind the lines in a snug hut, which he had made as comfortable as conditions allowed. He served his guests four-course meals and rested to recover his health. He was furious that they were sitting on their hands, because he thought that the Allies would soon withdraw and that they should be destroyed before they could do so, but he could not convince his superiors, who felt that they had already lost far too many men—they would wait for overwhelming artillery superiority. Kemal announced that he would resign if they did not attack; Liman persuaded him to go on sick leave instead. In early November he left for Constantinople to recover his health and to spend his back pay. A little more than a week later the British, led by a new commander, General Munro, evacuated Suvla Bay and Anzac and a few weeks later withdrew from their other toeholds. Astonishingly the evacuations were achieved without a single British casualty; finally a substantial British victory. The Ottomans had fair warning because the House of Lords had been told a week previously that they would withdraw—this astonishing security lapse was interpreted as a ruse. We can only speculate how it might have gone had Kemal been on the scene. The first successful operation showed that Liman was inattentive; the second suggested incompetence. He was relieved as army commander. It is likely that Kemal was glad to see him gone. On Gallipoli, the British and French casualties were about 265,000. Ottoman figures were kept loosely—the total was probably about 300,000, though the British prefer 460,000.

The British Official History says of Kemal:

> Seldom in history can the exertions of a single divisional commander have exercised, on three separate occasions, so profound an influence not only on the course of a battle, but perhaps on the fate of a campaign and even the destiny of a nation.

It is only fair to note that, when this was written, Kemal was the leader of Turkey—but it is still hard to argue with the evaluation.

Harold Macmillan
September though December 1915

In France, Macmillan began to see his men as people rather than as matchsticks. Guardsmen fell silent when an officer was about—unlike the recruits in the Rifles who let their opinions be known by talking to be overheard—but when overseas, he had to censor their letters. He read about their worries—about the family at home, their financial problems, their dreams and their desires. He wrote to his mother:

Some of the older men, with wives and families, who write everyday, have in their style a
wonderful simplicity that is almost great literature.

Their letters un-blinkered his eyes and he began to see them as people when he inspected
or watched to make certain that they drank their rum ration—it was not to be hoarded.
His interest and solicitude were subtly communicated; soon, some of his men asked
permission to discuss personal problems with him. Word began to spread that he was
helpful and decent; his newfound regard for them had enhanced their respect for him.

All of the officers of the division were assembled in a village square for an address by
the corps commander. His audience included curious locals at the edge of the square and
village ladies listening from the comfort of their windowsills. The corps commander gave
all present a detailed briefing on the attack they were about to launch; the wags claimed
that a stream of messenger pigeons flew from the houses to spread the news. He concluded
by assuring them that all their generals were firmly behind them—the wags amended this
to "a long way behind them." The following day, Macmillan read to his platoon a message
of encouragement from the commander-in-chief, Sir John French, which began: "On the
eve of this, the greatest battle in history …" At this point in the reading, Macmillan was
interrupted by one of his old sweats, "now we're in for it, boys!" The lieutenant was too
amused to punish the infraction properly.

The "greatest battle in history" was to be a massive joint assault by the British and French
armies at carefully selected points. Joffre believed that at last they had sufficient artillery
ammunition to destroy the German positions before starting successive waves of infantry
forward; each wave would go as far as it could and then the next wave would filter through
the survivors to press on until they had sliced through the enemy front and were in open
country. The British government—desperate to help the floundering Russians—and Sir
John French signed on to Joffre's dream. The British First Army would make the attack.
Its commander, Sir Douglas Haig, inspected the ground they were to advance over. It was
an agricultural area; much of the landscape was bare and featureless—perfect for machine
gunners. Just behind the German positions, there was a coalmining district, spotted with
high mounds of piled-up slag extracted from the mines. Just behind the front where the
British were to attack was the massive iron framework for the wheelhouse and elevator of an
extensive mine. From a distance, it appeared to be two huge pylons—so the British called
it "Tower Bridge." The German observers perched on the bridge and on the slagheaps had
a clear view of the British lines, and for miles behind. If the British succeeded in breaking
through the front they would then have to battle their way through "intricate mazes of
mining works, slag heaps and villages." Haig thought it an unpromising place to attack,
but Joffre insisted that they strike there to support the French assault just to the south. The
British gave in. No sooner done than Joffre decided that the ground for the French attack
was better in Champagne, so their main push would be there.

Haig had excellent aerial photographs of the stout German defences. Since the spring attacks the Germans had doubled or even tripled the depth of their barbed wire entanglements. Their front line trenches were along a position chosen when static warfare began in late 1914; most were on a forward slope to give the defenders good visibility and fields of fire. Subsequently the Germans had learned that such exposed trenches were admirable targets for enemy gunners. A trench on a reverse slope was hidden from direct observation and attacking infantry could be wiped out with modern weapons even when the trench was only 150 metres below the ridgeline. The attackers made wonderful targets as they were silhouetted on the crest. On the Loos front, the Germans had built a reserve line roughly 2.5 kilometres in the rear, on a reverse slope beyond the range of most enemy guns, and wired it heavily. Between the front and reserves lines, in the intermediate zone, there was a strong point every kilometre or so, either a concrete pillbox or the strengthened cellar of a ruined house.

117 heavy British guns were sited behind a 10.2 kilometre length of front; each was allocated ninety rounds per day for the preparatory bombardment. The total artillery support worked out to a gun every 29 metres—a much lower concentration of fire than in the unsuccessful British attack at Neuve Chapelle earlier in the year. Each field gun was allotted 1,259 shells per day—all shrapnel. Haig would compensate for the diluted artillery by lengthening the preliminary bombardment to four days and by releasing a cloud of chlorine gas from cylinders in his front line, which he hoped would be pushed over the German lines by a 30kph wind. More than 5,000 cylinders were installed. The plan allowed a three-day margin for a suitable wind; if none came, the assault would be limited. Cavalry was assembled nearby; once the front was pierced, they were to advance 80 kilometres into Belgium. The Guards were held in reserve.

D-day was 25 September. The preliminary bombardment began four days earlier; it was so skimpy that the Germans suspected a feint. According to Frank Richards, a private in the Royal Welch Fusiliers, that evening a German called across No Man's Land, "You can come over on the 25th, you English swine, and send your gas over: but we'll smarten you up." As the sun first peeped over the horizon on D-day, Haig ordered an aide to light a cigarette and watched the smoke drift lazily toward the German line. He ordered the full scale attack. At 0550, the cylinders were opened. Robert Graves, a lieutenant with the Royal Welch Fusiliers in the assault trenches, reported that the release of the gas went slowly because many of the men responsible for opening the valves had been issued spanners that did not fit the nuts on the valves. Eventually they were opened with the few variable spanners on hand. The gas cloud drifted lazily into No Man's Land; when supplemented by smoke shells from mortars it at least kept the Germans from seeing the attackers groping their way toward them, their heads covered with gas masks with eyepieces misted over. The artillery blasted the German front line and then lifted onto the intermediate zone between the two German lines. In the northern part of the sector the German front line was taken rather easily. In the centre it was harder going because a section of the front line trench was on a reverse slope behind largely unbroken wire. After a series of bloody attacks this part was also occupied. After the front line fell the advance was checked by the machine guns in the strong points. Only one division made it through the intermediate zone; when they finally crested the slope in front of the German reserve line they were mown down. Two well-manned machine guns could take down 1,000 attackers.

Sir John French learned that German front line trenches had been occupied. Elated, he added XI Corps to Haig's command. It was made up of two divisions of partially trained Kitchener Army new men and the Guards Division. They were billeted far behind the front. By mid-morning they were pushing forward through the throngs on the roads. At 1500 Macmillan's 4th Battalion was ordered to the side of the road so that more urgently needed troops could get past—it was the Cavalry Corps. Some thought it a splendid portent when cavalry advanced while infantry waited; others had less faith in their leader's good sense. The Grenadier Guards were kept in ranks along the roadside; they stood or sat in formation for more than six hours while the rain poured down. They had no food, but finally their cookers provided tea. Most of the time the men sang—classic army songs, music hall ditties, love songs and so on. They watched the ambulances bringing back the casualties; many of the lightly wounded were cheerful and garrulous, some claimed that the enemy was running. When the 4th Battalion was allowed back onto the road the rest of their division had six hours' start on them, and no one knew where they were. Cyclists and signallers could not find them. The 4th Battalion marched until 2300 when they halted in a field. The rain had stopped, there was a lovely full moon, and stars were twinkling. They had hot tea and bread and cheese and could sit down. Forty-five minutes later they were on the road again, because they finally had been told where to go. Two hours later they reached a village where they were billeted in barns with plenty of straw for bedding. Reveille was at 0430; at best, they slept for two-and-a-half hours. After breakfast they sat down to wait. Macmillan wrote to his mother, telling her of the march thus far. That afternoon they moved on to a village closer to the front where Macmillan's platoon was allowed to shelter in an old French trench that ran through a graveyard, so macabre items projected from the walls. The lieutenant worried that his men might be depressed—they found it a jolly joke.

They had no news of how the battle was going; perhaps that was just as well. The two Kitchener Army divisions in their corps had been ordered to take the German reserve line and then to push on several kilometres further. They had reached the old British front line at sunset the previous day when the rain was changing from light to heavy. They waited there until morning. Some British batteries moved up at dawn but in the heavy morning mist they took an incorrect position, too far back to hit the section of the reserve line that was to be attacked. The Germans counter-attacked a forward bulge in the British line and recaptured a wood from which they could enfilade attackers. British observers reported that the German reserve line had been reinforced. The two inexperienced New Army divisions had been promised they would only be asked to occupy smashed enemy positions—instead, they were formed into ten columns, which then started to march toward the German reserve line. The Germans watched fearfully as they debouched in the far distance, certain that their trenches soon would be blasted by British shellfire. Scarcely a British gun fired as the columns marched forward. At 1,300 metres, the German machine guns started to rake the columns with short, intermittent bursts of fire, careful not to overheat their guns. One of them fired 12,500 rounds that afternoon. The columns continued forward. As they closed the German riflemen joined in, some leaping onto their parapets for a better field of fire. A six-gun battery over open sights fired shrapnel into the massed ranks; hundreds fell. The columns thinned but still came on. Some even reached the edge of the intact, dense band of barbed wire in front of the reserve line. They stopped briefly, saw no way through, and turned on their heels. The Germans stopped firing and looked on in astonishment and horror as the survivors picked their way back between the bodies strewn over the field; the Germans remembered it as the *Leichenfeld von Loos* (corpse field of Loos). The two attacking divisions lost 385 officers and 7,800 other ranks.

The next morning the Grenadier Guards were ordered to seize Hill 70, a knoll in the intermediate zone. It had been taken by the British and then lost to a counter-attack. Macmillan's company commander went forward to inspect their route. The 4th Battalion formed ranks on the road and started toward the front; none of the lieutenants were given any instructions. When they reached the crest of a rise they were ordered to redeploy into artillery formation, in which platoons formed loose columns, men four abreast, separated by irregular gaps, to minimize the number of men struck down by an incoming shell. Thus they started to advance across the fields. It was as if they were on a giant bare stage; the Germans on the 'bridge' and slagheaps admired how precisely they changed formation and applauded with heavy high-explosive fire. German prisoners later told them how thunderstruck they were by the stupidity of this performance. The Guards marched in perfect order through the geysers of erupting mud, every man in his place—now and again with a hideous gap. The Regimental History tells us that "Nothing more splendid has ever been recorded in the annals of the Guards." Macmillan drew on every reserve of will to appear unmoved and to keep his legs moving. The 4th continued on for more than 2 kilometres. It got worse as they advanced—the shells were joined by machine-gun fire from their right. Macmillan watched his men carefully to see how they were taking it. The only time he detected a tendency to break formation was when a hare ran across the gap between them and the platoon in front, some of the countrymen, were clearly tempted to have a shot. They were marching over ground that was speckled with dead, wounded and body parts from previous attacks and with small groups of master-less, demoralized men from the two Kitchener Army divisions. For Macmillan this march was one of the great horrors of his war. He re-ran it in his nightmares for years. He also probably thought of it when reading Wilfred Owen's lines:

> What passing-bells for those who die as cattle?
> Only the monstrous anger of the guns.
> Only the stuttering rifles' rapid rattle
> Can patter out their hasty orisons.

Finally, they reached the shattered remains of the village of Loos. The company commander was waiting for them; he ordered them forward on the double to shelter in an abandoned trench running through the ruins on the far margin of the village. Now they were struck by gas shells as well as high explosive. Their battalion commander was gassed; his second-in-command and adjutant were killed. The brigadier came galloping down the road through the village. He divided the Battalion into two groups. Macmillan's company commander was not to be seen, so he placed himself under the command of Captain Morrison. Morrison sent off four runners asking for orders—none came back. He decided that they had best move a short distance to the left, where they formed as the right flank of the Scots Guards. They advanced together in open order under heavy fire from shells and bullets:

> At the time, however, one does not notice these things. There is a kind of daze that makes one impervious to emotion.

The Scots Guards came under such heavy machine-gun fire that they were obliged to retreat. Captain Morrison, left on his own, ordered his grenadiers to lie down and take cover, but he was so corpulent that lying was not a plausible option, so he remained standing. Macmillan took his lead and also remained on his feet. They walked along the line of supine men, ordering them to crawl back to a road they had crossed over and to dig in there. Macmillan was forcing himself to walk casually. A shell fragment tore across his scalp, which bled copiously and hurt as though he had been branded. A bandage staunched the blood flow. The men now crouched along the verge of the road, scraping into the ground with their entrenching tools. While walking about encouraging them, Macmillan was struck in his right hand by a rifle bullet, which went clean through. It was dressed, but soon his arm began to swell. It was exquisitely painful. He was giddy with the combined effects of shock from blood loss and the concussion from the blow to his skull.

That night Captain Morrison ordered him to the dressing station. He remembered little of the next few days; he had "learnt the lesson of what was meant by the phrase 'the fog of war.'" In the Loos battle the 4th Battalion casualties were eleven officers and 342 others. The total British loss was about 60,000. As he later wrote home:

The act of death in battle is noble and glorious. But the physical appearance and actual symptoms of death are, in these terrible circumstances, revolting only and horrid.

According to friends, thenceforth an outstanding exploit would be rated by the 4th Battalion as, "almost as brave as Mr Macmillan."

In England he was treated in a makeshift hospital set up in the home of one of mother's friends—it was convenient for her to visit, only two streets away from Cadogan Place. His older brothers also dropped by now and again. The elder had entered the army but was discharged as medically unfit; the middle brother had epilepsy and had been rejected. Harold thought and read about Loos. Even the fragmentary accounts reinforced his conviction that it had been poorly conceived and poorly managed. He also learned about the death of Rudyard Kipling's only son, John, a second lieutenant in the Irish Guards, whose body was never found. Now his father wrote, "But who shall return to us our children?"

Charles de Gaulle
June 1915 through February 1916

De Gaulle left the hospital and returned to the 33rd on the Aisne front in June. En route he had a few hours in Paris; he went to a cinema at noon, ate dinner at home and afterwards his father and middle brother took him to the station by car. He was adjutant again, busy ensuring that everyone was prepared for a gas attack, that the cooking facilities were properly inspected, that there was more aimed rifle fire at the enemy and that men saluted officers when they met in a trench. The fortifications were much improved compared to his last spell in the line, with trench walls revetted to keep earth from spilling in, a second line and additional communication trenches. In September his captaincy was made permanent and he was given command of the 10th Company.

The 33rd Regiment was not involved in Joffre's attacks in September in Champagne, which were synchronised with the British attack at Loos. Like the British, they began by releasing a cloud of chlorine gas; but here the breeze was favourable and the cloud rolled into the German front line trench, which was sited just forward of the crest of a small ridge. The French infantry advance was also shielded by a smoke screen. The artillery observers in the German front line could barely see the attackers, and most were helpless in any event because their telephone lines had been cut by the French preliminary bombardment. By the first evening, the French had broken though extensive lengths of the German front, penetrating in some places for 2.3 kilometres. The chief of staff of the defending Third Army proposed to withdraw to a new position more than 3 kilometres further back. He was immediately relieved and replaced by Colonel Fritz von

Lossberg, who had been deputy chief of operations at Imperial Headquarters. Lossberg rescinded the retreat orders, went to the front and soon was "running from shell-hole to shell-hole" evaluating the positions and gauging the defender's resilience. They had been pushed into the rudiments of a reserve line, which was under construction on the reverse side of a slope. Lossberg stationed sentries on the crest of the ridge; they were to withdraw when attackers approached. He adapted his defence to his situation. Most of his infantry were ordered to shelter in dugouts toward the rear. If a length of the front line was taken then the German artillery shortened range and rained shells on their former positions. Next, the infantry from the rear counter-attacked over familiar ground—the combat was invisible to enemy artillery observers on the ground because it was screened by the crest of the ridge. Lossberg transferred the German artillery observers to the next ridge behind the front, where their telephone lines to the batteries were shorter and more secure and they were less distracted by the enemy trying to kill them. The French continued to attack for a month, gaining little, suffering much, and unable to counter the novel, elastic defence they faced.

In November, de Gaulle temporarily commanded the 3rd Battalion, charged with preparing them for a formal review by the division commander. In his letters home he approved of the withdrawal from Gallipoli—it was just a senseless diversion—and raged against ineffectual politicians. In 1915 the French had 1,350,000 casualties, almost 2.5 times the number of Germans lost on the French front.

Adolf Hitler
June through December 1915

After the abortive British attack, the List Regiment settled back into the steady attrition of trench warfare. By summer they told one another: "In the east the German army battles, in the west it stands as the fire brigade." During the summer the British mined busily. The Germans followed their progress with microphones and dug countermines. The British dropped propaganda leaflets on the German trenches; most men used the paper for purposes other than reading, but Hitler studied them carefully, angered by attempts to turn the Bavarians against the Prussians, but also with some admiration:

In that propaganda carried out by the enemy I found admirable sources of instruction.

He was less happy with German efforts—"Had we any propaganda at all?" He had a clear concept of what was needed. As he wrote in *Mein Kampf*:

The receptive power of the masses is very restricted, and their understanding is feeble. Such being the case, all effective propaganda must be confined to a few bare essentials and must be expressed as far as possible in stereotyped formulas.

The theme of German internal propaganda was standing by the Fatherland—Hitler thought instead it should incite hatred for their enemy, as the Allies were doing.

On 2 October, the List Regiment was in reserve, billeted in La Vallée. The alarm sounded at 1400. They packed up, marched off and were herded into unmoving railway cars until 0430, when they finally chugged off south. During their assault at Loos the British had occupied a small portion of a German position known as the Hohenzollern Redoubt, which was a salient projecting out from the German lines to hold high ground. Now the British were fighting to take the rest of the Redoubt; the List was to strengthen the German line. On 4 October at 0500 British infantry attacked. They were repelled, and the heavy British bombardment resumed. The next day they attacked again following drumfire, which "was like hell" and then the enemy released a cloud of gas. As the cloud started to drift across No Man's Land, emergency flares shot up all along the German front. The men in the List Regiment had only primitive masks—chemical-soaked pads tied over the nose and mouth. Nonetheless, the masks gave sufficient protection and they repulsed the British infantry, hurling volleys of hand grenades at the attackers. The 9th Company of the List suffered the most: they had 194 casualties. The Regiment was relieved on 8 October.

Benito Mussolini
May through December 1915

The Italian-Austrian border ran as a long convoluted arc from Switzerland in the west to the Adriatic coast, mostly along alpine crests. The most suitable region for an attack was in the east, where the border ran roughly north to south, starting at Mount Krn—at 2,259 metres, the highest point in the Julian Alps, it is perpetually snow-capped. The vivid, emerald-green River Isonzo forms in the heights and has cut a deep cavern in the first part of its run to the sea. The banks are gentler when it reaches the city of Gorizia (Görz), 35.5 kilometres south of the mountain, a pleasant community where many retired Austro-Hungarian officers and civil servants lived. South of the city, the river runs along the edge of a limestone plateau, the Carso. Once past the Carso, the Isonzo flows through relatively flat country until it enters the Adriatic. As the crow flies from Gorizia to the sea is 14.5 kilometres. From the river mouth, Trieste can be seen in the distance. The border ran roughly parallel to the river a few kilometres to the west, not far from the present Italian-Slovenian border. The Carso was the defensive key, because cannon on its summit could interdict both of the major passageways across the border—along the sea coast or through Gorizia. The plateau has steep slopes. Rain flows into the porous limestone, so the Carso is pitted with sinkholes—funnel-shaped indentations that lead into caverns. The sinkholes were excellent natural gun pits. The caverns were used as gigantic dugouts to shelter men and supplies. The population of the province east of the Isonzo, Küstenland, was 46 per cent Italian, and only 2 per cent German-Austrian. If the Italian army crossed the Isonzo they could liberate their fellows, capture Trieste, and then swing northward, through the passes in the Julian Alps, toward Vienna.

The Italian chief of staff, General Count Luigi Cadorna, set up headquarters at Udine, west of the midpoint of the Isonzo line. As the Italians counted down to war he called up a few reserves every day—a mobilization order would alert the enemy. When war was declared he was joined by the forty-five-year-old King, Victor Emmanuelle III, who looked and strutted like a bantam rooster and liked to say: "Italy was unified not by Dante but by bayonets." Nonetheless he had a better feel for reality than his top generals. Cadorna assembled an army of 900,000 men, including a division of *Bersaglieri* and fifty-two battalions of mountain troops—*Alpini*—supported by 2,000 guns and howitzers. He had only 618 machine guns and his artillery was short of what they needed most: mountain guns and heavy guns. His field guns had only shrapnel shells and stocks were low. Italy manufactured only 2,500 army rifles per month, too few to make up for wastage. The Italian military attaches in France provided Cadorna with detailed intelligence about how trenches had changed warfare—he paid little heed.

Immediately after the declaration of war, Mussolini requested active service. He was told he must wait until the older reserves were called up in a businesslike sequence. Cadorna did offer a poet, the fifty-two-year-old Reserve Lieutenant of Cavalry Gabriele D'Annunzio, carte blanche to go where he wanted and to write what he pleased. Presumably Cadorna had in mind a poem describing the conqueror triumphantly riding his charger into Trieste. D'Annunzio would to do more as a poet without portfolio than the most optimistic general could anticipate, including dropping leaflets from the air over Trieste and Vienna, bombing the naval base at Cattaro, and attacking shipping in a Croatian port with a torpedo boat. He lost his right eye as his head hit a machine gun when his aeroplane made a crash landing.

Italian prospects were dazzling if they moved immediately. Austro-Hungarian strength on the line from Mount Krn to the Adriatic was only 25,000 men and 100 guns, but after the Italian declaration of war two corps moved from Serbia to Isonzo. Command of the new front was given to General Svetozar Boroević, a Serb from a warlike family. He was well trained, fiercely determined, intelligent, experienced and pig-headed—a more desirable characteristic for defence than offence. The Italian declaration of war had a remarkable affect on the Austro-Hungarian Army. All of the soldiers felt it was a stab in the back. Slavs, reluctant to fight Russian and Serbian "brothers," were now defending their homes; even Czechs and Poles were ready for a go at the Italians.

Boroević entrenched lines and sited guns. At the end of May the Italians advanced across the border. Their first objectives were the mountains and ridges along the upper Isonzo, which were defended by the 3rd Mountain Brigade, made up of German, Czech, Polish, Ukrainian, Magyar and Romanian mountaineers. The Italians established a bridgehead across the River. *Il Popolo* heralded a triumphant advance—waves of Italian attackers ran as best they might up the steep ridges and were shot down. Some of the fighting was above the snow line, exploiting the skills of the mountaineers on both sides. It was difficult to evacuate the wounded; many froze to death where they fell.

The invading Italians razed villages where snipers sheltered and shot hostages—Belgium in miniature. On 16 June the *Alpini* took the peak of Mount Krn. Italian morale soared and *Il Popolo* had banner headlines—but too soon. The Austro-Hungarian line held firm, bent around the eastern slope of the peak. Five days later Cadorna ordered a general advance on Gorizia and Trieste. The defences of Gorizia were commanded by an Austrian general who was a trained engineer. He had finished the initial stages of a defensive line by blasting into rock and erecting parapets of sandbags filled with stones. The Italians bombarded for five days. Their enemy were traumatized by the incessant shelling, but their rudimentary entrenchments reduced casualties and shrapnel did little damage to the works. Italian infantry attacked on each of the next seven days. Many of the sorely needed, professional Italian field officers fell; but Boroević's line was scarcely dented. It was named the First Battle of the Isonzo. Neither Cadorna nor Boroević ever visited the front to see what their troops faced, hence their inflexible tactics—frontal assault by massed formations against a continuous trench line that was to be held to the death.

When the first attack failed, *Il Popolo* urged patience, determination and resolution. Cadorna brought up replacements and built up his supply of shells; the Austro-Hungarians redoubled work on their defences and dynamited out dugouts in the Carso. Even the heaviest shells could not penetrate five feet of limestone, but dugouts took time to prepare, and when the Italians attacked a second time, many of the 100,000 defenders were not adequately sheltered. In July, the Italians captured the height of San Michele, regarded as the key to Gorizia—*Il Popolo* exulted, but again, too soon. The height was recaptured by ferocious Bosnian troops wielding knives and battle clubs. The Second Battle ended in early August.

Three weeks later the class of '84 was called up and Mussolini was ordered to report to the barracks in Milan. It was a deliverance, because his old socialist comrades and their newspapers had baited him relentlessly as a slacker—"Why is not the famous interventionist off to the war?" He bade farewell to Rachele and at least two lovers in Milan. One was Ida Dalser, who kept a beauty shop before working at *Il Popolo*. The other was Margherita Sarfatti, the Jewish wife of a socialist lawyer; she was *Il Popolo's* art critic. After busy farewells, Mussolini joined the 11th Regiment of the *Bersaglieri*, where he was pleased by the frame of mind of the class of '84: "Men of thirty who understand the necessity of the hour." He started a war diary, which was published in sections in *Il Popolo*, and in later years became required reading in the Italian schools. After two weeks of retraining he was sent to the front as a replacement. They took a train decorated with greenery to Cividale.

The next day at 0600, they started marching—400 men each lugging 30kg of gear. They crossed the old frontier and then passed through the pleasant, tidy town of Karfreit, which the Italians called Caporetto and which is now Kobarid Slovenia. We shall use its Italian name. Ahead of them loomed the snow cap of Mount Krn, which to Mussolini was *"il fameoso e misterioso Monte Nero."* They crossed the Isonzo, "wonderfully blue," on a bridge and started climbing. Everywhere he saw evidence of the massive Italian war effort. Italian engineering was first-rate; their new roads snaked up seemingly impassable slopes. Along the roads were mule teams and a few Fiat trucks, sturdy and reliable, the vanguard of the thousands that were to come. The replacements stopped to gape at a platoon of forty-six prisoners whose commander was a cadet not yet twenty years old and who "could barely restrain his tears." According to Mussolini his classmates now regarded him as their leader.

With scarcely a breather, they started up the mountain on a mule trail; wounded Italians and enemy were coming down. An exploding shell covered the *Bersaglieri* with dirt and leaves; one man's collar bone was shattered. They slept in the open near the battalion kitchens; dinner was "spaghetti, broth, a slice of meat." The next morning they were apportioned to companies; Mussolini and the others assigned to the 8th company climbed up a steep mountain trail for three hours, passing fresh graves along the way. They were now at 1,900 metres; the air was thin and freezing. The exhausted replacements panted desperately as they pulled themselves up the last few metres. By early evening they reached the line; men were lying on their bellies and sheltering behind rocks. An officer ordered them to load and fix bayonets for action. They opened fire at 2200; it was promptly returned, and both sides tossed a few grenades. The battlefield was illuminated by rockets. The man beside Mussolini was hit by grenade splinters in both arms; Mussolini covered him with his blanket. After two hours a section of the Italian line erupted in a shower of flames and sharp rock fragments; it had been mined. The firefight slackened off toward dawn. When it was light enough for observers to register their fire the Italian artillery opened up on the enemy trenches. The *Bersaglieri* pulled in their wounded and dead. They had lost about thirty men, for no gain whatsoever. It is hard to imagine the exhaustion of the replacements after the long, arduous climb capped by a night of battle.

When the news circulated that Benito Mussolini was in the 8th company three officers from the regiment stopped by to embrace and congratulate him for leading the struggle for intervention. Similar episodes occur frequently in his diary. Most of his fellow soldiers were peasants; Mussolini lauds their spirit and dedication, but many of them regarded him with suspicion and few thanked him for getting them to war—and he found them rather dull. On 20 September the company commander took Mussolini up to the advanced outpost, close to the enemy line. A Sicilian *Bersaglieri* jumped up and started hurling grenades; an enemy bomb wounded him in both legs. Mussolini and three others carried his stretcher down to the aid station.

The class of '84 learned how to live at the front. The enemy were on higher ground, looking down on them. Popping one's head into view for an instant might mean death. The Italian fieldworks were meant to be temporary staging areas for assaults, not a defensive redoubt. The Italians had "… mere holes dug between the rocks … everything is temporary and unstable." Water was short; there were few springs on the mountain sides and as winter neared, the streams had dried up. Clothes went unwashed; lice multiplied. The latrines were open excavations and many had diarrhoea, so the facilities were busy and odoriferous. The stench of bodies drifted in from No Man's Land; rats thrived. When the Italian soldiers saw photographs of trenches along the western front they envied their comfort and security. At the front the *Bersaglieri* wore tight woollen skull caps, not their traditional felt hat with its ornament of feathers, and they were permitted to talk to an officer without standing to attention. As he later wrote, "It was far away from our Garibaldian conception of what war was." The enemy was better off. They picked the best ground for defence, brought in well-trained engineers to design fortifications and built them with a will. Where practicable, pipelines brought water up close to the firing line.

A few days later Mussolini was ordered to present himself to the regimental commander, an hour's march down the slope. The colonel said:

> You must stay with me. You must relieve Lieutenant Palazzeschi in his official work and you must write, when you are off duty, the history of the regiment during the war. This is a suggestion you understand—not an order.

Mussolini respectfully declined, but asked for a transfer to the 7th company, commanded by one of the interventionist officers who had embraced him. When his mates asked why he had turned down such a plum assignment, he said: "I have come to war to fight, not to write"—not mentioning his diary in *Il Popolo* and the necessities of politics.

On 21 September, they were shifted to the slope of another mountain. As they settled in, Mussolini's platoon lieutenant was shot by a sniper. They slept in tents; they were at 1,897 metres and the angle of the mountainside was as steep as 75 degrees, so between headquarters and the firing line they hauled themselves hand to hand up along a rope strung on the slope. The line consisted of two-man foxholes. During the day the men crouched in their holes playing cards; Mussolini had nothing to read. Four days later they had the "mist, cold and rain of winter;" leaves fell on their tents "with a rasping sound;" the rain seemed endless. They wrapped themselves in their cloaks. Seven days later they were relieved and went down to a valley, where they slept in huts. The valley had been a battlefield and so there were bits and pieces of equipment, cartridges, empty meat tins and the like everywhere, interspersed with Austro-Hungarian graves. The rain kept on. The mail came, but none for Mussolini or his classmates—the post office had lost them. They were finally issued winter clothing.

On 6 October, they started for a new sector of the front. Along the way they stopped to clean rifles and to receive an issue of new shoes. The next day they marched for ten hours. Some fell out, unable to keep pace; Mussolini took a nasty tumble and smashed his wristwatch. The next morning, under fire from sharpshooters, they moved up the slope and scraped out foxholes. That night he slept for thirteen hours. The next afternoon they were shelled for an hour; a stout branch ripped from a tree fell across Mussolini's hole, but he was not hurt. Two men in the company were wounded. The following day their rifle clips were inventoried. Each man was supposed to have twenty-eight, those with fewer were disciplined. They were shelled again—two men were killed and nine wounded. They spent most of each day in tents or holes except for their turn in the front line. Mussolini bathed and washed his hair for the first time in a month. In the evening they could hear the enemy singing their national hymn and shouting: "*Bersaglieri* of the 11th, we are waiting for you" and "Italian scoundrels get off our land." Every day they had a ration of coffee, a little wine, a shot of *grappa*, a piece of cheese and half a can of meat, along with almost as much bread as they could eat. Many felt that they were short-changed in their precious coffee, and they griped that the "Government is a thief." Mussolini frowned on the issue of *grappa*; he had promised Rachele to drink little. A year later he would happily drink a half bottle of rum when one came his way. Every morning they watched the wounded and those with frozen feet limping or being carried down from the outposts. Mussolini was struck by their stoicism; they smoked cigarettes and most travelled silently. Each company received six steel helmets, on the front of each was emblazoned R. F., for *Republique Française*.

The next day they all longed for a helmet. Mussolini and his hole-mate Petrella were going about their morning routine when a heavy howitzer lobbed a huge shell at the Italian rear area; it passed over "with a ferocious hissing sound." Ten minutes later there was a second. Another ten minute wait. The third landed up the slope, closer to them; the fourth was closer still. Another ten minutes. They crouched in their holes, which were covered with branches.

> The hissing of the fifth … I could hear it above me. Very, very close—about seventy centimetres above our heads. Petrella and I crouched motionless on the ground. A moment's wait which seemed hours. The projectile exploded only three metres from where we were. The current of air had enough force to completely uncover our shelter. A hail of shell fragments and rocks. A tree was torn up by the roots. Boulders were shattered. We were literally covered from head to foot with earth and stones and debris.

The stock of Petrella's rifle was sliced in two. Mussolini's canteen was riddled with holes and his rifle strap severed. The trees about them were stripped of bark. A comrade was beheaded, but neither Petrella nor Mussolini had a scratch. They huddled in their hole, waiting with pounding hearts for the enemy to reload and reset their giant cannon; but there were no more shots that day. Later they inspected the enormous shell hole. Mussolini retrieved a 2-kilogram fragment of shell, still warm; it became a centrepiece in his collection of war relics.

At noon on 18 October, the Italian artillery opened up; more than 1,300 guns along a 48 kilometre length of front. Italian warplanes bombed the enemy aerodrome just east of Gorizia and then turned their attention to supply depots and headquarters. The *Bersaglieri* enjoyed it thoroughly. They had not realized there were so many batteries about them. They identified the calibres of their guns by their characteristic sounds. They sang and whistled an accompaniment, shouting "good luck" when a projectile roared overhead. The explosion of shells from the largest guns "made the mountains tremble." The bombardment continued all night and all of the next day. Mussolini was on a work detail bringing up empty sandbags, cases of hand grenades and a moveable metal shield that would be pushed forward to shelter the men who would cut the enemy wire. The chaplain came up to say mass. The bombardment continued for four days; they were told to be prepared to advance later in the day, when they would take position in the attacking line between two battalions who were already at the front. Mussolini was told that he had been proposed for promotion to corporal—it ultimately came through many months later. At midday the enemy artillery opened up; they had been saving ammunition until the Italian infantry attacked. The *Bersaglieri* hunkered in their holes, while the wounded streamed back from the front. They had made no progress—far too many Austro-Hungarian rifles and machine guns had survived—so Mussolini and his comrades stayed where they were. The next day the enemy exploded three mines under the Italian line, doing little damage, but in any event their assault was getting nowhere—it made little matter because they were merely a diversion.

The serious attacks were further south. After the first bloody day the Italian ranks were restocked with raw troops. The artillery returned to work for a few hours, and the assaults resumed near Gorizia. The following day the main thrust was along the Adriatic Coast. On the seventh day of the battle Mussolini's company had four men killed by a shell; they moved up closer to the line into holes far poorer than those they had left. The day after the battle ended the snow began to fall. One platoon from the company was posted in the front line, where they were shelled lavishly for the next two days. Mussolini reported that the Austro-Hungarians were so generous with their shells that they fired forty-seven shots at a single shelter.

When a newspaper with the official communiqué arrived at the front he could see how little had been achieved. Only Mussolini and one other enlisted man in the company read newspapers, though "for the most part" the men were literate—62 per cent of the Italians could read—but the men were interested only in news from their homes. Their pay was too paltry to feed a family—many had children with too little bread. Rachele and Edda were supplemented by a monthly stipend from *Il Popolo*. The days shortened, but only officers were permitted candles in their shelters; the men improvised lamps from a tin, some sardine oil or fat from the meat, and a wick of unravelled cloth so they could play cards or traditional hand games. Mussolini passed the long, boring hours studying his comrades. They never spoke of the goals of the war, the dreams that *Il Popolo* made so much of: "I have never heard one of these men speak of the subject of neutrality or intervention. I believe that many of the *Bersaglieri*, who have come from remote villages, are absolutely ignorant of the meaning of the words." The war was a disaster that they were forced to be part of. One song told all—"We must go to war, because of the King." Nonetheless, most would risk death or mutilation rather than hang back; religion had little to do with it—most wore religious medals, but few attended mass. Mussolini wore a ring made from a horseshoe nail; a talisman which he acknowledged was his equivalent to the image of a saint. The men were cogs in a society which, Mussolini knew, must be led by the natural elite.

They moved to another support position in early November. Their new shelters were pretty good, but soon there was mud everywhere—rivulets of ooze trickling between the holes. Late the next afternoon Mussolini's platoon was ordered to relieve the men on the front line; they went up in the dark through driving rain. Whenever the enemy lit the battlefield with a flare, they flung themselves into the cold, slimy mud. There were too few holes at the front, so most men had to lie on the open ground. They did not know where the enemy line was or even where their own line was supposed to run. At midnight, snow fell in a dense white blanket, piling up over the men hugging to the slope, afraid that any movement would attract an enemy machine gunner. They lay miserable and freezing; it was Mussolini's worst night so far.

The Third Battle finally ended; the Italians had lost another 67,000 men. The enemy lost fewer, but a higher per centage of their strength—their VII corps lost 85 per cent of its riflemen. Mussolini's platoon was relieved and headed back down the slope; a machine gunner spotted them and wounded seven men. At their bivouac, they lit enormous fires, the sun came out, and they cheered up. Mussolini's company was set to work excavating dugouts, but division ordered Mussolini and four other men to report to the rear. The five marched three weary hours to a town where they tried to sleep in a noisy barracks on mattresses stuffed with straw from wine-bottle covers. The next morning they continued on their way, pausing to examine the cemetery of the 6th *Bersaglieri*; more than 100 grave stones and a large cross in the centre. It "made me silent and melancholy." As they neared Caporetto, the scene changed; along the road they met elegant officers in immaculate uniforms, "well-fed, rosy-cheeked," and on well-groomed horses. When they passed through town the bystanders stared at these filthy, muddy, ragged apparitions: "We are, modestly, proud of being the objects of their curiosity."

According to his published diary, he then hung about aimlessly for six days before being ordered to return to regiment—just another snafu. In his autobiography, he writes that he was supposed to enter officer candidate school, but had been blackballed because of his politics; he claims that the prime minister ruled that such a troublemaker should never be an officer. After his rejection he picked up his travel papers, his pay and a tin of meat and struck off back to the mountains. In Caporetto he visited the cemetery, where he helped bury two soldiers who had died in hospital. He went to church, which was crammed with troops. At the end of the service they sang a hymn new to Mussolini:

> O, Holy Mother
> Bless the Italians,
> Make our army victorious
> In the Holy name of Jesus.

He marched on by himself; his last stage was in the snow while a column of mules carrying men with frozen feet passed in the opposite direction.

Then there is a gap in the diary. He does not tell us that on 11 November his mistress, Ida Dalser, gave birth to a son, christened Benito. It was the day after the Fourth Battle of the Isonzo began; it was fought in the centre of the front, and was as bloody and fruitless as the previous attacks. During the Third and Fourth Battles the enemy used 37 million small arms rounds, 706,000 shells, 76,000 hand grenades and 13,500 mortar shells.

At the end of the month, Mussolini fell ill with typhus. He was evacuated to the military hospital in Cividale and from there to a Milan hospital, where his brother Arnaldo could visit. When he could get about he was given a month's leave. He went to Forlì, where on 16 December he married Rachele in a civil ceremony. Returning to Milan, he saw young Benito and Ida, resumed their affair, and made financial provision for the son (who died in an institution during World War II). He spent his days at *Il Popolo*, adjusting its political line and finding some hours for Margarita Sarfatti. He warned against "the insidious and subterranean propaganda of the priests and socialists … working for peace at all costs, a peace of compromise."

Gustav Mannerheim
July through December 1915

The Russian army continued to retreat throughout the summer. Warsaw fell on 5 August, losing Mannerheim his home and goods. Inevitably, the enemy pursuit slowed as their supply lines lengthened. At the end of August Mannerheim's rheumatism flared up again, his joints were swollen and so painful that he could scarcely walk—riding was torture.

The divisional doctor prescribed treatment in the hot springs at Odessa. He took medical leave and travelled by rail the 600 kilometres to the shores of the Black Sea. Odessa was a beautiful, rich, modern city, built up after the Crimea had been taken from the Turks. The wide city streets were lined with splendid palaces, homes, handsome apartment buildings and elegant shops. There are gracious parks; along the cliff overlooking the harbour there was a splendid walkway, connected to the shore by the impressive, giant Potemkin Stairs. His sister Sophie, who was a senior sister at the Surgical Hospital in Helsinki, came to Odessa to nurse and keep him company. Their family had not allowed her to study nursing, but after a brief marriage and divorce, she pulled free to attend the Nightingale School at St Thomas's Hospital in London before embarking on a noteworthy career in the profession she loved.

General Mannerheim was warmly welcomed by Odessa society. Though a bit creaky at present, he was the epitome of the dashing, heroic, handsome, aristocratic cavalry officer, sporting the Sword of St George along with his collection of lesser decorations and known for his explorations. It was less pleasant when he talked war with wounded officers recuperating in the city—the situation seemed even worse than he had thought. The depots behind the lines were overflowing with conscripts; almost six million men had been called up, but without trained officers or NCOs, the conscripts idled about in training camps and indulged in subversive talk. In the past year the army had lost half a million trained men. Enormous quantities of stores had been destroyed or captured in the retreat; the factories were behind in replacing what had been lost. The only bright spot was the defeat of the Turks in the Caucasus. Public outrage had led to the dismissals of the effective minister of war and of the commander of the eastern front, the Grand Duke Nicholas, who was respected in the army for knowing his job and for making decisions. Now the Tsar held the reins.

The idea of the Tsar as Supreme Commander was ludicrous to all who knew him; he was far too dim, retiring and indecisive and was incapable of touching men's hearts. He had no political sense either, for instance when the war came he sent the Duma home—he would rule by *ukase*. Then he recalled the Duma in February 1915, only to dismiss them after three sittings because they criticized him. When he recalled them a third time a progressive coalition demanded a parliamentary government and amnesty for all political prisoners. The scandalized Tsar sent them home yet again.

Mannerheim returned to his division at the end of September, spending the autumn of 1915 in defensive operations to keep a corner of Galicia in Russian hands, with the usual "at any cost orders." The strategic aim was to prevent the enemy from occupying the region of the Ukraine north of the Romanian border. When the fighting died down in December the 12th Cavalry Division had a few weeks' rest, before marching 200 kilometres north to the railway junction of Luck (366 kilometres due west of Kiev).

Herbert Hoover
July through December 1915

Hoover had found money and a passageway through the blockade; now he needed sixty ships to carry the food. He had twenty Belgian vessels, requisitioned by their Government for the duration. After most tedious negotiations, he contracted to charter thirty German merchantmen, stranded in neutral ports. They were to be operated by Dutch companies with Dutch crews. At the last minute, the French Government vetoed the scheme. By the time the French were persuaded to relent, the Germans realized that leasing their ships would give the equivalent extra tonnage to Allied shipping, so they withdrew their offer. The needed ships had to be leased at a higher cost from the scarce world stockpile. Each ship displayed on its side "Belgian Relief Commission" in letters that could be read from far off and each flew the CRB flag. The Germans maintained a mine-free channel into Rotterdam. When they altered its course, they informed the Dutch who then passed the information along to the CRB skippers. At first, the British insisted that all CRB ships sailing from North America stop at a port on the south of England for inspection, adding days to the voyage; finally the British agreed to inspect them before they sailed.

Hoover was surely startled and apprehensive when his old foe Kitchener asked him to call at the War Office. He could never have guessed why he was summoned. Kitchener pressed him to accept British Citizenship, so that he might do an unspecified "great service" for his new country. Hoover declined. One possibility is that they wanted him to direct their newly established Ministry of Munitions. Lloyd George became the minister; it is more likely that he wanted Hoover as his right-hand-man.

The CRB organization resembled a mini-state. Headquarters for Belgium and Northern France was in Brussels, where they leased six floors in a new office building; the Belgian National Committee occupied the other three. The French Committee was headquartered in Lille. There were local committees throughout territories served by the CRB, which managed all transportation and warehouses. When Hoover visited he would meet with the assembled local representatives, quietly listening to their ideas and problems. Many CRB workers came to idolize their boss, though once his mind was made up on an issue he was testy with any who persisted in trying to change it. Every recipient had ration cards—separate cards for each major commodity with squares to be punched when delivery was taken for the specified time period. Separate branches of the organization distributed food to those able to buy and to those relying on charity. The distribution points were run by local mayors. All of the harvest in Belgium in excess of that needed for the farm family was requisitioned and put into the food chain; this shut down the black market. To keep up production generous prices were guaranteed for future crops.

Northern France posed further problems. Local produce was used by the German Army and repaid with food from stores in Germany, but there were always disputes about the balance sheet. Most of the *maires* who led the 1,200 communes were gone, many of them serving in the French Army. There was no lawful mechanism for replacing them, so the CRB assumed the authority to appoint replacements—soon more than 40 per cent of the *maires* in Northern France were women. The CRB, acting as an intermediary, paid the allowances from the French Government to families in the occupied areas who had members serving in the French armed forces. Soon there were too few French francs circulating in the occupied area to sustain these transactions, so the CRB printed its own currency. The Germans seized some of these notes as reparations and used them to purchase items they wanted. To stop this, the CRB issued a distinct currency for each commune—1,200 different ones. Each note had to be signed by the *maire*. Another problem in France was that people would not abandon their homes located just behind the firing line, even though there were casualties. In desperation, the CRB forced them to leave by refusing them rations until they did so.

The *maires* raised money for charity by selling the empty flour sacks and condensed milk tins to the Germans. British attackers captured German trenches shored up with sandbags stencilled CRB and discovered homemade hand grenades assembled in the tins—there were howls of protest. The CRB responded by requiring each commune to deposit 10 francs for each sack or tin. The recycled tins were shipped to the Netherlands where they were melted down under the eyes of British agents.

The "benevolence" side of the operation provided the destitute with fuel, clothing, medical care, etc. In addition to the staples on the ration there were kitchens from which the needy received a daily bowl of soup. Hoover wrote:

> The emblem of Belgium during the war should have been a child carrying a soup bucket.

The CRB also paid teachers to keep the schools going and police to maintain order. Eventually 50,000 people, mostly women, were working for the CRB, in part paid with free ration cards. Children were a special concern, because for normal growth they needed fats and trace nutrients not found in the rations. A noon meal programme was established in schools and in public buildings; by 1918 2.5 million lunches were provided daily for children and expectant mothers (after the war children's health was better in Belgium and Northern France than ever before). The great cottage industry in Belgium was lace tatting; about 50,000 families depended on it for their livelihoods and the market collapsed with the war. The CRB bought the lace in exchange for ration cards and extras. Each item was labelled with the maker's name. After the war $40 million of lace was sold on the world market and the makers received belated dividends for their artistry.

In late 1915, Hoover resigned from all of his business connections, except for his personal interest in the Burma mines. That autumn the boys returned to live in England, where he claims they soon acquired Oxford accents. Lou was busy with the American Woman's hospital for treating British wounded and a knitting factory providing work for women left without funds because of the war. Wilson's adviser Colonel House stayed with them in the Red House when in London. Hoover gave him ideas about how Wilson might make peace. But he was deeply sceptical; they thundered out lofty phrases like "a just peace". It was all unreal. The hard facts were that the leaders on both sides had no idea of a stalemate; they wanted victory; they wanted world power, new territorial possessions. The masses in each country believed that they were fighting for defence of their firesides against monstrous enemies and were going to get full compensation and vengeance upon them. Hoover tried—unsuccessfully—to show House that "Total war produced total hate," and that "In this furnace of hate statesmen were no longer free agents."

V

Verdun to Brusilov's offensive

Herbert Hoover
January to June 1916

Hoover travelled constantly; during the war, he crossed the North Sea forty times, reading as he went. He studied previous European famines. The worst of them, after the Thirty Years War, killed one-third to one-half of the European population. Surely the present war would also be followed by a famine, unless the world was organized to prevent it. While reading about the French Revolution he learned that almost all of the writings by émigrés about their experiences had been lost to history because they were discarded as valueless. To prevent such loss in his generation he set up a library at Stanford University to preserve documents on war, peace and revolutions.

He was bombed in Boulogne while on a visit to the King of the Belgians. His window was blown in and a shard of glass cut his arm. A cockney NCO pounded on his door, ordering him to the cellar. In the lobby he found the cockney now standing on a chair bellowing "Women, children foist." Terrorized women and children jammed the stairway; there was no man within metres, but the NCO kept shouting to pile on the panic:

> A Frenchman standing next to me said calmly, 'Shall we go over and kick him to death?' I felt like that too but instead went back to bed.

King Albert resided with his family in the tiny strip of Belgian territory along the Channel Coast still free of Germans. He told Hoover that the happiest period of his life had been when he worked in the States as a railway fireman. Hoover was bombed a second time when the packet he was sailing on from the Netherlands to England was captured by the Germans, who ushered it into Zeebrugge to search for escaped prisoners of war and Allied agents. A French plane dropped five bombs at them; the first knocked over and slightly wounded the Dutchman standing beside Hoover on the deck:

My neck had a crick in it for a week from the earnestness of my interest in the next four rounds from that plane.

The son of Colonel Marx, their German liaison officer in Brussels, had been killed or captured on the Russian front—the family knew no more. Hoover contacted the American ambassador in Petrograd (the name the Tsar gave Saint Petersburg at the outbreak of the war because it sounded less German). He was able to tell the colonel that his son had been wounded but was now recovered and was in a certain prison camp. The Americans conveyed messages from father to son and added small sums for the prisoner to buy extras. A few months later the CRB was notified that some of their staff were engaged in espionage and therefore must leave. Hoover rushed over to Brussels and called on Colonel Marx. The following day the colonel showed Hoover the German intelligence service report that was the basis for the accusation. A young American working in the Rotterdam office frequently travelled to their offices in France and Belgium; he thoughtfully provided the Germans with every anti-German remark uttered by his co-workers. Six men were accused and Hoover sent them home. He ordered the informer to report to him in London and he was arrested the moment he touched foot on British soil. After a week in jail, with assurances that he was likely to be shot in the moat of the Tower of London, he was deported to the US, where he disappeared from history.

Charles de Gaulle
January to March 1916

In January, de Gaulle fell ill with an infection, but he stayed at the front. He wrote to his mother that in February they would leave the line for weeks of rest and refitting. Falkenhayn had other plans—an attack on the fortress city of Verdun, a tempting target because its railway line had been cut by the German advance in 1914. He would strike on the east bank of the Meuse where dense forests ran almost up to the French lines, ideal for screening a build-up. He concentrated his air force there to prevent French aviators from crossing the line; winter mists helped also. The Germans built roads, light railways, supply dumps and airfields, all carefully camouflaged. Artillery positions were dug and the heavy guns were brought up at night—2.5 million shells were stockpiled. Large reinforced concrete underground bunkers called *Stolen* (tunnels) were constructed to shelter the attacking infantry, so there would be no packed assault trenches for the French artillery to batter. The infantry was beefed up with flame-throwers that poured out thick black smoke to make them even more frightening.

The French line on the east bank of the Meuse contained three concentric arcs of concrete forts built in the late nineteenth century by Italian labourers. The forts were kept up-to-date; the most recent upgrading was in 1913. Each had underground quarters, storage areas, a hospital and a chapel. Visiting the forts today gives little idea of the lay of ground then, because after the war the French planted trees around them to sanctify the site. In 1915 the ground around the forts was treeless and their vistas were awesome; each could support its neighbours. The exposed facades had embrasures for rifle and machine guns, and observation ports and retracting turrets mounting rapid-fire cannon sprouted from the roofs. After the Belgian forts proved to be death-traps, the French removed most of the guns for other uses. The forts were left with weak garrisons behind a trench line which now defended the city.

At dawn on 21 February, a giant 380mm German naval gun mounted on a railway car raised its muzzle to fire at its target, one of the bridges over the Meuse in the city of Verdun, 32 kilometres away. The shell struck directly in the courtyard of the Bishop's Palace, demolishing one corner of the cathedral—a titbit for Allied propagandists. Immediately thereafter, the 1,220 artillery pieces carefully sited along the 13-kilometre front opened up. The French artillery positions were covered by a cloud of poison gas, released from shells that exploded with a soft plop. Almost unnoticed in the hurricane of shells, a Krupp 420mm mortar fired an 800kg shell at the largest of the forts, Douaumont. The gunnery was tiptop—the shell struck the roof, penetrated and exploded. Inside the fort there was a crash like a dozen thunderbolts, the walls quaked and dust filled the air; but the occupants were unharmed. The shell had exploded in an outer layer; the inner layer was undamaged—the forts had been built with two plates of first-rate reinforced concrete, with a layer of sand four metres thick between them. During the battle, sixty-two of these huge shells hit Douaumont; the major damage they caused was knocking off half of the sign over the main gate. The carapaces of the Verdun forts were far superior to any the Germans had encountered previously—they were not dinosaurs after all.

At 1600, the German infantry came into action. Falkenhayn's concept was that they were to send out probing patrols; they should advance in force only where the defenders had been smashed—artillery would kill the Frenchmen. The objective was killing, not gaining ground. The army commander, the Imperial Crown Prince, had a contrary vision—he wanted a great victory and hoped to capture the city in three days. After the French line was tossed for hours into the sky by high explosive, the German infantry battalions emerged from their *Stolen* and advanced to occupy what had been French positions. They were met by Frenchmen who crawled out of the rubble and fought savagely, so the Germans paid for every metre they advanced. When it was dark the German artillery poured fire again on the line where the French survivors were sheltering. The scenario was repeated every day; the line of red balloons the German infantry flew above their first line so their artillery knew where they were crept forward until the French were pushed back to the old fort line. On the fourth day Fort Douaumont was captured by a handful of pioneers who slipped in through an embrasure and locked most of the garrison in their quarters. The French admitted that the fort had been taken, but claimed that it fell to a massive, suicidal assault and that the conquerors occupied only wreckage. All civilians were ordered to evacuate Verdun. The Crown Prince, although behind his time schedule, was ecstatic, even though his infantry had suffered heavily.

The French high command dispatched reinforcements and promised the local commanders that they would suffer if they gave way. Joffre gave the command of Verdun to Pétain. Famously, an aide ferreted out Pétain at the hotel *Gare du Nord* in Paris—where he was entertaining a lady. Pétain set up headquarters in the village of Souilly, 19 kilometres south of Verdun, astride the only road running into the city. He was stricken with double pneumonia but his spirit of implacable resistance nonetheless seeped down to the survivors in their shell holes, as did a new sense of decision, command, and planning. His first order reminded them: "France has its eyes on you." He traced the lines to be defended on a map with charcoal; the remaining forts were the linchpins in these lines. The French artillery fired according to an overall plan, with concentrated, localized barrages that cheered their infantrymen's hearts. A feverish Pétain would stand on the front steps of his quarters, watching two streams of lorries passing—fresh men heading into hell and the wounded and stunned survivors coming out, while thousands of labourers shovelled gravel to fill the ruts chewed by the tyres. In the first week in March, 190,000 men and 25,000 tons of supplies went up the road, which became known as the *Voie Sacrée*.

The 33rd Regiment passed through Souilly in the night and entered Verdun on the morning of 26 February. Three days later they moved up to the front, part of the way in a tortuous single file weaving through a carpet of corpses. When they arrived at their position, they could see Douaumont looming off in the distance—"there was no front-line trench, no communication trench, no wire, no sketch-map." The men sheltered in shell holes and behind low, broken walls—the shattered shell of a village. They were ordered to dig deeper, but they could not bring themselves to do so—too many decaying body parts were buried in the earth. De Gaulle was sent with a scouting party to establish contact with the French regiments on either flank. The night was quiet; he could hear enemy assembling for an attack. At 0600, the Germans started to shell. After two hours the firing swelled to a furious barrage, an absolute hell that continued for four and a half endless hours. Then the artillery fire lifted and a wave of Germans came toward them through the smoke and dust. De Gaulle's 10th company had only thirty-seven fighters left. They opened fire, the Germans fell back but then a second wave came at them. After the third or fourth wave was beaten back the attacks stopped. There was a second, violent bombardment. The remnants of his company huddled near the centre of their line; they had lost contact with the units on their flanks. When the shelling paused de Gaulle led the survivors off to the right to re-establish contact, running as quickly as they could over the shattered ground. Then a line of Germans appeared from the smoke; De Gaulle threw a grenade and leapt into a shell hole. Several Germans reached the same hole at the same time. One of them shoved his bayonet through de Gaulle's left thigh. De Gaulle shouted for his men to surrender, then, in blazing, unsupportable pain, he passed out.

When he came to, he was being cared for by two of the medical officers from his own battalion; they were all prisoners of the Prussian Guard. In three days the 33rd Regiment lost thirty-two officers and 1,443 others—about 60 per cent. The colonel survived and reported that de Gaulle had led the fragments of his company as a forlorn hope, charging directly into the advancing Prussians where his handful fought with rifle-butts and bayonets, "selling its life dearly and falling gloriously." De Gaulle was recommended posthumously for the *Légion d'Honneur* with the additional information that he had succumbed to poison gas following his bayoneting. The account was embellished for Pétain's signature and, perhaps with his input, described de Gaulle as a "company commander well known for his great intellectual and moral value" and "an incomparable officer in all respects." His family mourned.

Mustapha Kemal
November 1915 to July 1916

Kemal must have been taken aback when he returned to Constantinople to find that he was scarcely known to the public—his picture had appeared in the newspapers only once or twice during the Gallipoli battles, and he had scarcely been mentioned in the communiqués. The press interviewed him, but Enver Pasha forbade its publication and declined to promote him. Kemal gained renown by word-of-mouth when soldiers returning from the Peninsula passed on stories of his bravery and skill. He shared a house with his mother and sister; this was galling and constraining—his mother, as a fervent believer, did not approve of alcohol or staying out at all hours. When he had started school, she insisted that he receive a Moslem education. He was taken to the school in the traditional procession, but hated it. He always claimed that his willpower was such that he forced his parents to transfer him to a secular school, but in truth it may have been his father's choice. After his father died the family moved to the countryside, but Kemal again prevailed, returning to Salonica to attend a school which would prepare him for the military academy. Now in Constantinople, mother and son battled wills once again.

He fruitlessly pressed his political views in long detailed letters to the Grand Vizier and other ministers—the nub of his argument was that their country was being ruined by Enver Pasha, who was a cat's paw in German hands. Some of the best-trained and best-equipped Ottoman divisions had been sent as reinforcements to the Russian front, while the British and French were allowed to slip out from their snare on the Peninsula. Disgusted with home life, Kemal went to visit friends in Sofia. He instructed his aide in Constantinople to accept any reasonable appointment offered, thus he became the commander of the XVI Corps, which had been withdrawn from Gallipoli and was refitting at Adrianople. Six weeks later he marched his corps off to the Russian front in the Caucasus Mountains. Enver was planning another massive attack there as soon as the snow in the passes melted. Kemal was promoted to general, thereby acquiring the title of Pasha. Conditions were chaotic; there was insufficient food, ammunition and medical supplies. Contractors and procurement officers were corrupt; communications were primitive and the armies had negligible central direction. Enver planned his attack for July, but the Russians struck first, driving the Ottomans before them. Kemal, on his own responsibility, pulled his corps back to good defensive positions.

Harold Macmillan
January to June 1916

Macmillan was judged fit for duty shortly before Christmas 1915, though in fact he never recovered the full strength of his right hand and in his future political life some attributed his weak handshake to an effete nature. After leave he returned to duty with the Reserve Battalion. Now that he no longer thirsted for glory and felt thoroughly at home, life with them was much more agreeable than it had been the year before. Sometimes he served on the King's Guard, which was mounted at St James's Palace; from there a detachment marched over to Buckingham Palace (the Guard began to mount at Buckingham Palace some years later when it was found how well the ceremony drew tourists). Officers periodically made a round of the sentries, but mostly were at leisure to socialize and to read. They entertained women guests at lunch, so his mother could come by. In the evening they had male guests, all in highly civilized surroundings, with good food, delightful wine and service by elderly waiters who were part of the entertainment. He also visited Oxford and Eton, where his pleasure was dimmed by the long lists of killed or wounded schoolfellows.

With time, his fighting spirit revived, so he was game when sent to France with a draft of replacements in the spring of 1916, this time to the 2nd Battalion. In his reading about war he was impressed with a quotation from Pétain, the saviour of Verdun:

> The superiority of mind over matter, of the spiritual over the physical is indisputable and decisive.

He copied this maxim into his Field Pocket Book and resolved to follow it.

The 2nd Battalion was commanded by Colonel C.R.C. de Crespigny, who behind his back was known to one and all as 'Crawley.' The colonel was in constant pain from stomach ulcers, but managed to sustain a relaxed and light-hearted manner, which endeared him to all ranks. Crawley was never seen to read a book, "to all intents and purposes he was illiterate;" his interests were fighting, gambling and horses, a world apart from Macmillan—who adored him nonetheless. And by one of those interesting quirks of human nature, Crawley took a shine to the young fellow with the engaging grin who talked about literature or philosophy at the drop of a hat. On the parade ground the colonel was a strict and precise disciplinarian, but to his superiors in the military hierarchy he often seemed an anarchist. For example, the high command was vexed by poor sanitation in the trenches, so staff officers were dispatched to set things right. While the 2nd was in the line between Ypres and Poperinghe in Flanders they were ordered to take a census of their rat population. Crawley ordered a four-day shoot. All that were bagged were packed into sandbags and allowed to mellow for some days. Then the bags were trucked down and dumped against the front door of brigade headquarters.

A fellow officer in the 2nd was an old friend from Cadogan Place, Eton and Oxford, Harry Crookshank—now nicknamed "Lazarus". In the autumn of 1915 he had been with a working party in No Man's Land when the Germans exploded a mine nearby, covering him with a metre of loose earth. He was able to call out but no one responded. That night men were sent to dig him out. He could hear their chat as they worked, but they did not hear his now feeble moans. Several times they discussed giving up, but persisted and brought him out after hours of being buried alive. He was sent to the dressing station and was back in the trenches the next day. In later life Lazarus, who became a prominent MP, claimed he had been lucky, since in World War II he surely would have been sent on for psychiatric care and might well have been incarcerated in an asylum.

They marched up into the trenches at Wieltje, 3 kilometres northeast of Ypres, in early May. Charles Hamilton Sorley caught the mood:

> All the hills and vales along
> Earth is bursting into song
> And the singers are the chaps
> Who are going to die perhaps.

Packs were left behind; the men carried a light haversack stuffed with extra clothing, a groundsheet, chocolate and cigarettes along with rifle, bombs, ammunition and a gas mask. In most units the men were permitted to bring up surplus goods in a sandbag; but the Guards set higher standards. The communication trenches were in such a sorry state that they had to choose between wading up them in waist deep slime and slipping along the mud in the open. The relief was made without casualties despite the muck, almost a miracle because the Germans shelled most nights. Then the enemy must have learned who had come up, because the next day they shelled the Guards heavily and persist-ently, far more than a customary daily strafe, and they sustained their fire as long as the

Guards were in the line. What struck Macmillan about the battlefield was its seeming emptiness. Peeking over the parapet he could see only a few shattered trees, a few lines of elevated earth and sandbags and the tattered remains of a few blasted villages. It took a leap of the imagination to picture the hundreds of thousands of men lurking in the earth, "planning against each other perpetually some new device of death." He assured his mother that:

> If any one at home talks of peace, you can truthfully say that the army is weary enough of war but prepared to fight for another 50 years if necessary, until the final object is obtained.

Macmillan loathed trench life. Within hours they all were filthy; water was in short supply and strict water discipline was enforced—most clothing remained on as long as they were there. They arrived disinfected but were lousy almost immediately and there was little rest. Officers catnapped in cramped tunnels in the musty earth, men in small cubby-holes dug into the trench wall, three men in each, sitting together on a short bench, usually with torsos lying on thighs. The entrances were covered with groundsheets to block the light and to restrain the damp. Legs must be pulled in so not to trip men walking the trench. It was rare for a man to get more than two hours sleep at a stretch. At thirty minutes before dawn, all of the men were stationed on the fire step in groups of five, one group every 50 metres along the trench. Just after dawn they stood down, leaving one sentry per platoon, and had breakfast. Soon they had their daily issue of 71ml of rum; the officer watched each man drink his ration so they could not trade it or try to build up a stock for a real toot. The officers then wrote their daily reports, while the men cleaned their rifles and gear. Their officer would inspect them minutely to see that they and their equipment were in good order. Next, the platoon sergeant assigned tasks: going back for rations, working on the trench, sentry duty and the like. The day pattern ended at dusk, when they stood-to. After dark, rations were brought up and eaten. During the night, parties left the trench to install and repair wire, dig saps out into No Man's Land or to strengthen parapets. Early in the war the British prided themselves on the sharp alignment of the sandbags on their parapets. Finally, experienced hunters convinced them that precise lines made it much easier for German snipers to see a bit of man protruding over the top; subsequently they were deliberately made irregular. The days and nights in the trench combined danger, fear, little sleep, exhausting work, scant water and poor food. Siegfried Sassoon caught it well:

> Shaken from sleep, and numbed and scarce awake
> Out in the trench with three hours watch to take
> I blunder through the splashing mirk; and then
> Hear the gruff muttering voices of the men

> Crouching in cabins candle-chinked with light
> Hark! There's the big bombardment on our right
> Rumbling and bumping; and the dark's aglare.

They were relieved after four days and marched back to the prison in Ypres. The cells made fine billets; with heavy brickwork and windows plugged with sandbags, they were safe from all but the heaviest shells. Alongside was a grassy park suitable for drill; the men laughed because it was named the *Plaine d'Amour*, though they saw precious little of such activities out there during their stay. Macmillan and his fellow officers enjoyed boisterous and irreverent dinners with their genial colonel in the chair. They went into a different section of the line in mid-May. Macmillan thought their positions "had apparently been constructed by indolent pigmies," with sandbag parapets only waist high and not thick enough to stop a bullet. The surface of the ground was just above the water table, so they could not dig deeper. They filled thousands of sandbags to make the parapet thicker and higher and they also added eighty-four coils of barbed wire to their front; back-breaking night-work in which almost every man acquired a nasty gash or two. They left the trenches after six days and were taken by train to St Omer, where they rested until 7 June. From there they marched to Camp M, near Poperinghe, where the men were used to lay underground telephone cables. Life in Poperinghe was made more tolerable by a divisional theatre, seating 1,000 men, in which films were shown and band concerts given—the bands of the various Guards Regiments come out to France in turn. On 20 June the 2nd took over Lancashire Farm Line, which was in good condition, so despite heavy machine fire there were few casualties. As always when they arrived back in billets after their relief they were covered with mud that had worked through the layers of filthy clothing to coat their skin. A lovely little lake lay next to their new billets and the men were delighted when given permission to bathe. They were spotted; once the lake was filled with swimmers when the Germans dropped six shells into it, abruptly ending the party.

Benito Mussolini
February to September 1916

Mussolini's diary resumes on 15 February, when he returned from leave. He was in quiet Caporetto, housed in a large camp city on the outskirts. The Slovenian inhabitants were distant and enigmatic. The military cemetery had 600 graves—they were digging more—and was enclosed by a stone wall. There was an inscription on the chapel:

> To restore the sacred boundaries which nature has given to our country these intrepid men died a glorious death.

The next morning he went on to his company's winter quarters. Petrella kissed him, he embraced some of the old comrades—others still steered clear of the warmonger—and was introduced to their new officers. That evening they set out for the line, struggling up mule paths for two days. Their fortifications were abominable; Mussolini was shielded only by bags of frozen snow and a steel plate with a loophole, and their wire entanglements were buried beneath the snow. The enemy wire was 100 metres up the slope. Frozen corpses dotted No Man's Land. They were ordered to fix bayonets and to fire intermittently, to let the enemy know they were now facing *Bersaglieri*. It was bitter cold. Mussolini fired off a half-dozen clips during the night; the enemy fired rarely, but one Italian was wounded.

When the sun rose, they could see the Italian plain behind them, with Udine and the blue line of the Adriatic in the distance. There was desultory shelling, a few men were wounded and Mussolini was pelted with pebbles and sticks. The next day he was one of a working party hauling up food, he could walk on the icy slope with his nailed shoes; those with unadorned soles tied empty sandbags over their boots to gain traction. A friendly medical officer told him that there was trouble in the Italian cities, in Rome streets were barricaded. Soldiers' families were desperately poor and hungry; war workers were well paid and glad to be at home, but the shortage of food and fuel was provoking them also. Cadorna blamed the anti-war demonstrations on socialists, spies and pacifists. Mussolini was called in to meet their new colonel, who wanted to greet the famous interventionist. They were issued white coveralls as camouflage for winter warfare.

For the next few weeks, Mussolini spent twelve hours of every twenty-four in the front line, where they dug each night until they had a trench in which a man could walk its length upright. Just behind the trench was a sheer drop of 100 metres—there was no retreat. At the end of February he received his long promised corporal's chevrons. He was "dizzy with snow." Almost every day someone was lost by sniping or intermittent artillery fire. In early March they were relieved and Mussolini was given a short leave.

His diary does not mention the Fifth Battle, which began on 11 March. It was a gesture to the French struggling to hold Verdun—Cadorna knew he did not yet have enough heavy guns to break through. The Austro-Hungarians were alerted by heavy Italian radio traffic. The Italians bombarded for two days and then their infantry attacked for three days, without pushing any home. The enemy retaliated with the greatest air raid yet seen over Italy—seventy-eight aircraft—eighteen were lost and little damage done.

Mussolini was marched back to the front in a file of men guarded by two *carabinieri*. Italian staff work was so poor that they could not find their units, so Mussolini's file spent fifteen days wandering about. He found his battalion still up in the snow, but in a much better position, behind heavy barbed wire entanglements. The Bersaglieri front line had four redoubts made of enormous tree trunks; they had their shelters in a second line. The Italians were finally taking defence seriously. They used miners' drills to tunnel holes to hold dynamite to blast away the rock. Spring had added a new peril—snow slides; a stray artillery shell or nature itself would start ice and snow plummeting down the slopes—anyone in the avalanche's path was doomed. Every clear day a patrol with binoculars was sent to the top of the ridge line to watch the enemy blockhouses.

Mussolini wondered how long it would be before the *Bersaglieri* cracked. His assessment was that in his company of 250 men there were twenty-five like himself who understood the reasons for the war and fought with conviction. Twenty-five had returned from abroad to serve; they had initiative, determination and were splendid soldiers. Another 100 submitted to the war; they would rather be at home but did their duty. Forty were "brave or cowardly depending on circumstances." The remaining 60 were "composed of the refractory elements, the unscrupulous, the riffraff who have not always the courage to reveal themselves as they are, for fear of the military code." Their effectiveness was contingent on how much they feared their superiors. Soldiers convicted of cowardice were shot by firing squads, their shame was published in their home villages and their families deprived of their civil rights. Officers on the staff who questioned their superiors were jailed; it was different at the top. Cadorna delighted to repeat:

The superior is always right, even when he is wrong.

After more snow, a few days' bombardment, and endless hours, they were relieved at the end of April. Down in the valley it was spring. Mussolini ate a real meal in a little hotel and slept in a real bed. When they formed up the next morning some *Bersaglieri* were too drunk to move. Those sufficiently sober were marched up a magnificent new road, snaking up the mountainside, with frequent tunnels for shelter during a bombardment and periodic sentry boxes and drinking fountains. When they reached their new position they pitched tents and covered them with fir boughs. Mussolini was reading a gift from an interventionist, engineering officer: a collection of writings by Giuseppe Mazzini, the great nineteenth-century advocate of unification. Mussolini endorsed Mazzini's argument that Italian unification had taken so long because there were no leaders: "we lack the few that can lead the many."

At this stage, there is another break in his diary, so there is no mention of the Austro-Hungarian offensive from the Tyrol. The Austrian chief of staff, Franz Conrad von Hötzendorf, knew the area well and believed that an attack could take Padua, only 72 kilometres south of the front, and knock Italy out of the war. The Germans declined to participate and warned him that it was not feasible with the forces he could deploy—Conrad went ahead on his own. Four of the best Austro-Hungarian divisions were moved from the Isonzo to the Tyrol, others came from Galicia; all told, he assembled fifteen divisions and 1,000 guns, including 60 heavy batteries. They attacked in mid-May. The Italians had five defensive lines—but crammed most of their infantry into the first. On day one, Austro-Hungarian units broke through and advanced up to 8 kilometres. Then

THE LESSONS OF WAR

they slowed down, less from a strong defence than from the difficulties in bringing up replacements and supplies through the mountains. By the end of May, they had advanced 24 kilometres. They continued to inch forward, until on 4 June, a Russian offensive by the army of General Brusilov broke through the Austro-Hungarian entrenchments in Galicia. Conrad had to rush back divisions from Italy, where he had gained a "bridgehead to nowhere." His offensive did reshuffle the Italian cabinet; the new interior minister was Vittorio Orlando, who later became prime minister. The military command was unchanged.

Mussolini's diary stops in May and was not resumed for months. During the gap, he was sued in Milan by Ida Dalser, who claimed on the evidence of a hotel register that she was his legal wife and demanded more support for their son. The court ordered Mussolini to pay more, but did not rule that she was the legal wife. Furious, Ida went to Rachele's apartment to create a nasty scene. Some time during the war, Rachele purchased a house and farm near her home village with her "savings." Over the years it was built up as the family retreat.

Adolf Hitler
January to June 1916

The List Regiment began the year as division reserve in Santes, 8 kilometres behind the front. During the winter they welcomed back almost 500 men who had recovered from wounds or illness. The 1st Battalion paraded for King Ludwig III on 15 January. Back in the trenches they had sixteen killed and seventy wounded in two months. Their artillery was ordered not to shell houses behind British lines so they would not be shelled in theirs.

The regimental staff expanded to deal with the increasing complexity of the war. There was the commander and his adjutant Wiedemann, newly promoted to captain, Hitler's immediate superior. There were also officers for ordnance, machine guns, trench mortars, drainage, operations, telephones, mapping, observation and justice, assisted by NCOs and clerks. The runners on duty stayed at headquarters, where those interested might acquire quite a respectable military education by listening to the reports coming from the front and the directives passed down from corps, the discussions among the staff about appropriate responses and the orders issued. During quiet spells the duty officers often chatted about the course of the war and the news from other fronts. An apt student, as *Führer* Hitler unhesitatingly intervened in military decisions, ranging from orders given to army groups to those sent to individual battalions.

On 4 March, they were shifted to a nearby sector of the front, where they had to repair their fortifications. They dug additional deep dugouts, 6 or 7 metres down into the clay, and then boarded over the walls and installed sumps and pumps to keep them dry, electrical cables provided power and light; some dugout walls were even papered. The pioneers built reinforced concrete pillboxes, with prefabricated floors and walls; the roof was poured on site. The Bavarians built niches in their parapets for altars. Communication trenches meandered so they were more difficult for enemy artillery to hit and had periodic funk holes for shelter during a bombardment. The principal complaints were filthy weather and miserable rations. The men lost weight and energy, while the famished horses had to be lashed to their work. In April they had six dead and forty wounded.

In May an interesting novelty was detected—the English were wearing metal helmets, shaped rather like the barber's bowl worn by Sancho Panza. When spring sunshine dried the ground, patrolling in No Man's Land was stepped up. There were frequent clashes, largely fought with grenades. The British now had their oval Mills bombs. They were excellent for trench defence but were dangerous to the thrower in the open because the lethal circle from their fragments had a radius of 30 metres, almost as far as most men could throw them. The Germans had similar 'egg' grenades, lighter than the British and therefore with a longer throwing range, but they preferred their stick bombs, which had a heavier charge and could be thrown further thanks to the leverage of the handle. Some exploded on impact, others had 5.5- or 7-second fuses—the times were stencilled on their handles. They were armed by unscrewing a metal cap from the base of the handle and then pulling the string that was revealed. They did not fragment when they exploded and therefore had a smaller lethal zone. Both sides also had rifle grenades, which were attached to a metal rod that was inserted into the barrel of a rifle. The explosion of a blank cartridge sent the grenade toward the enemy. The Germans phased their rifle grenades out in 1916, because they were too inaccurate to be of much use. Later in the war a new, more accurate type was introduced. The British continually expanded their use of rifle grenades, positioning rifle grenadiers in each wave of an attack. Despite their popularity with both sides less than 3 per cent of the German wounded were hit by grenades, far less than the 44 per cent wounded by small arms fire.

In June, they heard a mine being dug toward them. Progress was followed carefully and countermeasures prepared. It exploded 20 metres short of the German front line. Both sides were thrilled and entertained by the battles overhead between the airmen. German air cover in their sector was led by their first ace, Max 'Tommy' Immelmann, who had become famous the previous autumn when it was announced that he had shot down four of the enemy. In January 1916 he had his eighth victory and was awarded the *Pour le mérite*. Everyone tried to spot his Fokker. He exploited its ability to climb high and then drove out of the sun toward his blinded opponent, when necessary dazzling them further with the lightning, twisting turn he had invented. Immelmann avoided girls, was devoted to his dog Tyras, who also became a celebrity, and to his mother, to whom he wrote daily—a personality remarkably similar to Hitler's. On 28 June Immelmann crashed and was killed; he had shot down fifteen. Soon the spectators cheered the next favourite.

Gustav Mannerheim
January to August 1916

Mannerheim's spirits revived during the winter. Replacements brought his units up to strength and they were armed adequately with carbines, guns and ammunition from Allied and American factories. General Brusilov was given command of the four armies on the Southwestern front, so Mannerheim was again serving under his old commander. Their front ran through the present-day Ukraine, roughly 100 kilometres west of the present Polish, Slovakian and Hungarian borders. Brusilov's predecessor believed that his armies were unfit to attack. Brusilov inspected them, reported that they could attack by May and demanded to be replaced if they were kept on the defensive. The Russian plan for 1916 was to attack the Germans along the northern part of the front while their armies in the south stayed on the defensive. Brusilov argued that they should attack at points along the entire front, so the enemy could not exploit their excellent rail network to rush reserves to a threatened point. Brusilov was permitted to attack also—but not given any additional supplies.

Brusilov wanted to surprise his enemy. To get infantry across No Man's Land it was essential to have an assault trench close to the enemy line. Such preliminary digging took weeks and was a sure giveaway that an attack was coming. Brusilov ordered assault trenches dug at numerous sites along his front. On D-day each army would attack from one of their sites; the army he had formerly commanded would be responsible for the actual breakthrough, but any successful diversionary attack would also be exploited. His army commanders were chary. He reminded them that the enemy was weaker because Germans were being transferred to Verdun and Austro-Hungarians to Italy; those remaining in the east were mostly manning the first trench line. He told his army commanders to be ready to attack in late May on a week's notice. The story of the offensive is told vividly in Sergeyev-Tsensky's novel.

The enemy positions were very strong. They had three defensive lines separated by 3 to 5 kilometres; each line had at least three trenches 50–100 metres apart with heavy wire in front of each. Some of the wire was electrified and in many places there were landmines in front of the first entanglement. The trenches were higher than a man and bristled with armoured emplacements and machine gun nests. They had deep dugouts, many with reinforced concrete roofs, and were equipped with stoves, heaters and often electric light. They were proud of their impregnable fortifications and exhibited photographs and maps of it in Vienna to raise morale on the home front. The Russians used aerial photographs to produce detailed trench maps that were issued to all of Brusilov's officers. The attackers were tutored by French liaison officers and by Russians who had served as observers in France. Infantry was rehearsed behind the line on reproductions of enemy trenches. They would not have much of an edge in numbers, about 600,000 Russians to 500,000 Austro-Hungarians—most of the Russian horde was in the north facing the Germans. Brusilov had 1,770 field guns and 168 heavy pieces. Artillery officers lived in the front line to meet the infantry and to study the landscape; most of the infantry sheltered in deep bunkers, leaving the front line lightly held. In places, they tunnelled forward so that the attackers could walk under their own barbed wire, so they would not need to cut lanes before the attack—another sure giveaway. Brusilov repeatedly visited every part of the line to inspect the works and watch the rehearsals.

To lull enemy suspicions and to avoid jamming the railways only a few cavalry divisions were positioned close to the front. Railways were a continual problem for the Russians. They were short of competent staff and top management was inept, and their headaches were compounded by a scientific miscalculation and by horses. The Russians believed that each soldier required 4,000 calories of energy from food each day. Other armies realized that 3,000 were enough, which spared a proportionate number of railway cars. Horses were even more of a problem—63 per cent of the food wagons arriving at the front carried fodder because the Russians maintained a huge cavalry force.

The enemy sat smugly on their hands. They detected the Russian activity, knew about the deep bunkers and did little to forestall the digging of the assault positions. Just before the attack, Russian deserters revealed that fresh underwear had been issued, a sure sign of an impending attack as it lessened the risk of infected wounds. The commander of the army group opposite Brusilov was the Archduke Joseph Ferdinand, a frivolous snob who refused to ride in the same automobile with his plebeian chief of staff, and who dawdled about with the privileged shirkers on his personal staff.

The Italians desperately needed help because the Austro-Hungarians were gaining ground in the Tyrol. Brusilov's artillery preparation began on 1 June, at four locations along his front, each about 30 kilometres long. The fire kept the enemy in their dugouts while their trenches were smashed and their wire breached. Three days later, while the Austro-Hungarians were celebrating their victory in Italy and Archduke Ferdinand's birthday, the bombardment reached its climax. Their lines were smothered in dust and gases. When the bombardment lifted, the defenders could not see what was coming at them. Their weak reserves were in a tangle; they had been shifted here and there as the commanders tried to guess where the main attack would come. The first Russians came as 'testing' patrols—where they could slip into the enemy trench they signalled for their comrades to come forward. In the first two days the Russians took 50,000 prisoners and seventy-seven guns.

The Russian cavalry's task was to slip through the breaches to take the enemy rail junctions. On the night of D-day Mannerheim's 12th Division marched 20 kilometres closer to the front. The next afternoon they were ordered to move north to where the infantry had made a breach. Because of jammed roads it was dark before they started to trip their way through the former Russian and Austro-Hungarian lines—they were confronted with smashed wire and trenches and deep shell holes. Mannerheim was with his advance guard. His troubles really began when they were through the battle zone; he had good knowledge of the trenches but only pre-war maps of the rear. Since then villages and forests had been obliterated and a maze of new roads constructed. His division, stretched out in column, had to stand in place until he could find out where he was and how to get to their objective. At dawn they encountered the enemy rear-guard, which had pulled back over the river Styr and destroyed the bridge. Mannerheim surveyed the ground with his binoculars. The river was 90 metres across and marsh extended for at least a kilometre on either bank; beyond the marsh on the far side was a manned trench. From Imperial manoeuvres twenty-five years previously he remembered a ford a few miles to the south, so he decided to try to cross there, moving his division down during the next night. When his artillery opened fire there was a prompt, fierce response from the opposite bank, and he could see two tiers of entrenchments. They could not cross there.

He received no orders from either corps or army command. Hearing that the river had been crossed 40 kilometres to the north, he started his division on their fourth consecutive night march. At their destination he found that the report that had brought them there was false—the intact enemy front was still being attacked. His men had spent five nights in the saddle. Two days later the Russians finally broke through and Mannerheim started his exhausted and depleted force toward their objective, the railway junction of Vladmirovka. They rode past fields of ripening maize and sugar beet, dotted with clusters of whitewashed peasant homes. They fought their way to within 20 kilometres and then met resistance too stiff to move with cavalry. He led his division onto a hill, which would be a good defensive position. Once there he made an unhappy discovery, so he immediately sent a message to the commander of the neighbouring infantry division, General Denikin, warning him to prepare to repel German infantry. Denikin scornfully replied that there were no Germans anywhere near; Mannerheim assured him that he could see them from his hill. The Germans had moved rapidly to save their allies' remaining chestnuts. That evening, Mannerheim was ordered to withdraw his troops from the hill. The Germans occupied it without opposition.

The next day Denikin was ordered to retake the hill and Mannerheim was to move to a position from which he could exploit Denikin's success. Mannerheim telephoned the army commander—who had lost an important battle in Manchuria—to suggest that Denikin was unlikely to take the hill and therefore it would be better to position the cavalry where they might move in several directions. "Have you heard my order?"—"Yes, sir"—"Well, carry on then." German heavy artillery blasted the roads and villages in the Russian rear, so Denikin's infantry attack was scrubbed. Mannerheim was ordered south and settled into weeks of position warfare. Brusilov continued to make progress in the north, where the battle went on until mid-August—recall that Brusilov's attacks were only a diversion for primary assaults against the Germans in the north. Few of these were even started and they got nowhere; the Russian supreme command was ineffectual.

The Brusilov offensive did not finish off the Austro-Hungarians, but they did have to give up their attack in Italy and bring men back to Russia. The Germans moved fourteen divisions from Verdun and the Somme east, and transferred fighter aeroplanes to stop the Russian aerial observers. Brusilov had taken 416,000 prisoners, 1,795 machine guns and 581 cannons and had moved the front west by an average of 50 kilometres—the furthest thrust was 95 kilometres. The victory tipped the scale for the Romanians who, with a sheaf of Allied promises in hand, declared war on the Austro-Hungarians at the end of August.

VI

The Somme to the battle for Romania

Harold Macmillan
July though December 1916

On 1 July, the Grenadiers celebrated the news that a massive attack had been launched on both banks of the River Somme; for the preceding week they had heard the distant thunder of a massive bombardment off to the south. In a few days, they read that the French attack south of the Somme had been wonderfully successful; so far the British had gained somewhat less ground. The Germans were said to be sustaining enormous losses; Macmillan suspected that the picture was too rosy. They were not told that on the first day of the attack the British had 19,000 killed—more men than the Germans had opposing them.

Seven days later, they took over the Irish Farm line—1,200 metres of mostly discon-nected shell holes. Here they met an especially nasty sort of unpleasantness. The Germans had trench mortars that shot huge charges, the size of a waste barrel, containing 90 kilograms of explosive. They travelled slowly, so you could watch them climb to their apogee, tumbling end over end and making a woof-woof sound. As they started to fall, you could judge where they would land. If your hole was threatened you jumped out and dashed for a safer one. This was nerve-wracking enough, but the Germans made it worse—when the mortar launched its bomb, their artillery fired shrapnel shells, so you ran a gauntlet if you changed holes. The tension was increased when they had a surprise inspection by the commander of the Guards Division, Lieutenant General Lord Cavan. He and his staff went through their positions with a fine-toothed comb, inspecting the men, their arms and equipment, trench stores, latrines and the like. Happily for Crawley everything was there, clean and in good order, only two mess-tins and three spoons were missing.

That summer, as the regimental historian put it, "The monotony of trench life was relieved by the exciting but dangerous ventures of patrols"—to Macmillan it was "patrol mania." On the morning of 19 July, Crawley ordered him to take out a corporal and a guardsman that night to capture a German, either from a working party between the lines, or by dropping in on the German trench; the difficulties were obvious. Both sides continually fired star shells and Very lights to illuminate No Man's Land and would fire at any moving thing not their own. The patrol had to pick their way through the sally port in the British wire, cross No Man's Land and, if there was not a convenient enemy out there, somehow get through the belts of German wire. Macmillan had a long, seemingly endless day to think about it; he does not tell us where he found the solitude in which to conquer his terror. That evening he and his two men were issued nasty looking wooden clubs as prisoner persuaders, their faces were blackened with burnt cork, their pockets emptied, and bayonets covered by an old sock. When there was a lull in the illumination, they were boosted out of the British trench. Macmillan led the way, successfully navigating the channel through their wire. As they stole across No Man's Land they were challenged by Germans in a listening post. Macmillan waved for his men to throw themselves down into the high grass; a German threw a hand grenade. It hit Macmillan on the head just before it exploded—almost miraculously his steel helmet saved him from serious injury. His eyeglasses were shattered but none of the glass was driven into an eye; a splinter gouged his left temple. The corporal charged and killed the thrower. "In the affray another German was killed or wounded"—perhaps by Macmillan, since I suspect otherwise he would have told us who had done it. Both sides retired from the field. In the morning, Macmillan felt as though he had the worst hangover of his life, and had difficulty walking, saluting or talking. When the patrol reported to Colonel Crawley Macmillan looked a sight with a sticking plaster over his gashed temple and with dulled eyes; his speech was incoherent. The colonel turned to the corporal for an explanation. After hearing about the bomb he asked the corporal, "What happened? What did you do when Mr Macmillan was wounded?"—"Well sir, I saw the German trying to run away. So I 'it 'im, and his helmet came off. Then I 'it 'im again and the back of 'is 'ead came off." Macmillan had complimentary words from his colonel, which he treasured, a second wound stripe, which he was pleased to wear, and a few days later a letter from General Pereira, the commander of the 1st Brigade, thanking him for the "most useful information they had brought in." Macmillan could recall no information whatsoever, but it was nice of the General to trouble to write. The medical officer thought he should be evacuated, but at the time, all of the hospitals were being cleared for future operations, so the wounded went directly to England. Macmillan opted to stay on light duty and to recuperate where he was.

The 2nd Battalion left the Ypres salient on 27 July and during the next days travelled by foot, train and lorry 150 kilometres south to a town in the rear of the Somme sector. After two days' rest they marched up to relieve the battalion holding the right sub-sector of the Beaumont-Hamel line. They were pleased to find the trenches there better than any they had occupied since Loos, neatly revetted and with the added luxury of real dugouts. After three days of heavy shelling they were relieved, and after a few days' rest, the 2nd

Battalion was detached from the Guards Division and marched to an area behind the 29th Division, where they dug a reserve line. Early in September they took a course on the latest developments in bombing and signalling; eight additional runners were trained in each battalion. All this time the attacks were continuing along the Somme.

Haig decided that considering "the deterioration and all-round loss of morale of the enemy troops" it was time to hit them with the final sledgehammer. HQ began planning for a battle already named "Flers Coucelette" in which they would unveil their secret weapon (the tanks), use their best troops, throw a massive preliminary barrage at the enemy and have the artillery lead attackers across No Man's Land with a curtain of fire moving stepwise ahead of them. They would specify every move. The 2nd Battalion practiced their attack on the outlines of the German trench system they would encounter laid out in white tape on a carefully chosen slope. They were taught to move forward along lines that would take best advantage of dips in the ground to shield from enemy fire. The major emphasis was on maintaining communications and coordination at all levels; they were not told about the tanks. Tanks required special planning because they could not travel over ground moon-cratered with shell holes. Therefore, they established 100-metre wide lanes that the artillery would not fire on; a lane on each flank of the Guards Division advance. The tanks must destroy the enemy in the lanes; otherwise, they would enfilade the Guards' advance.

The Guards Division would move forward in sixteen waves. The first wave of the attack was to be the Coldstream Guards. When they took their objective the Grenadiers would pass through them to fight on to their objective. Once there, the 1st Battalion of the Irish Guards would take the lead, with the remaining Grenadiers and Coldstream following in support. The attack orders specified exactly where the leading troops were to be at 1200 and at 1700 and the precise time when each objective was to be taken. They would be assisted by a contact aeroplane flying above them from zero hour to dark on the first day of the attack and from 0630–0900 on the second day, by which time all of their objectives would be taken. The contact aeroplane signalled to ground by a klaxon and could request the infantry to fire signals to show where they were. Red flares meant they were fighting enemy infantry, green that they had met cavalry. The infantry also communicated with the planes by signal lights or white canvas panels laid on the ground. Once the enemy defensive lines were occupied, the "Cavalry would advance and seize the heights ahead." There were rumours that the attack would be supported by some new and mysterious engine of war.

HQ believed they had thought of everything; they had no idea that German defensive tactics along the Somme had been transformed. Falkenhayn was bitterly criticized by his general staff officers for rigid defensive tactics. He bowed to the pressure in late July, appointing Colonel Lossberg as chief of staff of the German Army that the Guards would attack. He had accepted on condition that the attacks at Verdun would be stopped immediately; Falkenhayn promised to do so, but lied. Lossberg set up an elastic defence, which the British had not yet encountered—a defensive line became a series of trenches with outposts in front. A second defensive line was dug beyond the range of the enemy field guns. The defensive lines were connected by long, rambling trenches called switch lines, which were also excellent positions for enfilade fire in case of a breakthrough.

On the night of 12 September, the 2nd Battalion left their packs containing their surplus clothing and greatcoats at the transport line. They also left behind the men selected as 'battle surplus,' a cadre to reconstitute the unit if the attackers were wiped out. Its makeup was specified by regulations—the battalion commander or his second in command, half of the company commanders, two company sergeant majors, and one third of the runners, scouts, Lewis gunners and snipers; only twenty officers were permitted to attack. In the July attacks the men had struggled forward with full kit, moving at 3 kilometres per hour. Now they carried only gasmasks and haversacks, with a rolled ground sheet strapped below the haversack, and two empty sandbags between the back and the haversack, two Mills bombs, 170 rounds of ammunition, their precious water bottle and two aeroplane flares for company stores once they reached their objective. Encouraging messages from the higher-ups were read to the troops.

In the sector in which the Guards were to attack, the British line was indented by a small enemy salient, containing a machine-gun nest. Before the main assault, the Grenadiers were to reduce the salient by a night attack. Their artillery started the action by firing thirty or forty shrapnel shells. Then the 4th Company charged, took the nest and started to dig a trench across the base of the former salient. The rest of the battalion was to join them, moving forward company by company. The moonlight was bright, ideal for German artillery observers and machine gunners. Every enemy gun within range poured fire onto the former salient. Macmillan watched as the first company struggled forward, men dropping as they went. Then he had to lead two platoons of the 3rd company across the same ground. He lost men going forward and while they dug in.

The next day they huddled in the holes they had scraped during the night. They expected a counter-attack, which did not come, but shelling cost them a captain, two company sergeant majors and a number of other ranks. That night they were relieved and bivouacked near to the village of Ginchy. It was cold and they had no blankets or greatcoats, but they did get rations and rum. The day before the main attack dawned warm and inviting; the puffy clouds were bright white with reflected sunshine. Macmillan and an orderly were sent forward to contact the Coldstream Guards, who were to be the first wave. They would be closer to the front, hidden in holes in the desolate, blasted, featureless landscape. He vividly remembered passing a German corpse whose arm was extended upward in rigor, almost as though waving in welcome—his orderly reciprocated by giving the hand a hearty shake. Macmillan was glad for the corpse because it was a good landmark for his return trip; it was so easy to get lost. That evening at 1830 the officers synchronized their watches by telephone signal from division headquarters—zero hour was 0620. Their first objective was 1,200 metres ahead. From there they were to advance again at 0720 for another 1,500 metres; at 1050 they were to move on to the final objective, another 3,500 metres. The pauses would enable the artillery to lay down a wall of fire skipping in 90-metre steps into the German positions. During the night the troops of the Guards Division advanced into No Man's Land, lying down along pre-assigned assembly lines to spend the cold night in the open. The British heavy artillery bombarded the German positions throughout the night.

At 0515, secret weapons began to move forward on their left; Macmillan glimpsed only a shadow in the mist; aeroplanes swept low over the German lines to drown out the noise of the tank motors. There were three tanks in the lane on their left, but two broke down. The functioning tank, D-1, followed by two companies of infantry, cleared the pocket easily—most of the Germans surrendered when they saw the monster. Then D-1's steering was knocked out by a shell. The other tanks along the front also advanced along their pre-assigned lanes. Most of the terrified Germans hid safely in holes because there were no British infantry to net them; six of the ten tanks assigned to the Guards Division were incapacitated by mechanical problems. Meanwhile the infantry was issued a double rum ration. At forty minutes after dawn, the guardsmen rose to their feet. By a timing error the British barrage halted just as they stood up, so the Coldstream began to advance in disconcerting silence, moving "as steadily as though they were walking down the Mall." After a minute the barrage resumed. Half of the British guns dropped the shell wall in front of the attackers; the rest fired on the German front line. An instant later the counter-barrage started to ravage No Man's Land. The Coldstream encountered small groups of Bavarians, who were shattered by shelling from both sides and ready to surrender; they advanced through heavy machine gun and shell fire, leaving casualties strewn along the field like the bits of bread in the fairy tale. The ground was so torn by high explosive that it looked like a turbulent sea. The Coldstream rallied to the blasts of a hunting horn and kept advancing. They occupied a sparsely held German trench and, believing they had achieved their first objective, pressed on toward the second.

Once the Coldstream had advanced 400 metres into the reeking, chemical-tainted smoke, the 2nd Battalion started after them, marching in artillery formation. They were led by Colonel Crawley who, true to form, violated orders by wearing his leather Sam Browne belt, a cap with gold decoration, gold spurs, and sporting a smart stick. They were almost overwhelmed by the blast and the smoke and dust thrown up by the enemy bombardment. Fortunately, most of the shells fell just beyond the danger range and many burrowed in the mud and did not explode; otherwise, their casualties would have been far heavier. They were also under random but heavy rifle fire from their right, from ground that was to be taken by a tank that never made it into position. At this stage the battalion lost a company commander and one of the young officers in Macmillan's company, along with an unreported number of other ranks. Macmillan was hit by a shell splinter just below his right kneecap, but he willed himself to keep up. They lost sight of the Coldstream—its scattered survivors had veered off to the left, pushed by their own barrage, which had not stepped far enough forward. The 2nd stopped. Colonel Crawley sent a message to General Pereira by pigeon; the general did not know what was going on either. After twenty minutes Crawley decided to advance again, even though they were now far behind their stepping barrage. They passed through a German barrage, and then took machine gun fire from the left front and, even more disconcertingly, from the right rear. Their scouts reported a manned German trench ahead—it must be their first objective. They deployed from artillery formation into line. They took the trench, clearing it with bombs thrown in each dugout; their wounded were sent went back with the prisoners. They established contact with the 3rd Battalion of the Grenadiers, which was on their right. Captain Raymond Asquith, the prime minister's eldest son, was leading a company of the 3rd Battalion when he was struck in the chest by a rifle bullet. He fell, lit a cigarette and died on the stretcher.

A German machine gun fired from their left. While the grenadiers regrouped Macmillan was ordered to take a few guardsmen and a Lewis gun to silence it. He led them toward the sound of the gun, half crawling and half crouching. He was struck by a bullet in his left thigh just below the hip; some of the fragments lodged in his pelvis. He felt little pain, but was knocked unconscious. When he came to he rolled into a shell-hole. He could hear the battle on all sides; the explosions made a tremendous uproar, but he had no idea what was going on. He later learned that his party had dealt with the machine gun, but then a German counter-attack came down the captured trench from the left, moving forward by bombing each bay in sequence. The Grenadier Guards were short of hand grenades, so they jumped out of both the front and rear of the trench and ran along it until they had pinched off the attackers. About forty Germans surrendered, so the first objective had been taken and secured. That was as far as the British advanced that day.

Macmillan was dazed, but in nothing like the excruciating pain he remembered from Loos. The heavy shelling continued; he comforted himself that he was less of a target in No Man's Land than in the trenches. Twice or three times attacking Germans ran past the lip of his hole; he also saw some of them as they ran back. They were very dangerous—if one of them saw him breathing he would be finished off. Two shells hit close to his crater, covering him with reeking earth, but now no one was running about no Man's Land, so he felt safe to take half a grain of morphia, and slept for a bit. Many officers carried enough opiates, purchased freely from apothecaries at home, to kill themselves if necessary. He lay there for more than twelve hours, "thinking of many things and nothing." In his pocket he had a Greek edition of Aeschylus's *Prometheus*—it was a favourite and the theme of the hero helpless to move seemed apt, so now and again he read a few lines. At least this is his self-portrait. He could not tell how badly he had been wounded; the numbness in his legs was a blessing, but perhaps his spinal cord was injured—if so, he was doomed. His most desperate physical problem was thirst—his water bottle had been splattered to bits by a machine gun bullet. Perhaps as he lay there he thought about his grandfather who had "... a touch, in fact, of the rare quality of what we call heroism." His grandfather had been the tenth child in a family of peasants on the Island of Arran, off the West Coast of Scotland. He was apprenticed to a bookseller at age eleven and, nine years later, suffering from tuberculosis, he moved to England to make his way in the world. While working in a Cambridge bookshop he started to publish. Soon he brought a younger brother down to work with him and together they created the great publishing house that has kept their name famous. It was comforting to be rooted in heroic stock. The wounded lieutenant kept hoping that the British would advance to take the ground he was lying on, but at 1500 they had been ordered not to attack any more that day.

After dark, his company sergeant-major, Norton, brought out a party to look for him; they had a fairly good fix on where he had fallen. They found him and the sergeant, with rifle properly sloped, said, "Thank you, sir, for leave to carry you away." Suspended between the shoulders of two guardsmen they brought him to Colonel Crawley. Macmillan was dazed; he could talk but could not move either leg. "Well," said Crawley, "I think you had better be off." He and another wounded officer were placed on stretchers and the party started to the rear; a dressing station was supposed to have been set up in Ginchy. The shelling was still horrendous, especially on the remains of the village. There was no dressing station there; the stretcher bearers were exhausted and terrified. The two wounded officers agreed that it would be wrong to risk injury to four needed men, so they ordered them to return to the front. This done, they helped one another along; Macmillan must have recovered some leg movement. Soon they threw themselves to the ground to evade shell splinters and they lost one another in the dark. Before his troops, Macmillan could play the role of the staunch, fearless officer. Alone in a crumbling village erupting in a torrent of shells, he was in a wild, unthinking funk: "you could cry if you wanted to." He was so terrified that he walked despite his wounds, at one stage even managing a shambling run. A short way out of the village he collapsed and rolled into the ditch along the road.

He did not know how long he lay there; it was a day or perhaps two, unconscious much of the time, before he was picked up. At the dressing-station he had a brief conversation with the chaplain from Balliol College, who was at the front as a padre. Then he had a vague recollection of travelling on a canal barge; his first clear memory was of the ward of the French military hospital in Abbeville. He begged them to let his mother know he was alive. Overwhelmed by the torrent of casualties pouring in from the Somme and desperately short of physicians, they gave him an anti-tetanus injection and washed and bandaged his wounds. They were too pressed for time to operate to insert a tube to flush the wound continuously with antiseptic Carrel-Dakin solution to prevent infection. His infection formed abscesses deep in his flesh; he lay there for weeks with a raging fever, drifting in and out of consciousness. He retained a vague memory of a hospital ship, and then being placed on a train for Victoria Station. Once in London, he was carried to an ambulance that was to drive him to a hospital in Essex. He promised the driver that he would be rewarded if they drove by 52 Cadogan Place. His mother came to the door; she ordered the ambulance to remain for a moment. She telephoned an illustrious surgeon and then climbed into the ambulance and directed the driver to proceed a few blocks to a private hospital on Belgrave Square. There she had her son carried in and dismissed the driver with suitable rewards. Macmillan was rolled into the operating theatre, the surgeon arrived, opened up the infected wounds, and began to drain the abscesses and cut away the dead tissue. When finished he assured mother that if she had not acted her son would surely have died. It was the first of a series of operations, and also of a series of bureaucratic tussles with the War Office concerning this irregular episode, in which Nellie Macmillan gave more than she got. As Macmillan put it:

> No one who has not experienced it can realize the determination of an American mother defending one of her children.

His mother was born in an Indiana town where her father was the doctor. She was christened Helen but was always known as Nellie. At nineteen she married a musician, but in less than six months she was a widow. Her father helped her to move to Paris, where she studied sculpture, exhibited at the Salon, and also studied voice and performed at concerts and in churches. Harold never knew precisely how, where or when she had met his father, who was shy and close-mouthed. Nellie was a success in London society, cultivating contacts like those that helped her youngest son in his military career. Harold loved her deeply, but recognized that she was also "a formidable character" who demanded "high performance," especially from her children—she must know everything they did and tried to know everything they thought. During World War II, while serving as the British minister-resident in North Africa, a plane carrying Macmillan crashed and burst into flame; he fought his way out of the wreckage, badly burned. In the French hospital in Algiers his first request was that they let his mother know he had survived—she had been dead for seven years.

Macmillan was in the hospital in Belgrave Square for many months; he was operated on repeatedly until most of the metal bits were found and removed. Gradually the infected area shrank, but there were frequent relapses. His life was pain, opiates, visits, newspapers, magazines, books and gramophone records. He learned that the Grenadier Guards had lost heavily at Ginchy—eleven officers and 355 other ranks were casualties. His friend Lazarus had been castrated by a shell fragment and the Germans had learned about the tank. As Lloyd George later wrote:

So the great secret was sold for the battered ruin of a little hamlet on the Somme, which was not worth capturing.

The Grenadiers were beefed up with replacements and sent into a second attack ten days later, losing a further nine officers and 242 men. All told, in the Somme they lost 66 per cent of a battalion's nominal complement of officers and 61 per cent of the other ranks. As he heard the news and talked with comrades who dropped by when on leave, Macmillan accepted that he was lucky to have his 'Blighty' wound. He was still alive and had been spared the "signs of deterioration" so striking in those who endured years of the "dreary round of trench life." He scorned the British generals and their staffs but loved the Guards:

> … I gloried in the combination of the high sense of discipline within the Brigade of Guards and the attitude of rebellion against all authority outside.

Later life strengthened his scorn:

> The Second War was fought by great generals from their caravans. The First War was conducted by men of lesser quality from their châteaux.

Herbert Hoover
July to December 1916

On a visit to France in early August 1916 Hoover was invited to observe the Battle of the Somme. He was accompanied by Dr Vernon Kellogg, a Stanford scientist, who was 'ambassador' in Brussels. They were motored down to an observation point. An occasional shell flew by during the last part of the drive, but the road was so well camouflaged that they felt little alarm. At the observation post, "the constant rumble of artillery seemed to pulverize the air." Through powerful glasses they could make out the tangle of trenches and the "volcanic explosions of dust" thrown up by the shells. "Once in a while, like ants, the lines of men seemed to show through the clouds of dust." Hoover could appreciate what they were enduring. He had a vivid memory of advancing with a party of American Marines in an attack on a Chinese city during the Boxer rebellion; Hoover was there as guide. They were advancing across an open plain toward the city walls when they came under "sharp fire." The only cover on the plain was Chinese graves. Some Marines near to Hoover were hit and went down; he was "completely scared." He asked the Marine officer for a weapon and was handed a casualty's rifle. With the rifle in hand he was no longer terrified, though he never fired a shot. "I can recommend that men carry weapons going into battle—it is a great comfort." Four of the Marines were killed and twenty-one wounded in the attack. In the Somme the sights he saw in the rear were as emotionally draining as watching the attacks. In the right lane of the road an unending line of replacements plodded toward the front, marching in "sodden resignation." Moving in the opposite direction in the left lane was a queue of ambulances, interspersed with the bloody walking wounded. Even in the slaughter house they do not make the victims walk past the victimized. The elegantly uniformed, cigarette-smoking German officers escorting them were unconcerned; the enemy was losing at least two men for every German, so by definition it was a German victory.

Hoover does not mention in his memoirs that in October 1916 he and others conveyed a German peace feeler to end the war by restoring Belgian independence with indemnity and surrendering Lorraine to France. Lloyd George was not prepared to negotiate until the Germans were beaten to their knees.

Adolf Hitler
July through December 1916

In July the English facing the List were relieved by an aggressive Australian corps, seeing their first action in France. The year before the Germans had a single line fortified with sandbags; by this time there were several lines dotted with concrete pillboxes. Now and again the Australians released gas which shrouded the List trenches and rear areas in dense green-yellow clouds; all of the metal on their equipment blackened. The Bavarians now had leather gasmasks that sealed round the face with a rubber gasket and the air they breathed was purified by passing through a multi-stage filter. The Australians were ordered to keep pressure on the Bavarians so none could be sent south to battle in the Somme. The Australians raised the ante by obtaining permission to take the German front line. They concentrated 258 field guns and heavy artillery pieces and began to pound the enemy trenches, supply lines, gun lines and headquarter areas. On 16 and 18 July the artillery fire was heavy. On the next day at 0900, the firing began again, stronger than ever; the List sent fatigue parties to lug bags of grenades up to the front. At 1300 the intensity had reached the continual roar of drumfire and their front line was showered with mortar bombs; everyone except the trench sentries huddled in a dugout or pillbox. It kept on and on. At 1700 one of the sentries spotted an observation post in the Australian line. The German artillery observer called to his battery to plaster that area. Then the last telephone line from the front was severed—bad luck for the runners.

At 1645 red Very lights shot up all along the German line—that day's signal for an infantry attack. The opposing trenches were 150–400 metres apart, so the first wave of Australian assault troops had crept closer to the German line during the intense bombardment. As they jumped up to run forward a second wave of Australians popped out of their trenches to begin the longer run. The German artillery laid down a barrage and heavy machine guns in the rear began to traverse No Man's Land, which disappeared under a cloud of smoke and dust, while the Bavarian infantry raced to get their machine guns out from their deep dugouts and mounted on the parapet. They fired into the cloud of smoke. The Australian artillery set up barrier fire to prevent German reinforcements from coming forward; when the attackers appeared out of the cloud they were hit by volleys of grenades while riflemen tried to pick off the officers. The first wave was driven back. Then the second wave emerged from the smoke. They wavered in the face of the bullets and grenades, stopped advancing and threw themselves on the earth or into shell holes. The Bavarians watched an Australian officer running back and forth, rallying his men—no one could hit him. His men responded, rose and came forward, but they were mown down well short of the first German trenches. The attack had been repelled before it really began. In the history of the List Regiment this brilliant defence was regarded as the "personification of the German Army on the Western Front."

Most of the enemy artillery then shortened range to the German front line, but kept enough fire behind the line to block reinforcements. At 1900 the regimental commander learned that the enemy had broken through the regiments on the List's right and left flanks. Hitler and another runner were dispatched with instructions to block off the trenches on each flank, and then to counter-attack. Meanwhile the German artillery sealed off No Man's Land. The counter attackers, carrying sacks of stick bombs, slipped past their flank barrier and worked their way along the lost trench. Even in the dark they could spot the outline of the enemy helmets, which became the target for the attack leader's bombs; his supporters kept him supplied. A few of the attackers, armed with rifles, crawled along the shattered ground beside the trench, to shoot any Australian who climbed out. Soon they reached a pocket in the trench still held by men from Regiment 21; at 0200 the officer leading the counter-attack sent back the message that "spirits are excellent." By daybreak, they had recovered more than 100 metres of trench and by 0900 they had driven the last Australians out and had joined up with the rest of the survivors of Regiment 21. In the counter-attack they captured four machine guns and about 120 prisoners. The Germans would have suffered much more heavily if the English and American shells were better quality—unexploded shells peppered the battlefield.

The Australians asked for a truce to bring in their wounded. The Australian History describes the Bavarian lieutenant who received the proposal as being "immaculately dressed." After consultation the Germans agreed with the proviso that the Australians might bring in those in their half of No Man's Land; the Germans would take in those on their half. Work began. The Australians carried containers of gasoline and used it to burn corpses where they had fallen—thereby reducing the "Eau d'offensive." When British headquarters learned what was going on they forbade the truce. The Australian bearers were ordered in; the Germans continued clearing their half until stopped by sniping and surviving wounded had to be brought in at night.

The Australian dead were brought back from the front piled on the small cars of a narrow gauge railway while the Bavarians stood mutely watching the macabre shipment glide by. They learned that it all had been only a spoiling attack when a complete copy of the orders was taken from an Australian prisoner.

Hitler and his fellows now talked about how it had become a "material war," in which the individual mattered little; he was fascinated by the technology. He sought out men who could explain how petrol motors ran, how the artillery laid their guns, how a gas mask worked and the like. He had a remarkable memory, and soon knew the range of every type of gun, their weight of shell and a myriad of other specifications. It stood him in good stead when he commanded the German Army, impressing his generals with his knowledge of weapons, promoting technical developments and pressing his own ideas unhesitatingly.

The 6th Bavarian Reserve Division was congratulated by the Kaiser, the King of Bavaria, and Crown Prince Rupprecht for their victory at Fromelles. The 5th Australian Division was crippled, their casualties were about 7,000. The List regiment had suffered likewise—the 3rd Battalion with 156 dead; the 2nd with 122 casualties and the 1st with sixty-two. In the 2nd Battalion sixty-four of the casualties were hit by artillery, thirty-six by small arms, nineteen by hand grenades, and four by exploding mines. The advocates of the bayonet on the British staff would have been disgruntled, that is, if they had ever paid any attention to numbers— during the war only 0.5 per cent of German wounds were caused by edged weapons. The regiment had seventy-five concrete shelters along their front—fifteen were hit; nine were destroyed or seriously damaged. A few days later a patrol from the List captured an English newspaper—they made their way promptly from London to the front and were hawked by French newsboys at the entrances to the communication trenches. They chuckled at the *Daily Mail* on 23 July which headlined: "The Huns at Armentières surprised. Heavy losses of Bavarians." There was little fighting for the next few days, but the Germans were kept busy by the demands of bureaucracy—inventorying the trench stores. On 31 July the regiment received 300 replacements and on 9 Sept it received 150 more.

In August, Hindenburg and Ludendorff took command at Imperial Headquarters. They toured the Western Front, so different from what they had experienced in the east—for the first time Hindenburg saw men in steel helmets. He was appalled by the conditions the men fought in along the Somme:

> I could now understand how everyone, officers and men alike, longed to get away from such an atmosphere.

The new leaders had shown that they knew how to win; it remained to be seen whether they could do so against their western enemies. Corporal Hitler could never have conceived

1. Adolph Hitler (right), Foxl (lower right), Anton Bachmann (centre) and Ernst Schmidt (left) at rest quarters in Fournes in April 1915.

2. Hitler marching in field equipment, May 1915. This picture appears in the History of the List Regiment and is his only appearance in the book, even though he was a prominent political figure when it was published.

3. Hitler's sketch of the messenger's billet in Fournes in 1915.

4. Benito Mussolini in 1915, a *Bersaglieri* equipped for the front.

5. Just behind the Italian front line in the mountains along the Isonzo.

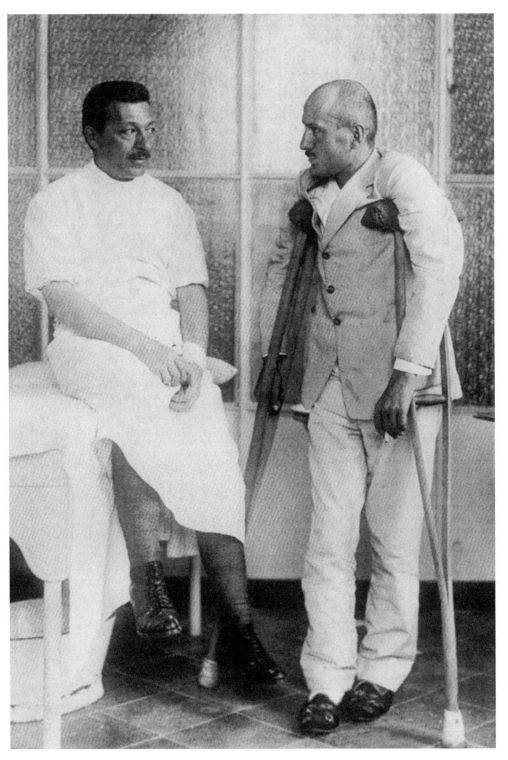

6. Mussolini (right) on crutches in the hospital in Milan, recovering from the wound he received in March 1917.

7 & 8. Mustapha Kemal as a major in the Ottoman army in 1913 (left) and costumed as a janissary for a ball in Sophia, Bulgaria in 1914 (right). He was serving as military attaché to the Balkan states.

9. Otto Liman von Sanders (left foreground) and Mustapha Kemal (right foreground).

10. Ottoman troops leave their trench to attack on the Gallipoli Peninsula.

11. Major General Gustav Mannerheim in Warsaw in 1914.

12. Gustav Mannerheim (tall figure in central foreground) leading his expedition to Central Asia in 1906. This is an example of the superb photographs that were taken along the way.

13. Gustav Mannerheim recovering from rheumatism on the seafront at Odessa.

14. Celebrating the Bolshevik revolution in Red Square, Moscow, in 1917.

15 & 16. Svetozar Boroević, commander of the Austro-Hungarian army on the Isonzo front (left) and Aleksei Brusilov, who lead the Southern Army Group in the great Russian victory (right).

17. Mannerheim as Regent of Finland in 1919.

18. Harold Macmillan shortly before the attack at Loos in 1915.

19. Captain Charles de Gaulle (right) in a German prisoner of war facility in 1917.

20. Charles de Gaulle (left) and his three older brothers after the armistice.

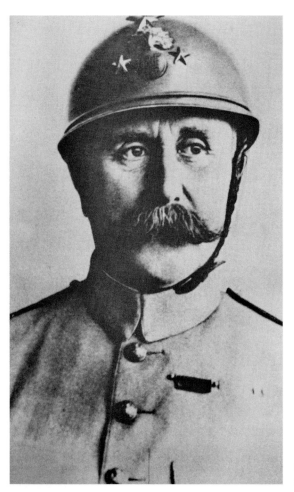

21. General Henri Pétain, the commander of the French Army, in 1918.

22. Herbert Hoover in 1917.

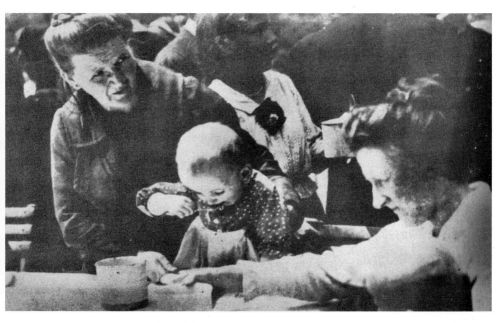

23. Feeding the starving children, Vienna, in 1918.

24. Hitler (right) and Mussolini (second from right) conferring during World War II.

25. Mannerheim (left foreground) and Hitler (centre foreground) meeting in Finland in 1942.

that in seventeen years he would take power in Germany by lying to Hindenburg, the president of the German Republic.

The List shifted their sector to the right of Infantry Regiment 21. They were welcomed by British trench mortars; in two days in mid-September they were hit with eighteen heavy, thirty-seven medium and 444 light bombs. They were issued steel helmets. After fifteen days they started toward the cauldron of the Somme, first by train and then on foot. At Bancourt, 3 kilometres due east of Bapaume, they were put to work digging trenches. As they toiled, off to the west they could see the flaming front and hear "rolling thunder." On 1 October the British took part of the first line held by other regiments of the 6th Bavarian Reserve division; the List would counter-attack the next night. They moved toward the front across muddy chalk land following lanes marked with white tapes. The regimental staff took quarters in Bapaume, while the rest went on to the front line, mostly miserable "mole holes," manned by six–eight men and covered with ground sheets—this was the worst yet. They were supposed to attack the English at dawn but had no hand grenades, so it was postponed for twenty-four hours. As they waited, three of their men were wounded by friendly artillery fire. Their attack got nowhere.

That night a shell smashed into the runner's dugout; six were wounded, including Ernst Schmidt and Hitler, who took a fragment in his left thigh—in trench lingo he had "a high iron content." When the stretcher bearers brought him out of the debris his first recorded words were:

It's not so bad, *Herr Oberleutnant*, eh? I can stay with you, stay with the regiment.

The pain had not yet begun; Foxl was safe, and Hitler did not want to leave him. Regardless of his protests he was evacuated to the field aid station, where the agony began in earnest, and then was transported by hospital train to Beelitz, a village 18 kilometres south of Potsdam, where there was a Red Cross Hospital. His wound healed without complications, leaving him with a depressed bean-shaped scar on his left thigh. He was furious at fellow patients who bragged about how they were using minor injuries to keep away from the front. Surely he shed no tears when the Emperor Franz Joseph died, but he did worry whether his successor, his nephew Karl, had the guts to see the thing through.

When he could walk, he went briefly to Berlin where he visited the *Nationalgalarie* and saw some of the great buildings. His reaction was much like that of Princess Blücher, an English lady married to a Prussian and a fine diarist:

The architecture is new and painfully varied, almost every building bearing the stamp of some man who at the moment was seeking to make his impress on the sands of time.

There is no one great master-mind, but many lesser minds struggling for expression. [When he came to power Hitler spent much time master-minding a projected rebuilding of his capital.]

His sights of wartime civilian life were unsettling—long queues of grumbling, unhealthy-looking women inching their way to the grocery stores; pallid, lifeless children loitering about rather than playing. It was even worse at night. The streets filled with pleasure-seekers hurrying to the cabarets and theatres, profiteers in elegant clothes and industrial workers with money in their pockets strutting about while civil servants and teachers were impoverished. Hitler surely was offended by the large numbers of women, many soldier's widows or wives, who walked the streets, some wanting human warmth more than money. He sent postcards to Schmidt and to his sergeant, Max Amann.

Mustapha Kemal
August through December 1916

The Ottomans counter-attacked in August. Kemal's corps was successful, capturing the important cities of Bitlis and Mush, for which he was awarded the Order of the Golden Sword. Then the Ottoman offensive petered out.

Their winter quarters were in what once had been Armenia. The ancient kingdom had been divided in the nineteenth century between the Russians and Ottomans and so there were Armenian units in the Russian army. Some Ottoman Armenians had taunted and harassed retreating troops in the winter of 1914. The government ordered all Armenians to be moved to parts of the Empire further from the Russian border; Liman strongly but unsuccessfully opposed deportation. Ragged masses of starving Armenians were whipped along the roads, robbed, raped or shot as suited their guards and vindictive local Turks and Kurds. One unintended consequence was that Kemal's men spent a bitter winter on one-third rations in a district without farmers or food and with problematic transport. Many had only summer uniforms, so entire detachments died of cold and want.

Benito Mussolini
June through December 1916

At the end of June the Austro-Hungarians along the Isonzo released phosgene gas from 6,000 cylinders in a localized attack aimed at San Michele, which the Italians had captured a second time. The cloud of gas hid the attacking Hungarians, who were protected by gas masks. They retook San Michele. The Italians lost 6,900 men and the Hungarians lost 1,572. The gas stiffened Italian resolve to fight and the next Italian offensive began on 4 August 1916 with an attack on the Carso. Two days later the attack shifted toward Gorizia, preceded by an enormous bombardment. General Badoglio's men captured the key position of Mount Sabotino (in World War II Badoglio was a field marshal who then became prime minister and signed the armistice with the Allies after Mussolini's fall). Another important position on the northern Carso also fell; the enemy counter-attack failed. Boroević had run out of options. That night they retreated to the east bank of the Isonzo and blew up the bridges. Cadorna finally visited his front in order to savour victory. At the end of summer the water in the Isonzo was so low that Italian troops waded across and established bridgeheads. The enemy artillery had little ammunition, so they gave up Gorizia and withdrew to their second defensive line; Cadorna let them withdraw without pressing on their heels. When the Italians struck at the new line the Schwarzlose machine guns still mastered the battlefield. The Sixth Battle ended in mid August; it was hailed throughout Italy as a great victory—Gorizia was theirs! The number of Italian dead in the attack was almost exactly the city's pre-war population and almost half of the Austro-Hungarian front line troops were casualties in the battle.

The Austro-Hungarians strengthened their new fortifications; 20,000 Russian POWs were used as forced labour. The Italians refilled their ranks and replenished stocks of shells. The bombardment for the next battle built up gradually, becoming intense in mid-September; the infantry went over the top in late afternoon. That evening Italian long-range guns targeted the pumping station that brought water to the Carso, damaging several pumps—water was as vital as explosives. The following day six Austro-Hungarian naval flying boats bombed the guns, saving the remaining pumps. It turned cold and the heavens dumped on the wretched warriors; the Austro-Hungarians treasured the two cups of strong rum each man received every week. The Seventh Battle ended after four days. The Italians had gained little ground, but the pounding had wreaked the enemy trenches once again. Boroević was allocated two more divisions.

The Italian bombardment resumed at the end of September—1,000 guns firing for ten days. In some sectors, the Italian infantry fought their way 1.6 kilometres into the enemy lines, but then lost half of these gains to counter-attacks. When the Eighth Battle ended in mid-October the crust of the new Austro-Hungarian line was fragmented. The attackers had lost twice as many men as the defenders, but again the outnumbered Austro-Hungarians had lost a higher proportion of their fighters. Boroević pleaded desperately for men, shells, cannon, and steel helmets.

Rachele bore a son, Vittorio, at the end of September when his father was home to meet his new offspring. Mussolini's diary resumes at the end of November when he returned from his leave, which had created a fuss; indignant political opponents claimed that he was given special treatment. The question was debated in newspapers throughout Italy, which was to his advantage because it kept him in the limelight and reminded everyone that most of the time he was at the front. He rejoined his comrades at a position on the Carso that was illuminated at night by flares and searchlights. Whenever there was a break in the rain enemy planes hovered above—like raptors looking for prey. In No Man's Land there were two cemeteries and a number of decomposing bodies. The *Bersaglieri* were preparing to attack. Every few days the Italians opened a bombardment which then died off; their food ration was reduced and often did not get to them on time. Food came up to within 200 metres of their position by lorry, so they listened eagerly for the roar of the motors, while the men grumbled more than ever.

The enemy were only 30–50 metres away, but by tacit agreement, neither side fired. Every night both sides worked, listening to enemy mattocks striking into the red soil and the explosions as they dynamited into the limestone. On 12 December the *Bersaglieri* were issued new model gas masks, which Mussolini thought "more artistic than the Austrians." Men from other units came to meet Mussolini; now, their favourite song was:

> Oh, Gorizia, most beautiful
> Your name resounds afar
> Now that you are Italian
> You shall be protected by our valour

In mid-December he was issued a pair of socks, a pair of drawers and a shirt. The men talked vaguely about the German peace initiative. The rain continued so there were casualties both from cannon fire and from trench foot; it was a "lean Christmas"—his company made do with six buns and six bottles of wine sent by a charitable committee and a "festive meal of boiled fish and potatoes." Mussolini also received postcards of "the inevitable Christmas trees," but his spirits lifted when an officer admirer presented him with a roast chicken.

At the end of December, he wrote:

> I leaned over the parapet of our trench. About ten meters away two Austrian soldiers were having a peaceful talk. A little further off another soldier, no less peacefully, was making his morning *toilette*. He lifted his jacket, his woollen vest, his shirt, and set about to get rid of his lice. When this operation had ended, he stretched himself, gave a glance about him, and went off slowly to his shelter. I suddenly remember that I have not washed my face for a month. The lake water is contaminated, and the water brought to us in the bags is rationed off to us, and too precious to waste on one's face.

Charles de Gaulle
April through December 1916

De Gaulle was transferred to a hospital in Mainz. To look at the kinds of places where he would be imprisoned and to see how men lived there, watch Jean Renoir's film *La Grande Illusion*. However, de Gaulle had an advantage over the film's prisoners because he was fluent in German; some German was required for admission to St-Cyr, and de Gaulle had spent the summer of 1908 wandering through Germany to see the country and to practice conversation. When his wound healed he was sent to a prison camp at Osnabrück and then to a transit camp at Neisse, on the river Oder. He contrived a plan to escape by boat, but was soon foiled. This was attempt 1.

For attempting to escape, he was transferred to a reprisal camp in Lithuania in April 1916. The fifty-odd French hard cases there were led by a rough little marine lieutenant colonel named Tardieu, who so bedevilled the Germans that by the end of the war he had been sentenced to 100 years of detention. De Gaulle tried to tunnel out with his roommate, who spoke Russian, but they were caught and, as part of the punishment, deprived of their Russian batmen. Attempt 2.

A few weeks later, de Gaulle, Tardieu and the room-mate were transferred to a high-security camp—Fort IX at Ingolstadt in Bavaria. A.J. Evans, a British flyer, has left a vivid description of the Fort and its life. He wrote about Tardieu and other Frenchmen, but did not mention de Gaulle. It was one of a ring of fortresses encircling the city; the date 1870 was carved in the lintel of the gateway. From the outside the Fort appeared to be a mound of earth, surrounded by a moat screened by a low rampart. The countryside was flat, utterly uninteresting, and with few places to hide. The rooms were in brick edifices built into the walls, with barred windows overlooking the moat. The sentry walk was between the windows and the moat, and sentries frequently peered in to see what the prisoners were up to. The rooms were entered from a long passageway, stretching the length of the Fort—the latrines at either end tainted the air of the whole passageway. The rooms had arched ceilings, whitewashed brick walls and asphalt floors. About 150 officers were imprisoned there—most had tried to escape at least once from other prisons. Evans relished thinking of the place as an escaping club. Indeed, there was much of escape talk, but most kept any plans of their own strictly secret. Expert help was available—photographers who could copy maps, men who could transform an ordinary knife into a hacksaw, locksmiths and engineers to consult about tunnelling—it was impossible to tunnel under the moat because of flooding. All prisoners answered three roll calls a day; the first in bed in the morning and the next two in their rooms or in one of the courtyards. Later a fourth was added in the evening. The men would be counted and, if the count was off, as frequently happened in the courtyard where the officers milled about instead of standing in rank, the whole procedure was repeated amid howls of derision. The French troublemakers imprisoned there did everything they could to make their captors suffer; mattresses were set on fire and there were night-time concerts by banging on mess tins. Again, watch the film. The English did not approve of these activities, which kept the Germans alert, making it harder to escape, and which provoked restrictions on their time permitted for games. The favourite sports were hockey, tennis and football. Equipment could be purchased in the prison canteen; canteens were mandated by the Geneva Conventions. The Russians favoured music, theatricals and fancy-dress parties; their frolics were assisted by a prisoner who rented a piano. According to Evans the camp had the atmosphere of a boys' school teetering on anarchy.

In one way the French and British captives did better than their jailers. Prisoners received military rations as specified by the Geneva Conventions, but this was never much and eventually declined to a daily ration of one loaf of what was called bread, one bowl of cabbage soup and a single cup of acorn coffee with one lump of sugar and almost unlimited quantities of unseasoned potatoes. However, they also received parcels from the Red Cross and from home. Even when the guards' families were starving, de Gaulle never heard of a single food parcel withheld. The extra food was also handy for bribery. When asked, de Gaulle's mother also sent along new uniform jackets and trousers from the best Parisian department stores. The officers could also obtain money from home for purchases from the canteen to supplement the salary advances provided by their captors. Every day, a list was posted of those who had received parcels and each recipient was allocated a collection time, to avoid an unruly, jostling queue. The officer was shown the intact parcel which then was opened and rigorously searched. Learning from hard experience, the Germans opened all cans and prodded the contents, searching for a compass or other contraband. When the inspection was complete the contents were taken to the officer's quarters by a servant—a Russian or French prisoner.

De Gaulle could see no way out. Then he learned that the prison hospital was a special ward in an annex to the military hospital near the city. His mother had sent a small bottle of picric acid to treat his chilblains; he drank it down. The next day he was gratifyingly yellow and his urine was cloudy. At sick call it was decided that he must be hospitalized for jaundice. He was nonplussed when he found that the annex was surrounded by a guarded wall—it was another prison. The ray of hope was that treatment was given in the hospital, which was unguarded. De Gaulle teamed up with another French patient—a French electrician who worked about the military complex each day brought them some bits from their stores of food and some clothing that could pass as civilian. They bribed a guard with food to get them a map. Once they had the map the guard was at their mercy; he was blackmailed shamelessly. He bought them a German military cap and, after a strong defence, surrendered his own trousers. The next night the comrade, dressed as a male military nurse, marched patient de Gaulle out of the annex. They went to the electrician's hut, switched clothing, fastened on their knapsacks and walked out of the hospital complex. They were 190 kilometres by crow flight from Switzerland. On the eighth day of walking they entered a small town—it was Sunday morning. The road led through the square which was filled with a socializing after-church crowd. The filthy, bearded strangers—de Gaulle wrote that they looked like "gallows-birds"—drew unwanted attention. Attempt 3.

Gustav Mannerheim
September through December 1916

The Russians expected the Romanians to be a great help. To get them into the war the Russians promised to reinforce them immediately with two infantry divisions and a cavalry division. In August 1916 the Romanians invaded Hungary by way of the Carpathian passes. The Kaiser turned ashen when he heard the news, fearing that the scales had tipped and that the war was lost. Falkenhayn was dismissed. Hindenburg was offered the command, with Ludendorff as chief of staff. Ludendorff insisted on having the right to appeal if he disagreed with his superior; Hindenburg calmly agreed. One of their first decisions showed how wise they could be; Falkenhayn was given the command of the Germans and Austro-Hungarians assembling in Transylvania. By November, Falkenhayn's army had cleared the mountain passes and were advancing toward the Romanian oilfields. A second army moved up from Bulgaria to capture the largest seaport and then to bridge the Danube. Denikin characterized the Romanian Army:

> In matters of equipment and ammunition their levity was almost criminal ... the officers were effeminate and inefficient, the men were splendid.

Soon cholera and typhus were as dangerous as the enemy armies. Mannerheim's 12th Division started a 725-kilometre ride south, along "roads that no longer deserved the name." For once he gives us a casualty report; they did not lose a single horse on the journey, which speaks highly of the training and discipline of his men. When he arrived the Russian commander told him that the Romanian Army "is cut to bits. They are no longer an army." Bucharest fell on 7 December. Mannerheim was ordered to Focşani, a town 160 kilometres north of Bucharest, close to the Transylvanian Alps, to join the Romanian Second Army. The army commander told him that everything was quiet so they should recuperate for a few days. The same night Mannerheim rushed to the front to stem a German breakthrough. He was reinforced with a Romanian brigade; the whole was called Division Wrancza. He was responsible for 60 kilometres of line, in difficult country he had never seen, cut up by rivers flowing out of mountain passes. His Russian cavalrymen had no experience in mountains—they did well, but were too few. After a few weeks Division Wrancza had two Russian and two Romanian cavalry divisions, plus two Romanian infantry divisions and a brigade. Effectively he was now commanding a very large corps. The Romanian government was at Jassy, in the extreme north of the country.

Mannerheim placed a Cossack division on his left flank. A few nights later he learned that they had withdrawn from their position, which the Germans had occupied. The Cossack commander had issued the following order of the day to his men before they slipped off:

> Having lost all confidence in the Romanian Army, I have decided to lead the division to the nearest Russian Army corps and report there.

The Cossack general was not even reprimanded. After defending Focşani for a month, Division Wrancza was withdrawn for rest and reinforcement. The 12th Division was sent north to Bessarabia where there was ample forage. Much later Mannerheim received a Romanian thanks—the Cross for Bravery, 3rd Class, of the Order of Michael the Bold.

VII

The Russian Revolution to Passchendaele

Gustav Mannerheim
January to April 1917

Thirty-six Russian infantry and six cavalry divisions were shoring up the Romanians, grateful that during the winter there was little fighting. French advisors tried to pull the Romanian army together and the Allies provided supplies, but they reached the front slowly because the railways were chaotic—the Romanians had retreated with all of their rolling stock, which jammed the tracks in the remaining sliver of their country. The Russians gave them 60,000 captured Austrian rifles and Mannerheim was given leave. He arrived in Petrograd in the middle of February, staying as usual at the Hotel d'Europe. The Tsar had stormed out of headquarters in the middle of a conference with his army group commanders when he learned that Rasputin had been murdered; he was now at Tsarkoe Selo, his palace outside of Petrograd, comforting the Tsarina. Mannerheim went there to report, as expected of a *Gènéral à la Suite*. He described the situation on the Romanian front. The Tsar sat dull-eyed, twisting the end of his reddish moustache in the fingers of his left hand and yawning. Mannerheim visited the Tsarina the next day. She was frail and grey, but both she and the thirteen-year-old Crown Prince followed his account closely. When he praised a Romanian colonel named Sturdza she asked whether this was the man who had just gone over to the enemy. Mannerheim had been out of touch while travelling, but would "stake his honour" that this could not be. The next day he learned that Strudza had indeed gone over to the Germans, urging his troops to surrender before Romania was destroyed.

Petrograd was still wonderfully beautiful, but its spirit was dying. Food and fuel were scarce because transportation was breaking down, partly because of weeks of intense cold during which more than 1,000 locomotive-boilers had burst. Everything was blamed on the Tsar. Helsinki was a quieter, calmer world. A dinner was given in his honour, at which he spoke of his experiences; no one mentioned to this Russian general that 2,000 Finnish volunteers were training in Germany to be the nucleus of an army to free Finland when revolution erupted in Russia.

He left Helsinki on 9 March. The newspapers wrote that there had been riots in Petrograd, but he found it much as usual, except for more Cossacks patrolling and machine-gun nests at major street junctions. On Sunday 11 March, he was able to get a scarce ticket for the ballet. When the performance ended and the enthusiastic spectators poured out of the Opera House, they found the city eerily quiet; there were no pedestrians and no cabs. A fellow officer gave Mannerheim a lift in his motor. Soldiers were posted along the principal streets; not another soul was to be seen. At his hotel, he met a Swedish friend, Emanuel Nobel, the director of the Nobel Company. They strolled to a nearby club, where a sleepy porter told them that they were the only members in that evening.

When he rose the next morning, Mannerheim took in the scene from his bedroom window. There were crowds in front of the hotel; armed civilians and soldiers loitered near the lobby door and groups with red flags and armbands marched along the streets. Finally, someone noticed a man wearing a major general's three stars standing at the window smoking a cigar; he immediately started shouting and pointing. A porter pounded at his door to warn that officers were being arrested. Mannerheim pulled off his spurs and put on his fur coat and a hat without military insignia. He stopped by his aide's room, to warn him of what was afoot, hurried down the staff stairway and walked to the office of the Nobel Company. Nobel and a French colleague were there. They decided to go to Nobel's home across the River Neva and stopped their car en route to examine a burnt-out police station. A hand grabbed Mannerheim's shoulder; a patrol wanted to inspect their papers. The Frenchman complied. Nobel said he was a Swede; they could see his passport at his home. Mannerheim declared that he was a Finn just in from Helsinki and that his passport was in his luggage in the checkroom at the Finland Station. They were allowed to go.

That evening Mannerheim insisted on leaving Nobel's home, he would not put a family in danger. He walked to the nearby apartment of a friend, a former Finnish officer. The sky was bright with fires and "the hooting of fire engines came from all directions." At his destination, the door was opened by his brother-in-law, who had just arrived from Helsinki. The next morning they heard heavy firing from the centre of the city. The telephones were working; they learned that the police were being overwhelmed. The apartment was searched by a group of soldiers led by a civilian—they were looking for a general on the loose. They convinced the search party that they were Finnish civilians. The next day he telephoned his aide, who told him that loyal troops were protecting the guests at the Hotel d'Europe, so Mannerheim returned there. He learned that the Tsar had told the Duma to go home—they refused—and that the Tsarina and her children were under arrest at Tsarkoe Selo. A Soldier's Council or Soviet had been formed; they proposed to control all arms, ammunition and provisions. Saluting was banned.

Mannerheim left for Moscow on 15 March in a sleeping compartment on the night train. In Moscow, he saw the demonstration celebrating the abdication of the Tsar with massed red banners. From there Mannerheim took the train to Romania. He begged his commander to launch a counter-revolution but he would not. The field army was falling to pieces and the revolutionary government proclaimed freedom of the press, and gave soldiers the right to strike "as far as the service permitted." Courts martial and the death penalty were abolished. As the acidulous General Knox, a British liaison officer, later wrote:

> No one who has any acquaintance with the Russian character was surprised to find that 'freedom' was interpreted as freedom to talk without end and to do nothing.

However, "nothing" was imprecise; by the end of April 1 million soldiers had deserted. In the 12th Division, the men elected councils to deliver their opinions—but Mannerheim kept the upper hand. Amidst the turmoil the Russian Army was reorganizing—infantry divisions had fewer riflemen and the surplus men were formed into new divisions commanded by a ragtag cadre of officers and NCOs; they became hotbeds of discontent. Cavalry divisions now had three battalions of dismounted troopers, releasing horses needed by the artillery. Every unit assembled to swear loyalty to the Provisional Government. In June Mannerheim was given command of the VI Cavalry Corps and promoted to lieutenant general. One of his new divisions refused to go to the front. He had a few shells lobbed near their camp and they soon changed their minds.

Herbert Hoover
January to September 1917

The New Year brought Hoover a one-two punch of new troubles. First the British and French Governments warned the CRB that they would be unable to sustain their financial commitments more than a few months longer as they were on the verge of bankruptcy. Hoover hurried to New York to try to raise a loan secured by Belgian assets. He found that "America was moving steadily into the psychological rapids which lead to war."

In February, the Germans unleashed unrestricted U-boat warfare; up to then the CRB had lost nineteen ships. They deduced that three were sunk by U-boats and when they had conclusive evidence, the Germans paid compensation. Most of the rest were sunk by mines, which might come from either side. When the unrestricted U-boat campaign was announced, the sea lanes used by the CRB were in the prohibited zone from which ships were given three days to leave. Seventeen CRB ships were diverted, but nonetheless two were torpedoed, one with only one survivor. Hoover notified the German government that relief would have to stop. Afraid of public opinion in the still neutral US, the Germans urged the CRB to continue and compensated them for the two vessels sunk. Nonetheless, over the next few weeks, four of their ships were lost to mines or other hazards and eight torpedoed—U-boat captains were loose cannons. US protests lost force as the nation slid towards war, and rations in Belgium and Northern France were cut drastically as a result. The Dutch and Spanish ambassadors in Berlin delivered a blistering note from their governments demanding food for the occupied lands. The Germans asserted that the torpedo attacks were mistakes that would not be repeated—indeed they were not.

The crisis was magnified because the British would not allow the CRB to store more than a four weeks' supply of food on the continent; their nightmare was that the Germans would seize it. The CRB argued that even if this improbable event occurred it would feed the Germans for ten days only. The British were relentless; the supply line into the Netherlands had to be carefully regulated so that the stockpile did not exceed the limit.

Hoover travelled to France in March to attend a celebration for the ground reclaimed when the Germans withdrew to the Hindenburg Line. On 6 April the US declared war. They entered as an 'associate power;' Wilson would not become a party to the secret treaties that bound the Allies together. Hoover received a message from Colonel House in the President's name asking him to return to the US to organize food supplies. He was prepared. Dutch and Spanish diplomats agreed to see that the sea-lane was kept open and to distribute the CRB food. When Hoover landed in the US, he was feted as a great humanitarian, as one of the world's illustrious men. In Washington, Wilson asked him to organize US food production and distribution. Hoover agreed with conditions—no salary, permission to continue to oversee the CRB, and membership in the War Cabinet. Hoover conveyed a personal message from his friend, Admiral Sims, the US Navy liaison officer in London, begging the President to insist that the British set up a convoy system for ships crossing the Atlantic; otherwise, the U-boats would win. The British navy agreed to try convoying only after weeks of intense pressure from Prime Minister Lloyd George. The US agreed to buy the food needed in Belgium and Northern France, while the British and French paid for the shipping.

Benito Mussolini
January to May 1917

On New Year's Day, the *Bersaglieri* marched down into the valley for a rest, and Mussolini was given a short leave. According to Rachele he arrived with no buttons on his tunic—it was secured by short lengths of barbed wire. Back in the line, his diary entry for 27 to 28 January was:

> Snow, cold, infinite boredom, orders, counter orders, disorder.

The men returning from leave talked under their breaths about discontent, the wish for peace and dissatisfaction with "the Government of National Impotence." Mussolini was assigned to a trench mortar section, which gave him a welcome chance to learn something new. Mortars were splendid weapons for trench warfare and their numbers were skyrocketing in all of the armies. He was promoted to *caporalmaggiore*, equivalent to sergeant in the British Army. One memorable night he saw five cigarettes glowing in the enemy line. He launched a shell, there was a loud explosion, and the lights were gone. In February he noted that the soldiers' canteen was surrounded by barbed wire to protect it from hungry men. He had begun to smoke.

He was seriously wounded on the afternoon of 23 February. Typically, there is a choice of accounts. Some authors state that there was an accident during training behind the lines. According to his diary, he was bombarding enemy trenches. One case of shells had been fired and they were finishing the second; the last shell exploded in the barrel. Mussolini was thrown several metres and was "showered with fragments." In his autobiography, he wrote that his projectile burst in the trench; four died and "various others were fatally wounded." He told his lover Sarfatti that he had wanted to cease fire because the barrel was red hot and may have cracked, but his officer ordered him to continue. The officer was also badly wounded. Rachele gave the same account. All agree that he was placed on a stretcher, taken to the aid station and then to the hospital. Some accounts have it that several men refused to help to bear the warmonger.

In the hospital, he was anesthetized and a surgeon wrested the larger metal fragments out of his flesh. The wounds were left open and irrigated with antiseptic solution to minimize the danger of gas gangrene. He had two large leg wounds, each big enough to put a fist into; the total circumference of all of his wounds was 80 centimetres. His left thighbone was shattered. Every day or two the surgeon examined the open wounds, paring away dead tissue—a procedure known as debridement. Bacteria flourish in dead tissue; general anaesthesia always carries a risk and repeats are even more dangerous. Most debridements were therefore preformed without anaesthesia, which led some wounded to conclude that their surgeons were sadists. All told, Mussolini had forty-four pieces of metal fished out. Between examinations he was immobilized so his shattered bone could set. His wounds became infected and his temperature rose to 40°C. The hospital was shelled and most patients were sheltered in dugouts; Mussolini could not be moved. Sarfatti inflated the story, claiming that the hospital was shelled because an Italian paper had revealed that Mussolini was a patient there. In March the King visited the hospital; the visit was reported in the newspaper *Secolo*. The King, who had met him once before, asked: "How are you Mussolini?"—"Not very well," was the mumbled answer. The King extolled his service and bravery.

The Tenth Battle began in May 1917. The Italians inched forward, but the enemy held their crucial positions—by the skin of their teeth. D'Annunzio and a friend, a major of infantry, planned an attack that required their men to cross a stream on a single plank before forming. When briefed, the men refused to go, so they were lined up, counted off and every tenth man was marched off and shot—decimation as the Romans had done it. The cowed survivors crossed the plank, lined up and on signal rushed up the hillside. They were slaughtered, and so was the major.

Charles de Gaulle
January to May 1917

De Gaulle concluded that escape from Fort IX was impossible, and so for the next eight months he was a model prisoner. He spent most of each day at his desk, writing and reading, while the others socialized and played games. Again he was known as *le Connétable*. He read history, literature and geography and noted items of special interest in his journal, such as an eighty-nine-year-old man in Napoleonic times who embarked on a love affair. Precedence was given to German newspapers—as many as he could get. The German military communiqués generally stated the facts truthfully, and some papers also published the Allied communiqués. By careful study, he filled the gaps and figured out what was going on. He posted his own communiqués for his comrades. In the evenings there were lectures and de Gaulle organized one series and spoke himself. He remained uncommonly aloof. He alone did not use 'tu' and would not answer to 'tu'. He would not share the communal shower and was never seen naked.

In his lecture series, he gave his views on the war thus far. Naturally he hailed the Marne, but castigated the French offensives in 1915, in which their infantry were massacred on unbroken German wire and after which the survivors were excoriated as cowards. He rated Pétain's performance in 1915 as poor because his men had been slaughtered on the Lorette ridge; but clearly Pétain functioned on quite a different level in 1916 at Verdun, where he brilliantly organized the flow of supplies and men into the salient. He let the French line be pushed closer to the city rather than sacrificing thousands in counter-attacks to recover useless metres of shell-blasted ground. His force grew stronger every week, because they received more of the new, long-range French 155 millimetre guns. His artillery on the west bank of the Meuse blasted the German rear on the other side of the river, which forced the enemy to attack in March to take the French gun positions on the west bank, where topography favoured defenders—the Germans had to advance in the open over bare hills and gentle plains. Massed German infantry suffered horrendous casualties. By this time, both sides had lost almost equally—so much for Falkenhayn bleeding the French white. The French air force was concentrated at Verdun; flying new, superior planes, they took command of the air. Standing along his vital road Pétain studied the drained, shocked and uncomprehending faces of the men coming back from the battlefield. He established a rotation in which a fresh division would be brought into line, pay its sacrificial due and then—before they were completely demoralized—be withdrawn for rest and to assimilate replacements. Often they were only in line for a few days. German divisions were kept in the cauldron much longer.

Pétain's masterful leadership, professional competence and capacity for analysis impressed old comrade de Gaulle, but not the leaders of France. What Pétain thought realism, they thought pessimism. They wrung their hands over each metre of lost ground and were vexed when there were no counter-attacks. Pétain demanded fresh troops, but they were saved for the projected attack on the Somme. In April 1916, he was kicked upstairs to command an army group. General Robert Nivelle took over at Verdun—he had vigorously lobbied against Pétain. Falkenhayn's prestige was also ebbing. His great guns were wearing out from overuse or damaged by excellent French counter-battery fire. In May he ordered a massive infantry attack on the east bank. It took ground at great cost; the French were pushed to the limit, but held there. On 1 July the offensive on the Somme began. The British lost more men on that single day than the French had lost at Verdun during their worst month, but German guns had to be shifted from Verdun to the Somme. Verdun was a mind-shattering horror for both sides. In the fall Nivelle regained some of the lost ground by a set-piece attack. He maintained that he had discovered the tactics for victory. He also spoke excellent English and soon convinced the Allied governments that he was the man to win the war. He replaced Joffre as chief of staff. De Gaulle had little praise for the Allied attack in the Somme. Falkenhayn was replaced in September, and the German attacks at Verdun halted. De Gaulle had high praise for Falkenhayn's successor, Hindenburg's leadership qualities:

> … due still more to the disinterestedness of his character, to his profound calm, and to that obscure awareness of the downtrodden masses that he was a sympathetic and compassionate man as well as a resolute leader.

Mustapha Kemal
January to September 1917

During the fearful winter in the mountains Kemal was promoted to command the Second Army, in which his corps was serving. The revolution in Russia in March 1917 saved them from another attack and the Russians pulled back to their frontier. Kemal worked on rebuilding the health of his troops and improving the decorum of his officers—one of his rules state that they were to dine bareheaded in the mess, not in their kalpaks.

Before long, he was in political trouble. His story was that before the war an officer was sent by the CUP to assassinate him. Kemal saw what was up, greeted him with a revolver on his desk and calmly discussed his political ideas; the prospective killer left as a supporter. Now the same fellow was arrested for plotting to overthrow the government. He advocated a separate peace negotiated by a new government in which Kemal would be minister of war. Kemal admitted that if the plot had succeeded he would have taken the ministry—but only after he had hanged the plotter. The plotter was executed and Kemal was kept under surveillance.

In the spring, Kemal moved to Syria to take command of the larger Seventh Army, which was assembling in Aleppo. The British were beginning to drive up into Palestine. An Arab uprising had cut off the Ottoman garrison in the holy city of Medina, where the Prophet is buried. Enver ordered Kemal to relieve the city and then to evacuate the garrison. Kemal refused—it was a hazardous operation in which an army might be lost and any officer abandoning the holy site would be execrated by the faithful for all time. In fact, the officer commanding in Medina refused to surrender the city even after the armistice until firm commitments were made that it would be occupied only by the devout.

Enver's next project was a counter-attack to retake Baghdad, which had fallen to the British. Liman had been given command in Mesopotamia, but now the operation would be directed by General Falkenhayn, who commanded a newly formed, small but grandiosely named German Asia Corps, which had only a handful of Germans—his muscle was Kemal's Seventh Army. Kemal saw that retaking Baghdad was impossible: there was no railway line and they had no shipping on the Euphrates or timber to make barges. Falkenhayn imaginatively proposed to float supplies down the river on inflated goat skins. At the planning conferences Kemal quietly demolished Falkenhayn's fancies with chilling reality. Then Falkenhayn was given a tour of the front in Palestine by an astute staff officer, Major von Papen (who later became an important German politician and the German Ambassador to Turkey during World War II). Falkenhayn saw that the British, now commanded by General Sir Edmund Allenby, might break through in Palestine and sweep north to cut off an army moving into Iraq. Consequently, Enver and Falkenhayn gave up on Baghdad; instead, they would drive the British back to the Suez Canal and then out of Egypt. The Seventh Army was moved to Palestine. Kemal told Papen that he was disgusted by these fantasies. The British were building a rail line and a water pipeline north from Egypt, to sustain a large army. Kemal wrote a long memorandum to the government about their desperate situation: starvation, corruption, and the breakdown of law, order, and economic life. In many divisions, half of their men deserted or fell sick on their way to the front. Arab regiments faded away. The Turks should eject the Germans, adopt a strictly defensive posture, and husband what remained of the Turkish army. He asked to be relieved unless they agreed.

Harold Macmillan
January to April 1917

The other patients who passed through Macmillan's small ward did little to help him pass his long, painful days. For a time the man on his left was stone deaf from shell shock. He talked constantly but of course it was not necessary to respond in detail. Occasionally Macmillan would say, "Rhubarb, Mr Benson," just to keep up his side of the conversation. Correspondence was more interesting, especially with his great friend Ronald Knox, who had been his tutor when as a lad he had had to stay out of school because of a weak heart. They kept in touch while Macmillan was at Eton, and because Knox was a fellow of Balliol, they saw much of one another there. Knox was an ardent Anglo-Catholic. This did not suit Nellie Macmillan—although now an Anglican communicant she had been reared as a staunch Methodist. Knox tried to draw Harold towards his credo. In 1917 Knox became a Roman Catholic, hoping that some of his friends would follow. Macmillan replied:

> … while I am still lagging, timidly, cowardly and faint. I feel sure you are right.

He never did convert, but became even more deeply committed to the Church of England.

Adolf Hitler
January to June 1917

After his convalescent leave he reported to the barracks at the *Elizabethen* school in Munich, where he was even more shocked than he had been by Berlin: "Anger, discontent, cursing, wherever you went." The Bavarians blamed the Prussians for their miseries; Hitler blamed the Jews. He was desperate to get back to his regiment and to Foxl. He wrote to Captain Wiedemann begging to be ordered back so he could be with "his old comrades." He rejoined the Regiment on 5 March 1917 in a position they were holding near La Bassée, 10 kilometres north of Lens. Foxl "hurled himself on me in frenzy." He was welcomed back with a special feed, featuring jam; they filled him in on what had happened during the months he had been away—he had been lucky because it had been a bitter time. Just after he had been evacuated from the Somme they were attacked by the 23rd and 47th British divisions. The List beat back the attacks but conditions were dreadful—only cat naps, continual shell fire, little water, drenching rain and cold nights; no hot food. The wounded had to wait until it was dark and then faced a hazardous trip.

Infantry companies lost 25–30 per cent of their effectives. British aeroplanes hummed over the front, strafing men and circling above targets while honking their horns to signal artillery observers on the ground. Morale crumbled and all headquarters could do was to send encouraging messages. Their Regimental History states that this was their low point during the war. When they were relieved on 11 October their average front line company had only thirty-five men. In ten days the casualties were:

Officers: 7 killed, 17 wounded and 2 missing;
Others: 243 dead, 827 wounded, and 88 missing.

After Adi had been feasted, the comrades dropped off to sleep, but he stayed up playing at the old trench game, spitting rats on his bayonet in the glare of a flashlight, and caressing Foxl.

The Regiment had almost a month of rest and physical training. The role of the regimental staff had been adjusted to control fighting more effectively. Now the commander of the battalion on the front line was responsible for directing defensive battles, he could call on the other battalions for help if needed. Regiment was responsible for general administration and dealt with a constant stream of what they called "Ludendorff's paper barrage" or his "pearls;" his instructions and inquiries—some trivial, some profound—all a sure sign that a restless intellect had his eye on them. They were especially annoyed that each time an enemy was taken prisoner during the course of daily operations the report must include a sketch map of precisely where he had been captured. Ludendorff also signed the daily communiqués and relentlessly courted the press; soon it seemed that he was running the war. Hindenburg, with a character almost unheard of for a general, retained the final say, but let his talented and valuable subordinate grab the limelight.

The List moved into positions along the La Bassée canal, opposite the British 5th Division. It was another miserable spot; the trenches were ankle-deep in water. Much mining was going on so they were equipped with sensitive listening apparatus and the regiment was strengthened by two NCOs and sixty miners from Pioneer Mining Company 295. They were entertained by the air war. Von Richthofen was flying above them in his easy-to-spot scarlet Fokker—the French newspapers called them "red pirates." The Germans cheered his thirtieth kill.

The Germans began to withdraw from their salient in the Somme region to the reserve position that the Allies called the Hindenburg Line in March 1917. It would shorten their line and free up divisions. They thought that the public would stomach pulling back because they were still exulting over the defeat of Romania and excited at the prospect that unrestricted U-boat warfare would starve the hated British—just as they had been starved. Then the headlines were taken over by the Revolution in Russia. The List was not involved in the retirement—they were too far north—but the regimental staff followed the operation closely, and Hitler often discussed it during World War II. In exceptional circumstances, he was not opposed to shortening a front to free men to attack elsewhere, but he was certain the enemy should have been made to fight for every metre of ground, not allowed to walk in with only the minor inconveniences of booby traps, poisoned wells and delayed explosions. He concluded that it was impossible to get men to fight with determination to hold open ground when they had a well prepared fortification waiting for them in the rear. They were all astonished when the enemy slowly occupied the freed territory, leaving the German rearguard almost untouched.

The previous autumn the officers of the regimental staff had long discussions about the new directives from Imperial Headquarters on how fortified positions were to be defended. The publications incorporated Lossberg's ideas on an elastic defence, with the front line lightly held but to be retaken if necessary by counter-attacks. There was still a disagreement as to whether the troops in the front positions should hold where they were or if overwhelmed should be permitted to fall back to take part in the counter-attack. The general staff publication said that they should be allowed to fall back; but a month later, they also published Lossberg's contrary opinion (although Lossberg later changed his mind). As usual, the decision was left to the field commanders. Hitler was convinced that men who fell back under pressure would be useless in a counter-attack, so he strongly favoured the front line fighting to the death and never giving up ground. He never shifted his position, which caused Germans disasters in World War II, like Stalingrad.

On 9 March, 900 mortar bombs were fired at the Bavarian lines. Nine days later at 0500 a mine exploded under their position that dug a crater 30 metres deep and 60 metres across. Whimsically most of the earth thrown up was showered back on British trenches, giving them plenty of digging. Five days later, two mines were detonated simultaneously but the Bavarians lost no-one. When they left the line they polished up for inspection by Lieutenant General von Stein, the Prussian War Minister. Back in the trenches at dawn on 27 April, a fifty–sixty-man enemy patrol came running toward them. They were driven back by rifle fire and grenades. Four dead and one wounded Englishmen were brought into the German line. They were from the 66th division; the youngest was judged to be only sixteen to seventeen years old.

They were in rest camp when the British launched an attack near Arras, a diversion designed to draw away German reserves from the French front in Champagne before Nivelle's massive spring attack there. The German commander in the sector had not adopted elastic defence, and had packed his men into the foremost trench, where they were overwhelmed—which permitted the British also to burst through lines two and three. Ludendorff was too upset to attend his birthday party. The Germans were saved because the British had not assembled reserves to exploit success; their attack had been planned as a diversion. The Germans rushed men in to reseal their line. The List Regiment was moved down to Douai. After a few days they were marched 30 kilometres south to the sector where the British had attacked, but they were kept in reserve, and at the end of the month marched back to Douai. For once, they had been lucky.

On 3 May at 0330, they were aroused by the alarm. They moved to trenches just north of Gavrelle, which is 10 kilometres northeast of Arras. For the next two days they were bombarded and then it became relatively quiet. At 0700 on 12 May, the British threw drumfire at them; the attack came and an English company of eighty men with a machine gun occupied a 40-metre length of the List's line. The counter-attack eliminated the machine gun and the survivors ran the gauntlet back to their lines. Ernst Jünger vividly describes how German counter attackers bombed their way up the communication trenches. A second attack on the following day did not reach the German lines. Six days later they were relieved and had two weeks' rest. The Germans had beaten back Nivelle's huge attack along the Aisne, but the French did succeed in hiding the mutinies that had broken out in their army. Pétain was given command of the French army; he settled the army down by a combination of stringent discipline and satisfying just complaints, not attempting major attacks hoping for a breakthrough and waiting for the Americans.

Their next tour in the trenches was in a part of the line just a kilometre or so north of where they had been last; it was covered by a metre of filthy water and the British kept firing gas shells at them. After two weeks, they moved to the rear and set to work polishing their equipment and getting their clothing into shape. On 19 June they were reviewed by their army group commander, Crown Prince Rupprecht, in the park of an elegant chateau. He was a popular and respected soldier so they cheered from the heart when he presented the medals earned in the Arras battle. Of course, he did not tell them that he was privately warning the Bavarian prime minister that they were almost sure to lose the war.

Charles de Gaulle
June through November 1917

One of de Gaulle's fellow prisoners was a Russian nobleman, Lieutenant Tukhachevsky. Language lessons were a popular diversion; de Gaulle helped him to improve his French and they often discussed military problems. De Gaulle declined to attend English classes. In June, model prisoner de Gaulle applied for a transfer and was moved to an old fortress, close to Bayreuth, perched on a rocky peak and bristling with towers, much like the castle in Renoir's film. De Gaulle and three others climbed over two walls and across two moats and then down the sheer face of a cliff on a length of homemade rope—again, watch the movie. Ten days later, hungry, cold and completely miserable, they decided to shelter for the day in the loft of a pigeon house. They were spotted by peasants and were rounded up. Attempt 4.

Back at the castle, de Gaulle and a comrade resolved to have another try before they were transferred to a tighter prison. They sawed through a window bar and again went over the walls, across the moats and down the cliff. They walked to the rail station, hoping to catch a train heading west toward the Dutch border. Their absence was discovered, a call to the station was made, and they were retaken. According to Evans, British escapes were undertaken with "a sort of childlike exuberance, in which the comic element was seldom absent for long." It is unlikely that this is how de Gaulle thought of it. Attempt 5.

Mustapha Kemal
October through November 1917

Kemal's Seventh Army was holding the left of a 32-kilometre Ottoman defensive line, which extended from Gaza on the seacoast inland to Beersheba. This front had been stagnant for eight months. At either end the defenders were fortified in well-sited positions, protecting the coast road at Gaza and the vital wells inland at Beersheba. The centre of the line was desert, garrisoned lightly by both sides. Allenby was preparing a third try to break through. Crucially, a new shipment of aircraft gave the British air superiority for the first time, so the Ottoman flyers could not follow changes in the British dispositions. On the night of 30 October, Allenby marched 40,000 men from the coast over road-less and featureless land to Beersheba. They attacked the 5,000 defenders at early light. As Wavell puts it:

> It was like taking a county cricket eleven to play a village team; but the pitch was a difficult one, and there was much at stake.

The British infantry captured the chief defensive position, which was still well south of the wells, but then they were pinned down, unable to advance further. The cavalry corps swung through the desert around the open flank, dismounted, and attacked the well-entrenched rear. By late afternoon they had taken the outer crust of the Ottoman positions, but were still well short of the precious wells. With only an hour of daylight remaining, the Australian Light Horse, mounted on horseback, charged directly at the Ottoman trenches, sweeping over the defenders and into the town—capturing the wells before they could be dynamited (their charge is the climax of Weir's film *The Lighthorsemen*).

Kemal pulled his army back to set up a new line just north of Beersheba. The next day Allenby hit at Gaza, starting with a prolonged bombardment from land and sea. In three days the British made little progress. On 6 November Allenby's right jabbed through the desert west of Gaza, while his troops from Beersheba swooped behind the enemy line, aiming for the sea. Falkenhayn ordered a fighting withdrawal to a new line 10 kilometres to the rear. The bulk of the Ottoman forces fell back during the night, leaving small bodies behind to hold on as long as they might; on their right, the withdrawal was pressed so closely that they were pushed past the proposed second line. Overall the Ottomans lost 10,000 men and 100 guns. Kemal was able to withdraw deliberately, in short steps, gradually shifting back to form a new defensive line just south of Jerusalem. Some military writers regard this retreat as Kemal's most brilliant military achievement; it displayed how well he had learned to control an army.

When he reached his new position, completely disgusted, Kemal resigned from command of the Seventh Army, refusing to meet Falkenhayn to discuss the matter. He was given a month's leave before taking an appointment at the General Staff. He had to sell six of his horses for train fare to Constantinople. Once there he lobbied for an end to the war. Enver, harking back to Kemal's views on the separation of army from politics, mischievously suggested that he resign from the army and enter parliament. Kemal did not take the bait. In December 1917, the British marched into Jerusalem, which the Ottoman army had abandoned so that it would not become a battleground.

Harold Macmillan
May through December 1917

Macmillan was released after nine months in hospital, first on leave, and then for light duty at the Chelsea Barracks. Now and then, he returned to have his wounds reopened and probed for metal bits. Some bullet fragments remained embedded in his pelvic bones, so he shuffled when he walked—when he was prime minister, some of his political opponents scorned his shuffle as an effete affectation. For a time he was seconded as a drill instructor for Kitchener Army officers and NCOs. He was unable to stand King's Guard because he could not wear a sword over his still-infected left thigh. He was "haunted by memories and fears." There were so many dead; fellow officers, young men he had idolized as a lad, classmates at Eton and Oxford, even fellows in the classes behind his,· he had read so many of their names in the daily list that it sometimes seemed as though everyone he had known was gone.

He followed the political news carefully. He admired Asquith, who had treated him kindly when as a lad he had stayed at Number 10 as a guest of the youngest Asquith son, Cyril. He sympathized with Asquith's grief for Raymond and his fears for his middle son, Arthur, who had been wounded at Gallipoli and was now in France (where he became a general and lost a leg). Nonetheless, Asquith represented the "faults of the old world"—his tolerance and generosity permitted the follies of General Head Quarters to go unchecked, so Macmillan had been sanguine when Lloyd George came to power in December the previous year. Macmillan had breakfasted with him when he spoke at the Oxford Union. He admired him as "the rebel, the revolutionary, and, above all, the man who would get things done." But even the Welshman could not curb the generals. The government allowed the army to attack in Flanders, to draw the enemy away from the reeling, mutinous French. Macmillan shuddered as another 400,000 British men were consumed at Passchendaele. His political hero was Benjamin Disraeli, who wrote so well that Macmillan kept rereading his books—a conservative who agonized about the "two Englands," rich and poor, and tried to bridge the gap. Macmillan's men had taught him how wide the gap remained.

Benito Mussolini
April through December 1917

When Mussolini could be moved he was sent to a hospital in Milan, where Rachele, in nurse's uniform, could tend him. Ida came to visit—wife pummelled mistress. However, Ida soon left the stage; she was interned because she was a citizen of Austria-Hungary. When he left hospital he was discharged from the army and once again could play his violin to little Edda as she fell asleep in the evening. On 15 June he walked on crutches back into the *Il Popolo* office. The paper was failing—two issues a week rather than three, and down to two pages, it could not survive by foreign subsidies alone. Mussolini started a subscription campaign that raised circulation and improved finances.

The war needed all the support it could get. There were food riots in northern Italian cities and forty-one protesters were killed in Turin. In Parliament, a Socialist deputy proclaimed:

We will desert the trenches before winter comes.

There were 5,500 desertions every month. In the pages of *Il Popolo* the war hero demanded that the sacrifices of the soldiers should not be dishonoured by anything less than total victory. On 1 August Pope Benedict XV offered to mediate; the governments were exasperated by his intrusion and Mussolini was incensed. The Eleventh Battle began in August. The Austro-Hungarians were outnumbered 3/1 in infantry and 4/1 in shells. The Emperor Karl watched the fighting on the Carso, naturally from a comfortable distance. Across the lines, King Victor Emmanuelle watched and photographed the same action— hopefully, the last time two European monarchs will face one another on a battlefield. D'Annunzio was with the Catanzaro brigade; their attack was beaten back and they lost heavily. After a short respite the survivors were ordered to attack again but they refused.

The poet watched as they were decimated. The tenth men, peasants from Calabria and Sicily, sang together before they were shot—an uncanny, lugubrious chant. Much moved, D'Annunzio photographed the row of cadavers before writing a poem about dead men singing with dirt in their mouths.

The attack drove the Austro-Hungarians from the central part of their line on the Carso. They retreated to a new position that had been prepared about 6 kilometres to the rear, out of the range of the Italian field artillery. *Il Popolo* was ecstatic. The Italians followed their retreating enemy cautiously, giving them ample time to settle into their new line and to mount their machine guns. Cadorna shifted direction and assaulted a mountain near Gorizia. On the night of 26 August the troops in the sector heard martial and patriotic music, seemingly from the heavens. They were serenaded from the top of the newly conquered height by a band who had hauled their instruments up 690 metres. The baton was wielded by Arturo Toscanini, fifty years old, the most celebrated conductor in Italy and an ardent interventionist; he was rewarded with a silver medal for bravery. In later years, Toscanini was a bitter foe of Mussolini and became an exile.

Mussolini advised the government how to inspire troops:

> Tell those that fight that not in vain do they toil and struggle, tell those that suffer at home that their suffering will be turned into joy. Ancient Rome gave land to her legionaries. England today looks forward to a similar policy. Give the German gold to the families of the fighters! The land to the peasants!

Il Popolo lambasted the socialists for their international congress held in Stockholm, which was sponsored by the Russian Provisional Government. German and Austro-Hungarian socialists attended; Allied socialists were denied passports until the British broke ranks under Russian pressure. Nonetheless, the anti-war British Labour leader (and future prime minister), Ramsay MacDonald, was prevented from sailing by the British seaman's union. A cartoon of MacDonald sitting disconsolately on his luggage on the quay was gleefully reprinted by pro-war newspapers around the world.

The Eleventh Battle ended in early September with an Austro-Hungarian counter-attack that regained almost all of the lost ground on the Carso and took 6,700 prisoners. The casualties on both sides were the highest yet and the front had scarcely moved. Cadorna decided that he had too few men for another attack before bad weather, so he went on the defensive. *Il Popolo* promised, "wait until next year."

Their enemy was not waiting. Karl—throne slipping away—begged Wilhelm for assistance. Hindenburg agreed to lend seven divisions with 460 guns, 216 mortars, and sixty aeroplanes to become part of a temporary army with a German commander. The Austro-Hungarians contributed their best mountain troops; they would attack over the rugged terrain along the northern Isonzo. The guns were brought up secretly, hidden behind the high ridges along the river; their fliers kept Italian reconnaissance aeroplanes away. The bombardment began before dawn on 24 October. The Italian artillery line was saturated with gas shells and splattered with shrapnel and high explosive. Italian gas masks were effective for a few hours only. At dawn a huge gas cloud, released from thousands of mortar bombs projected from simple tubes dug into reverse slopes, engulfed the Italian trenches in the river valley. Many of these were manned by workers from Turin who had been called into service because they had struck their factories. The German and Austro-Hungarian infantry advanced in small units that slipped through gaps, bypassing well-defended positions. The mountain troops drove west along the lightly defended crests of the ridges. Thirty thousand Italians were captured in the first twenty-four hours and Cadorna ordered a general retreat.

The attackers reoccupied Gorizia. Cadorna's communiqué described it as "perhaps the greatest catastrophe in history." However, he was helpless, and he found that his army "was swarming with worms." Caporetto fell, giving its name to the battle. In days that followed the Italians lost everything gained from eleven offensives and 400,000 civilians were refugees. The attackers swept on over the Italian plain, taking Udine without a fight and occupying two provinces. Their advance stopped at the River Piave, 110 kilometres to the west of the Isonzo. They were stopped by the length of their supply line, rallying Italians, five British and six French divisions, and additional Allied artillery. The Italians lost about 800,000 men; of these 10,000 were dead, 30,000 wounded, 300,000 were POWs, and the rest simply left the front. Many of the deserters were rounded up by *Carabinieri* and placed in concentration camps for re-education. There is a graphic description of the retreat in Ernest Hemingway's *A Farewell to Arms*, although he was not there—he came to Italy in 1918. The Italians also lost 3,150 guns, 1,732 mortars, 3,000 machine guns, and 300,000 rifles. *Il Popolo* condemned the shooting of deserters—the soldiers were not to blame; it was the higher-ups.

A distraught Mussolini launched a "stand to the finish" campaign and organized demonstrations by wounded veterans demanding a new volunteer army, military rule of Northern Italy, and the suppression of the socialist newspapers. The advance into the abundant Italian farmlands was a Godsend for the starving enemy soldiers; their average body weight was down to 54 kilograms. For a few wonderful weeks, they had enough to eat. Ten thousand wagons hauled away the booty and the German divisions returned to the Western Front. Mussolini was invited to speak in the *La Scala* opera house at a ceremony to welcome the Allied reinforcements. He wrote:

> We must abandon the great phrase of 'liberty.' There is another which ... ought to be on the lips of the Cabinet when they address the Italian people, and it is <u>Discipline!</u> Either discipline today in order to achieve victory tomorrow, or collapse following upon defeat.

At a hastily convened Allied conference at Rapallo, Victor Emmanuelle, in excellent English, blamed Cadorna and his generals for the rout. Cadorna was made the Italian representative in France. The new commander, Armando Diaz, was a well-trained, experienced gunner—a model of pragmatism. He flushed out the staff and brought in competent men; Badoglio became an assistant chief of staff. Diaz replaced field officers only when absolutely necessary; he wanted stability—in the past year, Cadorna had fired twenty-four corps commanders and equivalent numbers in lower grades; one infantry regiment had forty-one commanders since the start of the war. Diaz also changed tactics. The Italian army would no longer hunker down in a single defensive line, attempt mass attacks in columns or tolerate inaccurate barrages. Infantry attacks were to emphasize firepower, machine guns and mortars. The troops were given a rise in pay and a free insurance policy so they would no longer despair about their families' survival. The money came from a tax on war workers. Leave was given more frequently and rations were markedly improved. The Italians also acquired a new, more energetic Prime Minister, Vittorio Orlando.

When the front stabilized along the Piave Mussolini wrote:

> Was it written in the book of fate that the defeat of Teutonism, begun beside a river of France, should be completed by the banks of a river in Italy? We should know in a few weeks or days. Meanwhile, courage!

He demanded a dictator. When the Bolsheviks seized power in Petrograd *Il Popolo* was quick to denounce "this unholy alliance between the German high command and the synagogue."

In truth, there was now a lot less to worry him on the home front. The invasion had metamorphosed the war from a questionable adventure for expansion into a struggle for national survival. Strikes and bread riots almost ceased. Speakers against the war were jailed and thousands of young middle-class men crowded the recruitment offices, donning the black shirts, ties, fezzes and daggers of the *arditi*—Italian storm troopers. The dagger was to show that they were ready for hand-to-hand combat. Their battalions had twice the usual number of heavy machine guns, six times as many light machine guns, more light mortars and two light infantry guns for direct support. Mussolini wrote:

> I am convinced that, instead of saturating the trenches with human blood … we should pin our faith on those men who make war with conviction and passion.

War production went into high gear, and lost guns, rifles, mortars, lorries and the like were replaced. It was a hard winter for all—bitter cold, little fuel, electricity frequently cut off, little meat and bread scarce. Despite it all, by spring Mussolini could "feel the Soul of Italy stretching toward victory." *Il Popolo* argued that only those who had experienced the trenches were fit to lead the country toward its future.

Herbert Hoover
August through December 1917

Hoover's job as US food administrator had "little humour or romance." He had to cajole Wilson into letting him run the enterprise, not sit as chairman of a board or commission—he insisted on controlling everything. Hoover would identify a problem, consult with his old boy's network, and then inveigle the best person for working it through to come to Washington; many came as volunteers. He rejected the idea of price controls, which he argued had failed in Europe; instead, he guaranteed prices at levels that would stimulate American farm production—$2.20 per bushel of wheat and $17.50 per hundred pounds of hog. The Food Administration would buy all produce at the price fixed and then the transporters and processors added additional fixed fees to the final cost to the consumer. A Congressional appropriation provided the capital to buy all of the wheat, peas and beans on the US market and all of the sugar on the US, Filipino and West Indian markets. He considered and rejected rationing the Americans, and instead pushed voluntary programmes for reducing consumption and waste. Households posted cards in their windows pledging to cut waste and were visited by volunteer ladies, dressed in neat uniforms, who suggested ways to save. The word "hooverize" entered the American lexicon—it meant to scrimp. His offices were initially in requisitioned hotels and later in a 'temporary building' which held 3,000 employees—it remained in use until after World War II. During the first weeks of the new operation many of its top men boarded at the Hoover's Washington home. When the Food Administration shut up shop, the Congressional appropriation was returned with a 40 per cent profit.

One of Hoover's quirks was displayed at a dinner where he sat next to General Peyton March, the army chief of staff. Hoover mentioned an incident that day on the Western Front. The General told him he was mistaken and corrected his account. Hoover replied,—

General, when you know me better you will find that when I say a thing it is a fact.

The answer was,—

Mr Hoover, when you know me better you will find that ... when I tell as a fact something about the military progress of the war, it is a fact.

After the dinner Hoover rushed home to check his files. Abashed, he wrote the General a note of apology and tells the story in his memoirs.

Adolf Hitler
July through December 1917

The List regimental staff moved up to Belgium, followed a few days later by the troops. By 13 July, they were near Gheluvelt, along the Menin Road, just where they had first seen war in 1914. Then it had been a gentle landscape of tree-lined roads, little woods and soggy green fields—now it was battered into chaos; craters everywhere, ragged stumps of trees, and a marsh which in many places could only be traversed on duckboard paths. The German fortifications were mostly concrete bunkers and pillboxes dotted about the countryside, sited to give interlocking machine gun fire across the ground the British infantrymen must traverse; German infantry sections were dispersed in fox or shell holes with "tin Siegfried's" in front of them—curved ovals of metal plate about a metre high with a firing slit. Dugouts had reinforced concrete roofs, two exits and were not as deep as in the Somme, where some had been death traps. The British artillery opposing them had 226 heavy guns and 526 heavy howitzers in addition to 1,098 18-pounders and 325 4.5" howitzers. The German advantage was that their observers were on high ground, with a clear view for 11 kilometres behind the front so they could bring down fire on anything that moved during daylight.

The volume of British fire gradually built up into the heaviest bombardment the world had yet seen. After battering the enemy positions, supply lines and headquarters for thirteen days the British began counter-battery fire. However, they had not located many of the German guns, because most had three prepared firing positions and shifted frequently from one to another; sometimes they would leave one gun behind, firing frequently to deceive British spotters. The firing was blind on 28 and 29 July when Flanders was shrouded in dense fog. After firing 4.3 million shells, the British infantry came forward on 30 July. In the first days they were scheduled to seize the high ground, then there would be amphibious landings along the coast, western Belgium would be liberated and the German Army crushed. After the infantry's disappointing first attack the heavens opened, and most of the subsequent fighting was in torrents of rain and the sodden ground became a dangerous sea of mud.

It was another execrable time for "the poor worms of the infantry," as Hitler called them. In their first ten days back at the Flanders front, the List Regiment lost 800 men, primarily to high explosive and gas. The runners had to be especially careful during the day, because British flyers would hover above, tracing their routes to headquarters, which were then targeted by artillery. During the last week of July the fighting was the bitterest yet seen, on the ground and in the air. On 26 July, just above the List headquarters, ninety-four single-seater fighters fought it out at elevations from 1,500 metres to 5,200 metres. Hitler often talked about this air battle in later years, lauding the bravery, skill and dedication of the German aviators. The British opened a "fantastic" bombardment on 31 July. They attacked Pilckem Ridge north of Ypres. Both sides suffered terribly, but the defensive system set up by General Lossberg, who had been transferred to Flanders, made the best of a bad thing. After each visit to the fighting zone—often he greeted dawn in the front line shell holes—he made tactical adjustments, but as before relied heavily on counter-attacks. The British lost fewer men attacking than when defending newly won ground, where they were battered by German artillery and then defied by infantry advancing skilfully over familiar ground.

Finally, the List's remaining men were transferred to a quiet sector in Alsace to recuperate. Along the way a railway man offered Hitler 200 marks for Foxl—he indignantly refused. Within hours, Foxl disappeared; Hitler was devastated: "The swine who stole my dog doesn't realize what he did to me." It was not the end of his dreadful journey. Next, someone—he was convinced that it must be a civilian—rifled his knapsack and stole his leather portfolio of sketches, watercolours and poems. He did no more painting and was not consoled for his losses by being awarded the Military Service Cross with Swords. Without Foxl to keep him at home, as he called his regiment, Hitler took his first leave. He and Schmidt went to Berlin to stay with the parents of their friend Richard Arendt, sending enthusiastic postcards back to the comrades.

The List Regiment moved on to Champagne, garrisoning a quiet part of the line near Laon. Hitler returned from his eighteen-day leave; it reopened the wound to be back without Foxl. On 22 October the French launched an attack with gas along the Oise-Aisne Canal, but they did not make significant progress and the List did not suffer badly.

Starting in summer 1917, troops were marched periodically to 'patriotic instruction;' a programme initiated by Ludendorff. Rudolph Binding, an author and mayor who was now an officer and a lecturer, described its goals:

> It must constantly foster and maintain affection for the Kaiser and the reigning Princes and strong German sentiment for the Fatherland and thus insure that a fight is put up against all agitators, croakers, and weaklings.

Whenever possible the troops attended compulsory lectures twice a week. Lecturers encouraged discussion afterwards and reported what they thought useful and acceptable to the higher-ups. Hitler must have enjoyed spouting his ideas. Sometimes films were shown or plays performed; they were popular with the troops. But the programme did not fit his ideas of effective propaganda—it overestimated the intelligence and attention span of the average man. The defeatist spirit of the new replacements coming to the front made him livid; they even infected some of the old comrades of 1914. To add to their misery, food was scarce and the men were scrawny; they had a watery soup at lunch time, later one-third of a loaf of bread with a tiny portion of a spread, usually some ambiguous variation on jam. The men hunted and ate dogs and cats—Hitler preferred the latter.

Gustav Mannerheim
July through November 1917

The Provisional Government appointed Brusilov as supreme commander-in-chief. He tried to keep the army together and to prevent the murder of officers. The Germans remained quietly where they stood; Hindenburg feared that a German advance would reignite Russian patriotism. The Provisional Government was committed to a military offensive to help the Allies win; the leading figure was War Minister Kerensky, an amateur politician and soldier. He toured the front, speaking to mass meetings. A splendid stump speaker, he managed to stir up some fighting spirit; volunteers—including the Woman's Battalion of Death—were formed into storm troops, wearing a red over black chevron on their right arms. Mannerheim—perhaps by hindsight—thought that the government should have focused on land reform and elections rather than military victory. Kerensky's offensive began in July in Galicia and Bukovina. They were supported by French advisors, British armoured cars and aeroplanes, and Czech, Serbian and Polish units. The principal attack floundered; the Woman's Battalion had 80 per cent casualties, but in the south the Eighth Army, led by General Kornilov, advanced 30 kilometres, so he was given command of the entire southern front. The enemy counter-attacked in Galicia on 14 July, the Russian front was broken, troops fled in disorder and the Germans advanced toward the Ukraine—the Russian front was pushed back 100 kilometres. The Romanian army attacked along a 24-kilometre front, and made a modest advance, which boosted their morale, before being stopped in their tracks.

General Kornilov was appointed supreme commander in August; Brusilov retired (and was later to serve in the Red Army). Kornilov was tough; patrols collared deserters, unsure officers were dismissed, soldiers' assemblies were banned, and their council's powers were diminished. At his insistence, the death penalty and courts martial were restored. It did not stop the disintegration. Mannerheim battled to keep officers who expressed anti-government opinions from arrest; every move required negotiations with commissars. Kerensky became prime minister. The Germans demonstrated their latent power by over-whelming the fortress of Riga, taking the fourth city of the Russian Empire. Dismayed, Kornilov attributed the defeat to treachery; the Provisional Government was "… acting in full accord with the plans of the German General Staff." He sent the Savage Division and a Russian cavalry division to Petrograd to arrest Kerensky. The commander of one of these divisions went alone to the Winter Palace to meet Kerensky. Exactly what happened between them is unknown. After the meeting, the general drove to his home and shot himself; Kornilov was arrested the next day. Kerensky took supreme command. Elections were finally held in late October 1917 and out of 36 million votes, the Bolsheviks had only 9 million; but before the newly elected assembly met, the Reds forcibly seized power. Soon Kornilov and Denikin were leading White armies.

The Romanian front was far from the capital and communications were so poor that the army there remained comparatively tranquil. Fate was on Mannerheim's side. On a cross-country ride in early autumn, his horse took a tumble; he was thrown and his ankle badly sprained. The doctor predicted that he would be laid up for several months so he asked for medical leave to recuperate in Odessa. He said his farewells, hobbled to his car and drove to the Hotel London in Odessa, where he took up with his old social set. In his *Memoirs*, he describes a tea party at which they were entertained by a clairvoyant. For Mannerheim it was much like Macbeth's encounter with the weird sisters—his fate was that he would be given command of an army and would lead it to victory; surely a stock vision for a seer to toss at a lieutenant general. But as he recalled it by hindsight much later, he was also told that he would relinquish this command of his own accord, then an important mission would take him to two Western countries, from which he would return to a higher position—you will see how accurate this was. Whenever he discusses this prophecy the chill rationality of his *Memoirs* slips away—he was fulfilling destiny.

He read about the Bolshevik takeover in Petrograd in the newspaper of 8 November. It was time to get to Finland. Normally the train from Odessa to Petrograd took two days, but now it was at least four days and the cars were so packed that passengers could only board or leave through the windows. Mannerheim asked an old comrade, now the military governor of Odessa, for a private coach—it was granted. He took with him his aide and his batman, two British Red Cross Sisters, a British midshipman, on his way home, and three Romanian doctors heading for Japan. The private coach kept breaking down, each time it was dropped off for repairs and then hitched to another train. Tired of this, Mannerheim bribed a coach-load of soldiers to swap equipment—his lovely blue first-class for their disreputable red fourth-class. When his little party pulled into Molhilev, where Supreme Headquarters was located, there was a pool of blood on the platform. The chief of staff had been bayoneted and clubbed to death by soldiers when he came to the station to meet the new Bolshevik commander-in-chief, Officer-Cadet Krylenko.

Krylenko was there to redeem the Bolsheviks' promise of peace. As soon as they seized power, they lavished money on propaganda promoting world revolution to end the war. For instance, 500,000 copies of their German newspaper, *Die Fackel* (The Torch), were printed daily, brought up to the trenches and distributed to the other side by Russian soldiers who were encouraged to fraternize with the enemy. The Bolsheviks also proposed that all belligerents meet in a peace conference—there were no takers. On 13 November, Krylenko sent three emissaries—a lieutenant, a surgeon and a volunteer—under a white flag to propose an armistice to the Central Powers. They agreed to meet at the citadel of Brest-Litovsk, as soon as five German, four Austro-Hungarian, three Turkish and two Bulgarian negotiators assembled there. The Russians sent twenty-eight delegates, including soldiers, sailors, women, workers and revolutionaries—one of whom characterized their delegation as a "menagerie." The Central Powers agreed to a twenty-eight-day ceasefire, but refused to facilitate the distribution of written materials among their troops. During the armistice, the Central Powers agreed not to shift troops other than those already under order to the western front. On 2 December, an agreement was signed for a month's armistice, with automatic thirty-day extensions unless there was a week's prior notification. The Romanians also signed an armistice six days later.

Mannerheim's carriage took six days to get to Petrograd. In the station he was disgusted to see soldiers loitering while generals carried their "own kit." With impressive size and icy blue eyes he soon had two soldiers saluting properly and then hauling his luggage. For a week he searched for a leading personality with the courage to fight the Bolsheviks. During dinner one night at the Hunt Club he sounded out two Grand Dukes, both with high commands in the Army; totally demoralized, both judged the game irretrievably lost.

Bolshevik policy was that Finland could become independent. Mannerheim told the General Staff that consequently he could no longer serve in the Russian Army. They agreed, but warned him that he would need a pass from the Bolsheviks to travel to Finland; he would not ask such scum for the slightest favour. Instead he went to the Finland Station and presented his army pass for the trip from Odessa to Petrograd to the soldiers who examined travellers' papers. They happened to be Finns whose Russian was not up to the technicalities, so after some pleasant exchanges in Finnish, they waved him through. He ordered two soldiers to carry his bags.

VIII

The Finnish Civil War to the Armistices

Gustav Mannerheim
December 1917 to April 1918

Mannerheim arrived in Finland in the middle of December. The turmoil in Russia had spilled across the border—revolution was in the air. The Red Guards were recruiting more men; there were demonstrations and some looting. Russian garrisons were still in the country. The Whites were forming paramilitary units called "Defence Corps" or "Fire Brigades." The Tsar's government had been replaced by a parliament, elected under the provisions of the Swedish-Finnish Constitution of 1772; in the election, the Social Democrats won 46 per cent of the seats. The head of the Senate was the leader of the White majority, P.E. Svinhufund. Physically he was a striking contrast to Mannerheim—a small, frail-looking fellow, with a wispy goatee. A leader of an underground association for Finnish independence, he had been jailed for years in Siberia—he detested Russians and was strongly pro-German. He cannot have warmed to a towering, formal lieutenant general with thirty years service in the Russian Army, but, recognizing his professional competence and knowing of his connections in Finland, Svinhufund asked Mannerheim to become a member of the Military Committee.

At his first meeting with the Committee Mannerheim learned that 1,800 young Finns had been secretly training in Germany, as the 27th Jäger Battalion, as a cadre for a Finnish Army. The government could provide few weapons—only the few that the Germans were willing to sell. Mannerheim asked the French Embassy for assistance with arms; naturally they would not help. Most of the Whites' rifles and small arms ammunition were bought from individual Russian soldiers. The Red Guards were armed from the Russian depots in Finland. There were about 40,000 Russian troops in the country, as well as units of the Baltic Fleet in Helsinki. At the end of his third meeting with the Military Committee Mannerheim told them that he was resigning.—

Why? Because you are dithering on inconsequential matters and soon you all will be arrested by the Reds. What did he recommend? That we all immediately proceed to the north of the country where we can set up a secure headquarters and get into action.

The chairman asked him to prepare a report to be discussed the next morning. Mannerheim silently lit a cigar and left.

The next morning several members of the Committee appeared at his house. They asked to see his report. "I did not prepare one. I already told you what I think." They were not to be surprised; they came prepared. They offered him the chair of the Committee and they assured him that the Senate would name him commander-in-chief. He went to talk it over with Svinhufund. Mannerheim assured him that the Finns could deal with both their Reds and the demoralized Russian troops, without troops from any other nation. Consequently, before becoming commander he required a commitment that if it came to war neither Germany nor Sweden would be asked to intervene, though volunteers from abroad would be welcome. He did not want the Russians replaced by another master. Svinhufund did not feel it necessary to tell him that the Germans had already refused to help, so Mannerheim became commander on his terms. That evening he met with the directors of the Private Bank, Finland's largest—he had known most of these men for years. He said he would leave the next morning to set up headquarters in Vaasa, a seaport 370 kilometres northwest of Helsinki. "If I arrive at my destination empty-handed, much time will be lost." They made no commitment at the meeting but in the morning, he was told that 15 million marks would be at his disposal in Vaasa.

On the railway journey, he was almost arrested by three Russian guards for travelling on false papers. They were fakes—his life was saved by a quick-witted Finnish conductor who persuaded the guards that his papers were legitimate. In Vaasa, he assembled the scattered ad hoc defence forces into a single command and enlisted every veteran soldier he could find. By coincidence, both sides went into action on 28 January 1918. In Helsinki, the Red Guard occupied the Senate, the Diet and the principal banks. A list of those to be arrested was issued and the hunt was on. Simultaneously Mannerheim struck in Vaasa. In the dark winter morning, the Russian barracks were surrounded by long columns of Finns and in the gloom, the Russians could not see that all of the armed men were at the fore of the columns; most of the rest were unarmed. The Russians surrendered; their weapons armed more Finns. Mannerheim issued a proclamation to the Finnish people stating:

> ... I had been compelled to disarm the Russian garrisons since the dregs of our population had joined them and committed acts of violence, murdering and robbing peaceful citizens.

He informed his government that military operations to secure the country would take three-and-a-half months; his forecast was dead on, almost to the day. He received valuable reinforcements from Sweden; eighty-four officers, thirty-four of whom were on the active list, formed the core of his staff. There was work for all and everything had to be thought of. For instance, Mannerheim personally commissioned a well-known Finnish artist to design medals. Compulsory military service was inaugurated, based on a law passed in 1879, showing that the government was confident that most Finns would fight the Bolsheviks. Mannerheim's ace-in-the-hole was the German-trained Jägers, 1,210 of their men had been fighting Russians; they arrived home at the end of February. They were assigned as officers and NCOs to eighteen newly formed Jäger battalions, making a force of 14,000 men. They must be ready to attack in mid-March.

On 3 March, the news came that the Bolshevik Russian government had signed a peace treaty in Brest-Litovsk in which they renounced claim to Finland. On the same day Mannerheim was thunderstruck when he was told that the Germans had agreed to intervene in Finland at the request of the Finnish Government, exactly what the government had promised their commander-in-chief they would not do. Mannerheim felt that he must resign, but lit a cigar and resolved to sleep on it. A night's reflection made him realize that if he left, the Germans would surely be credited with liberating Finland; if he stayed they could only claim that they had helped, so he swallowed his pride. He wired Ludendorff, thanking the Germans for the arms they had provided and requesting that the commander of their troops coming to Finland should be placed under Finnish orders and that they should proclaim that they were there to assist the Finns. On 10 March he had a telegram from Hindenburg agreeing to his conditions and requesting that the Germans be positioned on the Finnish right wing, so that they could easily be supplied by sea.

The Red Guards attacked from 9 to 14 March, moving north to clear the country of their opponents, but they were unable to break through the Whites' defensive lines. On 15 March, Mannerheim launched a counter-offensive to surround the bulk of the Red forces. Resistance was desperate—the Reds were steeled by their leaders, who told them that all prisoners were shot and that massive reinforcements were on the way from Russia. On 6 April, the Whites captured the key position, the town of Tampere, 160 kilometres north of Helsinki, taking 11,000 unwounded prisoners and 30 guns. The able Red commander, a former metal-worker, was among the 2,000 killed. The German Baltic Division landed in Finland; it entered Helsinki on 14 April. Then the Germans swung north to form part of the snare Mannerheim had woven around the major Red contingent. The Reds tried unsuccessfully to fight their way out and then surrendered on 2 May—25,000 were made prisoner. As usual, Mannerheim does not give any indication of the number of White casualties; other sources estimate that there were 4,487. About 20,000 Reds were killed; a large number in a small country—an equivalent loss for the British would have been almost 260,000 men. During the battles, medical care for both sides was provided by the Finnish Red Cross, led by his sister Sophie.

The Finns were still in a precarious position and there was little food. The Red prisoners of war suffered the most; by early summer the death rate in the camps was horrendous. The Government planned to try all of the prisoners in civilian courts; it would take years to work through the list. Mannerheim advised that all but a few leaders be freed at once, but the government considered sending them all to Germany as labourers. As the politicians talked, prisoners died. These deaths created a bitter divide that persisted in the country for years; many on the left blamed Mannerheim. The Senate voted to dismiss all of the volunteer Swedish officers from the Finnish service; they would be replaced by German officers and a German would be appointed as army chief of staff. He would draft a plan for the organization of the Army, which Mannerheim would be required to implement. In France the Germans were ripping through the Allies' lines and almost all of the prominent men in Finland looked at the world "through German spectacles;" Mannerheim was almost alone in thinking that the Germans were likely to lose. He requested and was given permission to address the Senate. He stunned them with his forthrightness:

> I lay down my command and go abroad tomorrow. I must request the Government immediately to appoint my successor, failing which I will hand over my command to the nearest officer.

Not a single man took his hand as he walked out of the Senate chamber and lit his cigar.

Harold Macmillan
1918

In the spring of 1918 Macmillan was back in hospital, feverish with his thigh swollen and throbbing. He was anxious, almost despairing, as he read about the German victories, and heartened when the Allies finally unified their command; scanning the long casualty lists for names of friends, and exulting when the Allies turned the tables. He was still hospitalized on 11 November, and could only walk supported by two sticks. He hobbled over to Hyde Park Corner to watch the crowd; all too aware of how many sad hearts were in the throng. Once again Rudyard Kipling expressed his mood.

> If any question why we died,
> Tell them, because our fathers lied.

Benito Mussolini
January to June 1918

In Italy the winter was bitter cold, there was little fuel, electricity was frequently cut off, there was almost no meat and bread was scarce. The children suffered and Rachele spent long hours in queues, but they could afford to purchase far better supplies than the poor. *Il*

Popolo went all out to fan the spirit of determination and victory, and by spring, Mussolini wrote the he could "feel the Soul of Italy stretching toward victory;" he exhorted his readers to settle for nothing less than total victory. *Il Popolo* kept reiterating that only those who had experienced the trenches were fit to lead the country toward its future. The paper's finances were no longer a problem because now there were subsidies from Italian industrialists as well as the Allies. One of the British intelligence officers stationed in Italy was Lieutenant Colonel Samuel Hoare. He was advised to subsidize Mussolini. He wired his commander for permission, assuring him that the French were also contributing and that British funding would be secret. Mussolini wrote to Hoare, promising that he would mobilize the *fasci* to break the heads of any anti-war demonstrators who dared to take to the streets of Milan. They did not meet at the time, but years later, when Hoare became British foreign minister, Mussolini enthusiastically remembered their collaboration in 1918 (Foreign Minister Hoare undermined efforts in the League of Nations to impose sanctions on the supply of oil that might have saved Abyssinia, now Ethiopia, from the Italian invaders).

In January 1918, a small attack by a detachment of *Arditi* was led by a seventeen-year-old volunteer, Roberto Sarfatti, the son of Mussolini's lover. When he left for the front, the boy visited Mussolini to say goodbye. He was slaughtered a few weeks later, becoming the youngest winner of the *medaglia d'oro*. Mussolini wrote:

Nor merely a drop, but all of my blood, not only part of my life, but the whole of my life, so that Italy may be safe.

In 1917, the Emperor Karl had launched a secret, private peace initiative, using his brother-in-law, Prince Sixtus of Bourbon-Parma, a Belgian who lived in France, as a conduit to the French President. The Germans learned about it and quietly stopped him. Rumours circulated, so in May 1918 the Austrian Foreign Minister admitted to the negotiations but claimed that they ended when Karl rejected French demands for Alsace-Lorraine. Premier Clemenceau riposted by publishing a letter in which Karl acknowledged France's "just claims" to the provinces. Karl lied, claiming that the letter was a forgery: "he was innocent as a newborn child." No one believed him, least of all *Il Popolo*, which campaigned relentlessly for total victory and for attaining the borders of the 'true' Italy. To preserve his throne, Karl gave the Germans control of many aspects of Austro-Hungarian life and promised a new offensive in Italy.

When Karl ordered his generals to attack the Italians they protested strongly—led by Boroević, who was now a field marshal. His army was starving once again. They lacked everything; guns could not be repositioned because they were so short of draft horses. Regardless, an attack was scheduled for mid-June and planned as meticulously as ever. Guns and supplies were brought up to the front at night and skilfully camouflaged, but Italian intelligence learned the date for the assault from deserters. The attackers crossed the Piave at a number of places, but resistance was strong, and where they took the Italian front line, they were then stopped at a well-manned second line. Allied artillery fire was devastating and 80 per cent of the bridging the Austro-Hungarians thrust across the Piave was destroyed by Allied air strikes. Within days the Austro-Hungarians were forced back across the river. They had lost 118,000 men; the Italians about the same.

Boroević knew that they could not just continue to sit along the Piave. He planned to hold the Italians there just long enough to withdraw the bulk of his army back to the River Tagliamento. They no longer had supplies for their troops, not even shoes for men serving above the snowline. Their medical service was collapsing. In 1917 the Austro-Hungarians had 7,392 doctors in the field; by April 1918 there were only 4,870. Malaria was a major problem. Tens of thousands of men were infected and because of the blockade they had no anti-malarials, which came from South America. *Il Popolo* scented victory.

Charles de Gaulle
December 1917 to July 1918

Back in Fort IX, in solitary confinement, with no reading materials and only thirty minutes of exercise per day, de Gaulle's morale sank to rock bottom. He wrote to his parents:

> ... a sorrow more bitter than any I think I shall meet at any time, is wringing me more severely than ever.

This was in December 1917. In a sense it was bitter news when Tukhachevsky escaped. He had been warned by his fellow prisoners that once back in Russia he would be immediately shot because he was a noble. He promised that, on the contrary, he would be a general at twenty-five.

In May 1918, de Gaulle was transferred to an eighteenth-century fortress to the west of Nuremberg, so he missed the denouement at Fort IX. An NCO who was overseeing the change of the guard saw a group of French officers laughing; thinking that they were mocking him, he ordered his men to fire over their heads. The French retaliated with curses. The outraged NCO then commanded a guard to shoot a French lieutenant. He missed the officer but shattered a chimney pot. Fourteen Allied officers submitted affidavits about the incident, demanding an inquiry. The Germans shut Fort IX.

At his new prison, de Gaulle and a comrade broke into the tailor's shop and stole a German uniform. The disguised comrade escorted de Gaulle out of the main gate. They marched off, slipped into a patch of woods, and emerged dressed as civilians. They were captured the next day by a patrol. Attempt 6.

On the morning of 7 July, as usual, the huge, padlocked laundry basket sat unattended for a few minutes, waiting to be escorted off the premises. Two well-practiced prisoners slipped in to remove the pins from the hinges. Some laundry was extracted and de Gaulle, in mufti, took its place. The pins were replaced by lengths of steel cable, the ends of which were thrust through the wickerwork into his hands. De Gaulle slipped out on the loading dock of the washhouse. Two days later he was apprehended by a patrol when he boarded a train at Nuremberg station. Attempt 7.

Mustapha Kemal
December 1917 to August 1918

The Kaiser invited the Sultan to visit Imperial General Headquarters. Too old to travel, he sent the heir apparent, his younger brother, Prince Vahid-ed-Din, fifty-six years old, with Kemal as his aide. When they were received in December, the Kaiser recognized Kemal's name and discussed in some detail and with great approval his defence of the Anafarta ridge. Hindenburg and Ludendorff were outwardly optimistic, though the latter seemed nervous and troubled. They had defeated the Serbians, Romanians and Russians, now they only had to fight on the Western Front, where they outnumbered the British and French. They were planning a great offensive. Kemal asked Hindenburg, "for my ear alone," what was their strategic objective? Hindenburg rose and offered his guest a cigarette. Kinross tells us that Kemal later described Hindenburg as "a man whose eyes see to the heart of things and whose tongue knew the value of silence." Kemal concluded that they simply planned to pound away at their enemies, hoping they would throw in the towel.

When they toured the front, Kemal saw tattered, emaciated infantry, cannon with rifling almost worn smooth, and the bones of the horses' ribs—the Germans would not win. In Berlin, he saw the frenetic gaiety of the wealthy, filling the theatres and nightclubs, while the starving middle class shuffled palely about the streets on their perpetual quest for food. In the hotel each guest received their daily bread ration in the morning. On the trip home, Kemal unsuccessfully tried to persuade the Prince to save the Empire by ending the war.

Back in Constantinople in January, Kemal had a recurring problem—severe pain from an infection of his left kidney, probably an after-effect of gonorrhoea. He obtained permission to go to Vienna for specialist treatment and then spent a month recuperating in Carlsbad. While he was away, the treaty of Brest-Litovsk returned to the Ottomans all of the territory they had lost to the Russians in 1878; Enver happily reoccupied it. The treaty also established a Democratic Republic of Armenia and the Ottomans agreed to the return of Armenian refugees and exiles. The Sultan died in July and was succeeded by the prince, who became Mehmed VI. Kemal was eager to have his ear, but his trip home was delayed by another hospital stay in Vienna, this time with the influenza that was sweeping over the world. When he returned to Constantinople in August, Enver, Djemal and Talât ruled the Sultan, who personally ordered Kemal to retake command of the Seventh Army in Palestine. Kemal dare not reject a direct order from the Sultan but regarded command of a disintegrating army as a snare to ruin his reputation. He told Enver that he had "taken a fine revenge."

Adolf Hitler
1918

Morale in the List picked up during the winter; the weather was exceptionally fine and the news excellent. The Russians and Romanians were negotiating peace. The U-boats were ravaging Allied shipping. The German army was massing in the West so finally numbers would be in their favour. The great victories of late 1917 at Riga and at Caporetto proved that German offensive tactics could slice through enemy fortifications and, at about the same time, the army in the West had been buoyed by the Battle of Cambrai. It had started disastrously. The British completely surprised the defence, attacking without a preliminary bombardment and using a wave of tanks to trample the barbed wire. The British smashed through line after line. They were almost in open country. Then the remaining tanks encountered a motorized anti-aircraft gun, which knocked out the three leading tanks and forced the rest to retreat. The same gun drove back the cavalry that came up to exploit the breakthrough. The British paused and the Germans counter-attacked; within days, the British were driven back to their starting line or even beyond, so what started as a defeat turned into a notable victory.

Hitler was fired with enthusiasm and optimism, chiding his war-weary comrades, and he carefully followed the preparations for the offensive. Selected men were sent to training courses in offensive warfare and more light machine guns were issued, including excellent Lewis guns captured from the British. Storm units were equipped with automatic pistols in ingenious wooden holsters that could be slipped into an attachment on the pistol grip to become a stock, so they need not carry cumbersome rifles and could lug more grenades. Another advantage of the pistols was that they were less likely than rifles to be gummed up by mud. Bayonets were replaced by entrenching tools honed to a cutting edge or by daggers. In some divisions, steel helmets were covered with netting to hold twigs and sprigs of grass as camouflage. Assault infantry were trained to advance as scouts, locate strong points and then call up specialized troops with heavy weapons to deal with them. Assault cannon were brought into the front line—some were specially-built 37mm guns, but most were modified German 77mm guns or captured Russian field guns mounted on carriages that could be manhandled across No Man's Land. The British saw them and decided that they were anti-tank guns. There were thousands of light mortars, which were carried in two pieces and then snapped together. They fired rapidly with a range of 300 metres; their grenades had a sensitive impact detonator that hurled razor-sharp splinters over a wide field, but the grenades weighed only 2 kilograms, so a good supply could be lugged up to the firing line. The British had studied and tried to imitate German defences, apparently not considering that German fortifications were designed to counter Allied offensive tactics. The British constructed strong points behind the front line; some critics thought they would be traps—they became known as 'birdcages.' The Germans removed their metal unit identification marks from their uniforms and replaced them with coloured cloth patches. The List was trained as an assault division, but never served as such, because they were not allocated enough horses to make them mobile. The Americans were in the back of everyone's mind, but most accepted the official line that they would not arrive in time and anyhow were only an amateur army. It was already becoming clear that the navy's promise that they would sink all of the American troop transports was a fantasy. One way or the other, the war was going to be settled.

In January, they read about strikes in the factories at home and in Austria-Hungary. Hitler called it "the biggest piece of chicanery in the whole war." He cheered when the strikes were broken by the threat of military call-up, but he would have preferred to have the lot of them shot. On 18 February 1918, the Regiment was inspected by the Imperial Crown Prince and General Ludendorff. Bands played almost daily and the men cheered their comrades marching back from their courses. Regimental staffs focused on training; the stream of Ludendorff's paper barrage about offensive tactics was discussed while interested runners listened.

At 0440 on 21 March, there was a crash as if the world was ending; 6,608 German guns fired almost simultaneously along a 75-kilometre front running north from the river Somme. Firing as rapidly as they might the German gunners pounded the British artillery positions, on a strict schedule alternating between shrapnel, gas and shells containing both high explosive and gas. Overall, one-third of the shells the Germans fired that day were gas. The British artillery lines were kept saturated with gas, so their gunners worked in masks and their horses were withdrawn to safety. After the first hour more fire was directed at the British fortifications. The heavy fog that morning made it unnecessary to fire smoke. The List was too far away to hear more than faint thunder, but before nightfall, they were told that the British line had been pierced. The Germans succeeded in ending the stalemate of trench warfare—not with novel weapons but with innovative tactics. In the next days, the List marched through the former front, past devastated British trenches and smashed birdcages. Next they went through the area shattered in the withdrawal of 1917, and then through the Somme battlefield, which brought back terrible memories. Along the way they relished a match played on a former British army football ground. By 1 April they were west of Montdidier, at the apex of the deep salient driven into the Allied lines. They were fired on from three sides. Some of their foes were French Zouaves—Algerians or Moroccans; the Germans were always furious when they had to fight "savages" (they also fought a British division in which Anthony Eden was a staff officer. Years later, when Eden was foreign minister, after a day of negotiations he spent an evening with Hitler drawing trench maps on the backs of match books).

The German supply line was stretched too far and passed over too many former battlefields. The List arrived too late to take part in the looting of the rich British supply dumps, so five to seven men shared a loaf of bread for a day and the artillery was short of ammunition. Rudolph Binding, whose division was nearby, wrote:

> The physical exhaustion of the infantry …was so great that finally the men could hardly fire their rifles; they let themselves slowly be wiped out by the enemy artillery fire almost without caring, and would hardly move from the spot. They were just like used-up horses which stand fast in the shafts and dumbly take the blows of the whip without a movement.

For meat, Hitler and a comrade would reconnoitre for a dead horse that did not smell too bad. The List Regiment arrived in the salient with twenty-three officers and 1,123 men. In the next six days they lost 153 dead, 632 wounded and 338 sick.

Depressed and thoroughly spent, they moved to a rest quarter along the Aisne, a front known as the Chemin des Dames because that road ran along the crest of the heights. They took over 4,300 metres of front line on 3 May. Six days later, Hitler was awarded a regimental diploma for signal bravery in attack and nine days later the black wound insignia with sword. During their eleven days there they were attacked by two strong French patrols. They were cheered when told that their comrades had broken through the lines in Flanders held by the British and Portuguese along the river Lys. Within days, the Germans retook all the ground lost the year before in the Passchendaele offensive, but the attack was blocked short of its goal, the railway hub of Hasbrouck—if it had been taken the Allies would have lost Flanders. The troops were assured that the enemy was to be knocked out by a series of punches, not a hay-maker or even a one-two. The next German attack was along the Chemin des Dames, beginning on 27 May. They were supposed to make a limited advance to draw Allied reserves south, so then the final blow could be delivered in Flanders. Years later Hitler lectured his generals with:

> Something just occurred to me because people are always whining about getting reinforcements too late. For the second offensive in 1918, we started out marching on the evening of the 25th. We spent the night of the 26th in a forest and on the morning of the 27th we attacked. We marched at 5:00 a.m. The afternoon of the day before we received our reinforcements for the great offensive at Chemin des Dames.

The 6th Bavarian Division was with the reserves on the right flank. The night before the attack they moved up close to the front. Soon after the hurricane bombardment they started forward, passing walking wounded boasting of their success and French prisoners—some disconsolate, some relieved. They crossed the Oise-Aisne canal dry-shod on newly built bridges. They were nearing the battlefront. Their storm spearhead consisted of a captain, a lieutenant, a doctor, fifty-six men and three machine guns. The regiment followed them through an area shown on their maps as the *Potzdamer Platz*. Horse feed was too bulky for the feeble supply network—supplies were hauled on men's backs. They marched along roads targeted by the French artillery. Now and again they were held up by small groups of enemy who had to be dealt with. On the first day the List had fifty-nine men killed. The next obstacle was an embankment for a rail line that paralleled the road—it bristled with machine guns. The regiment deployed to attack and began to soften up the enemy position with machine guns and mortars, but mortar grenades were used sparingly because they were in short supply. Then a German field artillery battery galloped up the road, wheeled into position in open fields 700 metres from the embankment—just like a nineteenth-century battle painting. The infantry cheered; the surviving French fled. The List continued to march toward Paris. The attack was so successful that Supreme Headquarters gave up the idea of a limited attack and ordered them to go as far as they might.

The following day the List crossed the Marne battlefield of 1914, but that afternoon resistance stiffened; their right flank was in the air. When they reached the River Aisne the bridge was still intact. Their vanguard was within 100 metres when the bridge was blown sky high. In the first five days of the offensive they had captured 400 men, fourteen field and two 150mm guns, about 100 machine guns, a car and three trucks, fifteen ammunition wagons and all sorts of supplies. They had also advanced 30 kilometres. On 3 June, they came up against a firmly held line, which their trench mortars could not dent; their artillery was far behind. The List dug fox holes and waited for help. Several days later they were reinforced by an officer and forty-eight men from the Seventh Army Storm Battalion, but what they needed was heavy artillery. For the next three days they were battered by rain and enemy artillery. Many men were sick in their holes with "hollow cheeks, glazed eyes, and pale countenances."

On 12 June, the List Regiment was relieved and marched back across the Marne where their lightly wounded and sick went to hospital. On 26 June, they had a sports day. Two days later, they moved west to a camp at Passy-sur-Marne where they received 573 replacements. It was supposed to be a rest camp but sleep was difficult because they were bombarded at night with gas shells. There was no more rubber, so the replacements carried leather gas masks that lacked the edging to seal it to the face—close to useless and they all knew it. The high command prepared for a final attack to take Paris, which required a second railway line to bring supplies into the Marne salient. The List moved into position on the night of 13 July. The next day was muggy and threatening. They were receiving fire on their right flank from Allied guns near Chateau Thierry. The German bombardment was scheduled to begin at midnight on 15 July; the first shot was from a 42cm mortar dug in close to regimental headquarters; it turned night into day, the earth heaved, the trees shuddered. The first wave of assault troops filtered through the List lines. Two hours later the 1st Guards and two other infantry divisions assembled in bridgeheads on the far side of the Marne. The German barrage started to roll forward at 0450 and by 0645, the Germans had occupied the heights above the Marne, which were covered with a cloud of smoke and dust. They attacked Americans in the first defensive line, French in the second. The List Regiment hid in a forest during the first day of the offensive. The next night they marched down to the Marne and crossed newly-laid bridges at double time. They continued forward through orchards and vineyards.

Dawn brought a burning July sun. Things were not going well in front of them. The French had anticipated the attack by removing most men from their first line, concentrating them to meet the attack in their second position, which was beyond the range of the enemy field guns. A stream of 2nd Grenadiers was coming back, some of them unwounded. The List Regiment went into action piecemeal to help units stalled at the front and the supply service was straining its utmost just to bring up schnapps and cigarettes. The French prisoners wore new uniforms, sturdy men between twenty and thirty-five years old, while their guards looked like skinny scarecrows. The French infantry tactics were skilful; it was hard to move them. Their artillery was also good, but the intensity of their fire was tolerable. The large French bombing planes were another matter—they roared over in flights of twenty-five to thirty dropping bombs everywhere, driving the Bavarians almost crazy with fear and exasperation. German fighters shot down three of them, but there were too few fighters to meet each wave. The medical support services retreated to the north side of the Marne to escape the bombing. On 19 July, the List Regiment also withdrew to the north bank. Soon the entire army was in full retreat—they had played their last card. Once again their losses had been terrible; the 12th Company went into the battle with ninety-eight men and came out with eighteen.

On 1 August, the List Regiment moved to a camp near Le Cateau where they were to be part of imperial headquarters reserve. The following Sunday there was a parade for awarding the distinctions earned along the Marne. Hitler and a fellow runner received the Iron Cross First Class, on the recommendation of Lieutenant Hugo Gutmann, a Jewish officer; it was "for personal bravery and general merit." The regiment commander at that time, who maintained the highest standards, recalled "that there was no circumstance that would have prevented him from volunteering for the most difficult, arduous and dangerous tasks." There are different versions about what earned him such a distinguished award. One is that the medal was promised to the runner who would carry a vital dispatch to the front through enemy drumfire at a critical stage in the offensive. German school books later asserted that Hitler had taken fifteen Frenchmen prisoner. Some historians claim that he never received the Iron Cross First Class. The consensus from his former officers and comrades was that Hitler was exceptionally brave and coolheaded in battle, though this testimony was largely collected after he had become a major figure in Germany.

There also have been questions about why Hitler did not become an officer. Famously, Captain Wiedemann testified at the Nuremberg trial that the officers thought he lacked leadership ability. Considering that Wiedemann served for several years as an adjutant to the Führer of the Third Reich there is more than a trace of irony in this claim. To attend officer candidate school Hitler would have had to leave the List Regiment. Some historians argue that his strong ties to the regiment stopped him from trying for a commission. It is more complicated than that. Max Amann testified at Nuremberg that Hitler turned down promotion to NCO in charge of the messengers, declining on the grounds that: "without braid he had more authority than he would with braid." Amann probed as best he might but could not get Hitler to tell his real reason. This pattern in Hitler's behaviour will be discussed in the final chapter.

There were too few replacements to meet the demand, so they merged with Infantry Regiment 6 and became part of the 10th Division. Defeatism was spreading and sometime that summer Hitler beat up a telephone operator who was advocating immediate peace. They were assigned to XVIII Army Corps in mid-August and taken by motor lorry to the Cambrai region. On the evening of 20 August, the "black day" in the history of the German Army, the British broke through the German defences near Amiens; their attack was a complete surprise. The British had moved up their best assault troops—Canadians and Anzacs—just the night before the attack. The Germans had shuffled their batteries about in the foggy days that preceded the assault but the British had located them by flash-spotting and sound-ranging, so they were struck by a torrent of well-directed fire. Tanks ripped great gaps through the German wire. The attackers penetrated 10 to 13 kilometres and in three days captured 21,000 Germans, while suffering only 20,000 casualties themselves. The Bavarians were alerted and on the next night were in the line once again. On 23 August they came under drumfire and half an hour later the British infantry attacked unsuccessfully. There was a second attempt later that day. The British were short of tanks because so many were put out of action by mechanical failures and by German machine gunners firing armour-piercing bullets. The Bavarians were pushed back into the shattered remains of a town where they stuffed their packs and bread bags with grenades and then formed a defensive line. Their new regimental commander, Major von Baligrand, impressed his men when he personally dressed the wound and put on a stretcher one of their Australian attackers.

In late August, Hitler was sent off for a week's course on telephones conducted in Nuremberg, and then was given an eighteen-day leave, which he spent in Berlin. It gave him the opportunity to criticize such examples of German domestic propaganda as a poster showing two children hand in hand gazing over a meadow and cows; the stirring caption was:

> Little ones, do without milk so we can keep our colonies.

He rejoined his regiment toward the end of September. While he was away they had lost 700 men, a battalion commander and three company commanders. They were briefly rested and then taken by train to Belgium where they received replacements from a recruit depot. They were still so short of men that four companies were dissolved. They took over a battalion from Infantry Regiment 17, which was dissolved. Many of the replacements were men called up from work in industry or boys who had no heart for a losing war; they were surly and disruptive—Hitler wanted them shot. The Allied propaganda was having effect, telling the Germans they were fighting an aggressive war on foreign soil—not defending their homes— and printing menus of the meals provided to POWs. Some days all they had for dinner was cucumber. Supreme Headquarters worried about the propaganda; they paid 30 *pfennigs* for each propaganda leaflet turned in. According to a comrade, Ignaz Westenkirchner:

> Toward the end of the war, when to the rest of us the game seemed to be up, he [Hitler] would go wild if anyone expressed doubts about victory. He would stick his hands in his pockets, pace up and down with huge strides, and rage against pessimism.

The regiment was now holding part of the line near Messines; old scenes from 1914 and 1917. They were attacked by thick rows of Tommies on 28 September. The attack was beaten back with heavy losses. Hitler was unshaken:

> For him the heavy attack in Flanders by the English … was a proof that our submarine campaign was succeeding.

In this spell at the front they lost another 200 men. After a brief rest they were back in the line in front of Comines, along the River Lys. On 12 October they sent a patrol over the river, a cadet officer, an NCO and three men. They came back with eighteen prisoners and suffered no losses. The next night the irritated British bombarded them with shells containing mustard gas, which they had just brought into use, long after the Germans introduced it. Hitler recalled:

> On a hill south of Werwick, in the evening of October 13th, we were subjected for several hours to a heavy bombardment with gas bombs, which continued throughout the night with more or less intensity. About midnight a number of us were put out of action, some forever.

Towards morning I also began to feel pain. It increased with every quarter of an hour; and about seven o'clock my eyes were scorching as I staggered back and delivered the last dispatch I was destined to carry in this war. A few hours later my eyes were like glowing coals, and all was darkness around me.

Mustard gas kills cells in the cornea of the eye, leaving an opaque scar. At the aid station they bathed his eyes, swabbed the traces of gas off of his skin, gave him opiates for the searing pain and disposed of his contaminated uniform. He was transferred to the hospital at Oudenaare for further assessment. From there he was brought to the Ghent railway station.

He spent the next five days on a hospital train, dressed in a patient's white uniform with blue stripes and sitting on a hard wooden seat for the entire trip. The trains were in miserable shape; because of the shortage of oils none had been repainted for four years. He was brought to the hospital at Pasewalk, 120 kilometres northwest of Berlin; it had once been a brick factory and then a combination restaurant and rifle range. He was unable to read the newspapers, but his mates read the reports of civil disturbances in Germany. He was recovering:

> The burning pain in the eye-sockets had become less severe. Gradually I was able to distinguish the general outlines of my immediate surroundings. And it was permissible to hope that at least I would recover my sight sufficiently to be able to take up some profession later on. That I would ever be able to draw or design once again was naturally out of the question.

In fact eyes injured by mustard gas usually recovered completely when the cornea regenerated. In hospital on 2 November he dictated a poem, *Quiet Heroism*.

One day in November:

> Sailors came in motor-lorries and called on us to rise in revolt. A few Jew-boys were the leaders in that combat for the 'Liberty, Beauty, and Dignity' of our National Being. My first thought was that this outbreak of high treason was only a local affair. And so I could not help believing that this was merely a revolt in the Navy and that it would be suppressed within the next few days. With the next few days came the most astounding information of my life. The rumours grew more and more persistent. I was told that what I had considered to be a local affair was in reality a general revolution. On November 10th the local pastor visited the hospital for the 'purpose of delivering a short address.' The reverend old gentleman seemed to be trembling when he informed us that the House of Hohenzollern should no longer wear the Imperial Crown, that the Fatherland had become a 'Republic,' that we should pray to the Almighty not to withhold His blessing from the new order of things and not to abandon our people in the days to come. It was impossible for me to stay and listen any longer. Darkness

surrounded me as I staggered and stumbled back to my ward and buried my aching head between the blankets and pillow. I had not cried since the day that I stood beside my mother's grave.

He was discharged from hospital on 19 November and two days later was back in Munich where the streets were patrolled by Red Guards. The King and Crown Prince had abdicated from the Bavarian throne, the new government was dominated by Bolsheviks and the barracks were ruled by a soldiers' council. The rest of the regiment and his surviving old comrades came in several weeks later. They marched from Belgium to Aachen, crossed the Rhine at Cologne and then on to Munich. The last regimental orders were issued on 12 December at Ebersberg—a village 30 kilometres west of Munich. During the war they had seventy-five officers killed, 112 wounded and eleven captured. 387 under-officers were killed, 1,006 wounded and eighty-two captured. Of the men, 3,289 were killed, 7,670 wounded and 678 captured. At peak numbers, the Regiment fielded about 4,000 men, so the total casualties were 3.3 times its normal complement.

Benito Mussolini
September through December 1918

Boroević must get his army out of Italy. In mid-October he exhorted his troops: "Our honour and the salvation of our fatherland demand that we preserve the foundations of an honourable peace." The Allies were nagging the Italians to attack, as support for the offensives that were pushing the collapsing Germans back in France. Diaz was cautious. By mid-October he had 51 Italian divisions, three British, two French and one Czechoslovakian and 7,700 guns with a reserve of 6 million shells. Bulgaria was out of the war and the Allied army based on Salonica was advancing through the Balkans toward Hungary. Finally Diaz set his attack for 24 October, the anniversary of Caporetto. Meanwhile his enemy was falling apart. On 16 October, Karl proclaimed the Empire to be a federation with self-government for each nationality—exactly what the murdered Franz Ferdinand had planned. Now it was too late; the Hungarians were breaking away. On 21 October, the independence of Czechoslovakia was proclaimed, followed shortly by the formation of a Yugoslav National Council; understandably, Czech, Slovene, Croat and Bosnian troops refused orders to return to the line in Italy. On the morning of 24 October, two Hungarian divisions simply left their trenches and started walking toward home.

As they walked away, the British bombarded their positions. When the British infantry advanced there was little effective opposition and they were soon across the river. A counter-attack was stopped by British machine guns, artillery fire, and aerial strafing.

The Italians attacking along the rest of the line made little progress; the offensive was renewed in late evening two days later. The Allied infantry pushed a gap through the defensive line, cleaving between two divisions. As the enemy retreated, the RAF machine-gunned the roads, so the men fanned out across the countryside to escape. The roads were clogged with abandoned transport, dead horses and guns, which slowed the pursuers. The headlines of *Il Popolo* were rapturous.

Boroević requested an immediate armistice on 28 October, but there was no response. The next day Hungary left the war. Two days later the Austro-Hungarian battle flag was lowered on the flagship of the Adriatic fleet and the new Yugoslav flag was raised in its place. The Italians permitted an Austrian delegation to cross the lines. On 2 November, the Austrians agreed to an immediate cessation of hostilities, promising promptly to evacuate Italian territory, which was defined as including the Tyrol and the province of Trieste, and guaranteeing the Allied armies right of passage across Austria so they could attack Bavaria. Nonetheless, the Italians continued to round up largely unresisting enemy formations as prisoners. Mussolini wrote: "… we must give them their own Caporetto." By 4 November, when the Italians stopped their advance, they had taken 360,000 prisoners (30,000 of these men died in captivity). Such was the great victory of Vittorio Veneto.

Boroević managed to withdraw part of his army to southern Austria; it was the only military formation remaining intact in the former Empire. His army dispersed and the men went home. None were welcomed by crowds, bands, flags, or cheers—they found fraying cities and towns and pallid, lethargic, starving people who feared the ragged, hungry wraiths that their warriors had become. Looking back over the three years that these soldiers had served on the Isonzo, one can only marvel at their willingness to stand. Now they returned to homes in Austria, Hungary, Czechoslovakia, Poland, Yugoslavia, Romania or even Italy. The victorious Italian army marched into Vienna. *Il Popolo* had another banner headline. The interventionist leader strutted, chest puffed out; he was soon attacking the socialists who were trying to help their starving brothers in Vienna.

Charles de Gaulle
July to December 1918

Even when the Germans seemed able to break through the Allied lines in France wherever they chose, de Gaulle remained serene; at least, so it seemed to his parents and his listeners in the fort. He argued that Ludendorff was destroying his army. When it became clear that he was not over-optimistic, he began to fret about his own future—he had sat out half of the war. His punishment for the last escape attempt was twenty-five days in a military prison. He was jailed with German enlisted men; after three days of vigorous protest, he was transferred to a prison that had a precinct for officers. When he was released on 10 October, he learned that the Germans had asked for an armistice six days previously.

During his years in prison, he spent hundreds of hours perusing the German newspapers. We know what he learned from them, because a few years later, after he had digested the German memoirs written for the post-war market, he published his ideas in *The Enemy's House Divided*. It is a vivid, interesting and largely forgotten book, especially fascinating from our vantage point, knowing what he would go on to do; the only one of the seven who left an explicit account of some of what the war had taught him.

The book starts on a military topic—the German doctrine that higher commanders should set goals and that their subordinates should use their initiative to achieve these goals. French officer training included courses on the philosophy of war, so it is not surprising that de Gaulle analyzed the doctrine from this standpoint, rather than as a pragmatic response to the limited information exchange possible on battlefields. He wrote that initiative was counterproductive because Nietzsche had taught the Germans that any man could be an *Übermensch*—a green light for subordinates to rate their own ideas too highly. He gives examples in which he thinks such actions served the Germans poorly in the Great War. I wonder whether in later life he ever read in Field Marshal von Manstein's memoirs about the qualities of the German army that defeated France in 1940:

> Individual leadership was fostered on a scale unrivalled in any other army, right down to the most junior N.C.O. or infantryman, and in this lay the secret of our success.

What de Gaulle might have criticized was the chain of command the Germans used to implement the Schlieffen plan. The seven armies involved reported to Imperial Headquarters, which had to be far behind the front because it also directed operations against the Russians. Wireless was the primary communications link. Messages were slowed by coding and decoding, and had to wait their turn on the single frequency available. The French used their transmitter on the Eifel Tower to jam transmission; many messages had to be re-sent. Later in the war, the Germans placed army group commands between the field armies and Imperial Headquarters, to coordinate operations locally and avoid the need for another Colonel Hentsch.

De Gaulle's second chapter is about the "direct cause of the German defeat," the declaration of unrestricted submarine warfare that brought the USA into the war. He traces in detail the political manoeuvrings and explains how "an exasperated America … [brought] to the Entente an endlessly expanding military assistance and, above all, a decisive moral reinforcement"—hard to argue against that point.

The third chapter is ironic in light of de Gaulle's own future career. It is about the prickly interactions between the Austro-Hungarian and German armies. Much of his evidence is true, but he ignores such successful joint attacks as Gorlice-Tarnow and the conquest of

Serbia. After Falkenhayn was replaced, the Austro-Hungarians, Bulgarians and Ottomans agreed that Hindenburg would establish "the conception and execution of a common programme of operations, to fix, in particular, the objectives, the importance of the forces to employ, to resolve questions of command. They then worked together to finish off the Romanians, the Russians and to smash through the Italian lines at Caporetto. The collaboration faltered when Emperor Karl tried to abandon the sinking ship. It was spring 1918 before Foch was appointed to coordinate the Allied and American armies. In addition, as a prickly personality, de Gaulle was heads above those he wrote about so scathingly.

His fourth chapter analyzes what he regarded as the last chance for the Germans to establish a government that could cope realistically with the world about them. Matthias Erzberger was a leader of the Catholic Centre Party in the Reichstag. When the war began, Bethmann-Hollweg made him responsible for propaganda abroad; he travelled to Rome, Constantinople, Bucharest, and Switzerland for quiet, fruitless discussions with Allied representatives. In the spring of 1917 he decided that the war must be ended. The Vatican believed that if Germany promised to free Belgium then peace would follow. In Stockholm Erzberger met representatives of the new Russian Provisional Government—they were ready for an armistice. Imperial Head Quarters (OHL—Oberste Heersleitung) was not interested and Bethmann-Hollweg refused to push them. Erzberger decided that he must become chancellor to mobilize political and public opinion for peace—he would need at least tacit support from OHL.

Out of the blue, on 10 June 1917 Colonel Max Bauer called on Erzberger. Bauer's job at OHL was to requisition arms and other materials required by the Army. Erzberger was astounded by Bauer's pessimism and erroneously concluded that OHL would support his push for a negotiated peace; therefore he left the government and joined the opposition. In fact, OHL wanted to oust Bethmann-Hollweg so they might wage total war. Three times a year the Reichstag was required to vote continuing credits for the war. The next vote was due in July; hitherto credits had been rubber-stamped. This time the Social Democrats proposed to vote against them; they held almost one-third of the seats. Bethmann-Hollweg was not too bothered—he thought it was simply a tactical political manoeuvre aimed at reforming the Prussian franchise, so the rich no longer had three votes to the common man's one.

Erzberger needed the centre parties to join the vote against further credits. The first step was to persuade a significant number of the legislators serving on the Principal Committee of the Reichstag, which framed the questions on which the entire chamber voted, to push for peace. Erzberger reminded them that from the beginning the Kaiser had "no desire for conquests" and hinted that that OHL no longer thought conquest feasible. For six months, there had been unlimited U-boat attacks. He compared the German Navy claims for vessels sunk with the substantially lower British figures—their own navy was lying to them.

Now do you want another year of war? Yes or No? If yes it will cost at least 50 billion in new expenses for Germany; and who can measure the extent of the irreparable losses in men?

They must have a parliamentary government. The war minister claimed that all was going well but Erzberger argued that only Hindenburg could give them a true picture— confident that the field marshal would echo Bauer's pessimism.

Hindenburg and Ludendorff came to Berlin to push the legislators back into line. The Kaiser did not tolerate this end run; he called them in to assure them that they had no business in Berlin, and must return to OHL, "where they would certainly be much better occupied." Erzberger and his allies wrote a resolution for peace "without annexations or indemnities." The legislators blamed the generals' retreat on Bethmann-Hollweg; he submitted his resignation, which the Kaiser refused to accept. So the generals played their next card—if the chancellor stayed, they would go. The chancellor went. Then the Kaiser selected the next imperial chancellor, Georg Michaelis—a civil servant with little political experience or talent. On 19 July, the Reichstag by a vote of 212 to 126 passed the peace resolution—but they also voted for the war credits. The new chancellor promised to support the resolution "as I understand it" and a few weeks later rejected Pope Benedict's offer of mediation. The Germans had lost their chance to negotiate peace while they were strong. What did de Gaulle learn from this? In his own political career, he sidestepped parliamentary political manoeuvring—he settled crucial questions by national referenda—and he fought to keep the French army out of politics.

De Gaulle's final chapter is about the German collapse in 1918. The year started well for them, with victorious peaces with Russia and Romania. The war credits were voted without discussion. Ludendorff said to the press, "I promise you, gentlemen, a rapid and complete victory." The Germans successfully attacked the British in the Somme and then in Flanders, then they broke through the French along the Chemin des Dames. In June, it all began to turn to dust. The next offensive to take Paris failed; the Austrian war budget was not passed and there were armed uprisings in Budapest. The German people had expected food from the Ukraine to end their starvation. A poor harvest, peasant opposition and transportation difficulties dashed their hopes; the bread ration dropped from 250 grams to 200 grams. On 18 July, Pétain launched a counter-offensive that caught the Germans completely by surprise. Toward the end of July Foreign Minister von Kühlmann told the Reichstag that it seemed improbable that a solution could be reached by arms; OHL forced him to resign. The Kaiser disappeared from public view. On 3 September, Ludendorff left OHL for psychiatric treatment; the Reichstag was silent. The right-wing press called for a German Clemenceau to take the country in hand. In Berlin marauders and the police exchanged gunfire nightly. The Spanish influenza was raging— 2,000 a week died in Berlin alone. At the end of August, in preparation for retreat, the German wounded were evacuated from occupied France and Belgium; hospital trains and ambulances flooded Germany. In the last days of September Bulgaria capitulated. Prince Max of Baden became chancellor; Erzberger and the socialist Scheidemann joined his government. On 30 September, Ludendorff demanded an immediate armistice. The Allies advanced relentlessly and the Kaiser remained silent. The rich rushed to spend their marks before they became worthless, there were large demonstrations in the cities, and the fleet mutinied. It was the end.

At the end of August, de Gaulle wrote home asking his mother to send him a horizon blue jacket with the ribbons for the Croix de Guerre with a palm and the *étoile d'argent*. We do know how he celebrated the armistice. On 2 December, he crossed into Switzerland, where a French officer loaned him the 1.90 Swiss Francs needed for a train ticket to France. Resting in the family house in the south of France he was photographed with his three brothers, all in their officers' uniforms. Within weeks he was attending a school to instruct officers who had been imprisoned about how the Army had changed—new weapons, new tactics and new organization.

Mustapha Kemal
September to December 1918

Three Ottoman armies held the line in northern Palestine; one had its right flank on the Mediterranean. Kemal's Seventh was next, with its left flank on the River Jordan and the third was responsible for the far side of the Jordan. By this time, Ottoman army was no longer an appropriate description. Jews and Christians had never served; they paid a special tax instead. The Arab and Kurdish regiments had faded away; Turks and a handful of German allies remained. From Kemal's viewpoint the only good news was that Falkenhayn was gone and Liman was back commanding the army group. The soldiers were emaciated from months of reduced rations and all replacements were sent to the Caucasus, where Enver proposed to exploit the disorder created by the Bolshevik revolution to pursue his dream of a new Turkish empire. In Palestine the British outnumbered the Ottomans by two to one and their superiority in artillery and in the air was even greater.

Allenby decided to end the contest by encircling the three Turkish armies. He would break through along the seacoast, where they would not expect the attack, and then send his cavalry and armoured cars sweeping inland to cut the Ottoman supply lines. First he would deceive the enemy into believing that Kemal's Seventh Army would take the brunt. A hotel in Jerusalem was requisitioned as a sham headquarters. New bridges were thrown across the Jordan and new tent camps were pitched in the river valley and stocked with 15,000 canvas horses. Mule-drawn sledges raised the dust clouds expected when horses were taken to drink. The real attackers hid in orange and olive groves along the seacoast. The deception was brilliant, but the day before the attack an Indian deserter revealed the precise time and direction; Kemal's men faced only a short bombardment and a brief skirmish. The British broke through easily along the coast and their cavalry flooded into the enemy rear across the plain of Megiddo. The RAF swept the Turks off the roads by bombing and machine gunning. Liman was almost captured in bed with his trousers off. Kemal's army lost the regiments on his right and he hastily pulled back the rest before the enemy cavalry cut them off. He was becoming an expert on retreat.

They withdrew through village streets lined with people dressed in their best clothes, gathering to welcome the British liberators. The Turks on the east bank of the Jordan were harassed by Colonel T.E. Lawrence, who struck with coordinated attacks by Arab cavalry—many mounted on camels—a handful of British machine gunners and mortar men, a few armoured cars and RAF planes machine gunning and bombing. After a desperate week the remains of Kemal's army forded the waist-high water of the Jordan. Liman ordered him to fall back to Damascus. In the city the flags of the Arab leader Feisal were hanging from the windows and gangs of armed Arabs patrolled the streets. Kemal was ordered to hand over command of the remnants of the Seventh Army; he was to proceed to Rayak, where he was to marshal the Turkish army units milling about in that area. He collected this ragtag and bobtail and, on his own responsibility, moved all of the Turkish troops in Damascus further north, to Aleppo—abandoning most of Syria. He now commanded the remnants of the three armies from Palestine.

His kidneys brought him into the Armenian hospital in Aleppo. Most of the British were far behind, but their armoured cars kept snapping on the Turk's heels. When they arrived at the outskirts of Aleppo the Arabs in the city rose up, seized the principal buildings and sniped at Turkish soldiers. Hearing shooting, Kemal went to the hospital balcony. He saw his men milling about while an Arab mob gathered at the end of the street. Kemal grabbed his riding crop, drove the Turkish sulkers out of the hospital lobby, set up a line of men to block the street and machine guns to meet a charge. He stood there slim, perfectly dressed, smoking a cigarette and calmly setting things right. Then he called for his car and drove about the city, issuing orders to suppress the uprising before evacuating the city that night and moving to a defensible ridge. The British had an unpleasant surprise when they ran into them two days later.

Enver, Djemal and Talât fled Constantinople. The Sultan appointed a new government, some of whom thought along Kemal's lines. Kemal hoped to be named minister of war, but was passed over. The new government began with a clever move. Sir Charles Townshend, a British general who had been captured in Mesopotamia, was in comfortable imprisonment on an island in the Sea of Marmora. They conceded to Townshend that the Turks had made a great mistake when they went to war against Great Britain; now they were ready to stop and make amends—confident in British respect for their military honour. Townshend and a Turkish delegation sailed on a tug to British headquarters. An armistice was signed on 30 October 1918. In the six weeks before the armistice, the British Army in

Palestine captured 75,000 prisoners and 360 guns while advancing 565 kilometres. Their 5th Cavalry Division had covered 885 kilometres. Total British casualties were 5,000.

The Turks gave up Mesopotamia. Kemal's forces were defending the hills north of Aleppo. He succeeded Liman as army group commander. When they met, Liman concluded a gracious speech:

From this moment on it is you who is the master: I am your guest.

They sat together silently and each smoked a cigarette. That night there was a party for the departing German officers. Kemal said:

The war may be over for our allies. But the war which concerns us, for our own independence, begins from this moment.

Kemal evacuated Syria and concentrated his command at defensive positions along the Turkish frontier, replaced unreliable officers and issued arms to reliable civilians who would fight for their country. They had been at war for four years; no one anticipated that it would require almost five more years to make peace. At the end of November, the Allied fleets, in a file 26 kilometres long, sailed through the Dardanelles to anchor off the Golden Horn. French troops made a triumphant entry into the city, led by a general riding his horse without reins, as the Ottoman conqueror had done almost five centuries before. The armistice specified that Turkey would not to be occupied as long as law and order were maintained, but the French settled in Stambul, the British in Petra—neighbourhoods in Constantinople—and the Italians further up the Bosporus. Unwilling to follow the Sultan's policies, the government resigned and parliament was dissolved.

Herbert Hoover
July through December 1918

As the elections of 1918 approached, Wilson appealed to the voters to elect a Democratic congress to support him, although many Republicans had strongly endorsed the war and his handling of it. Hoover wrote a letter to the newspapers urging voters to elect those who supported the President regardless of party. The Republicans won control of Congress and Hoover was in bad odour with the leaders of both parties.

After the Germans launched their 1918 offensives, the Allies needed every American soldier in France. Shipping was at a premium, and the transport of food to Belgium, Northern France and the neutrals was cut back. Hoover successfully fought to maintain part of his supply line and also managed to lease some Swedish vessels. The problems were then compounded when the Germans began to retreat and many civilians fled the new battle zones. Millions were close to starvation.

On 6 October, Wilson received a request from the new German Chancellor, Prince Max of Baden, for an armistice. The Central Powers accepted Wilson's fourteen points as the basis for a peace settlement. Hoover watched with admiration as, step by step, Wilson made it clear that his points included the principles he had enunciated in later speeches as well, raising the total to twenty-five, that they must have democratic governments, must agree to evacuate all occupied territories and that the Germans must remove the Kaiser. Simultaneously Wilson pressed the allied governments to endorse unambiguously the twenty-five points—their responses were grudging and incomplete. Wilson told the enemies about the British reservations about the freedom of the seas and other such information. The German revolution, the break-up of Austria-Hungary and the armistices were a great personal triumph for Wilson. Hoover arranged to get food into parts of the fragmented Austro-Hungarian Empire even before they signed their armistice. Shipments to the neutrals were also high priority—the hungry Netherlands, Denmark and Switzerland were on the brink of revolution.

Hoover and other close advisers urged Wilson to travel to Europe to establish his ideals clearly in the minds of the peoples, to meet the Allied leaders to evaluate how firmly they might resist a just peace and to access their weak points for the bargaining to come. Then he should return to Washington, above the fray, and leave an American delegation, including prominent Republicans, to negotiate the treaty. Flexing their economic power, the Americans should get most of what they wanted. The charter for a League of Nations should be kept separate from the peace treaty. Negotiations should be in a neutral city, to shelter the delegations from the passions of the public. Major sticking points would be referred back to Wilson; he could respond from on high after time for consultation and reflection. Wilson did not agree; he led the American delegation, refused to include Republicans, agreed to a conference in Paris and insisted that the League should be the cornerstone of the treaty.

On 17 November, Hoover and a small group of associates left for Europe to set up an organization for relief and reconstruction, to feed 400 million people in what soon would be twenty-eight nations. In the coming year, Europe would need 31 million tons of food—32 million tons would be available, 18 million from the US. In London he had a further education in "national intrigue, selfishness, nationalism, heartlessness, rivalry and suspicion, which seemed to ooze from every pore—but with polished politeness." The British, French and Italians were prepared for economic battles. Step one was to insure that food was controlled by a council with a member from each of these three plus the US, in which decisions must be unanimous. They wanted to keep blockading food shipments to the enemy, the neutrals and the liberated areas—for two reasons. First, to use food to bludgeon the enemy into accepting dictated peace terms. Second, to limit the demand for American food products and thereby drive prices below the levels Hoover had promised to the producers. They tussled with Hoover for days but he would not budge. Without any agreement, Hoover moved to Paris and began operations on his own authority, in a fifty-room building at 51 Avenue Montaigne. Most of his workers came from the CBR or the US Army; soon he had about 2,500.

By mid-December, more than 100 ships loaded with food were at sea. The US Navy took the stance that the Allied blockade of the liberated and neutral countries did not apply to ships flying the American Flag, and made it clear that they were willing to deal with any interference. For instance, they escorted to Finland shiploads of food Hoover borrowed from the Swedes and Danes, and then brought in US food to repay the loans. The Finns paid with credits from the US. They managed to get a small amount of food to Austria, the enemy country suffering the most. Vienna was starving and many survived thanks to a food train from the Swiss and another sent by the grateful parents of British soldiers who had been treated decently in Austro-Hungarian prison camps. Hoover sent envoys to evaluate need and set up operations in eighteen liberated and enemy countries and six neutrals. When their reports came in, Hoover learned that the children in Belgium and Northern France looked well—this was truly gratifying. The German children were in a dreadful state. The abominable conditions in Germany did prove that CRB food had not gone to the enemy. Hoover had never endorsed a food blockade; he did not think starving civilians was an effective way to shorten a war and knew it would cast a long shadow over the subsequent peace. He argued that if the Germans had been free to import food they would have used up their gold satisfying their civilian's hunger and would have gone broke.

Wilson arrived in Paris on 15 December. Hoover was named Director of Relief and Rehabilitation. He would have an advisory council and would report directly to the leaders. This advisory council soon proved useless, so the leaders agreed to replace it with a coordinating council made up of men of ministerial stature. This council's minutes fill volumes, but they were little help. Hoover also became one of the seven members of Wilson's Committee of Economic Advisers, who kept him close to the peace negotiations. His organization brought Europe 27 million tons of food and 420,000 tons of clothing and medical supplies. Operations were financed by loans from the US and by cash and goods from the countries served. Only the Finns repaid their loan, which surprised Hoover because he thought that none of them would settle their accounts. He insisted on loans rather than gifts because it moderated the demands of the governments. Four per cent of the goods came from the Allied countries, for which they were almost entirely repaid.

Gustav Mannerheim
May through December 1918

Mannerheim, true to his word, left Finland the day after his speech to the Senate. His possessions fitted into two suitcases; he was accompanied by a small entourage and his brother John, now a successful businessman in Sweden, organized the needed monies. He was welcomed in Stockholm as a hero. King Gustav presented him with the Grand Cross of the Order of the Sword, which delighted Mannerheim by the delicate blue of its sash. Nonetheless, he could not resist telling the King that he already wore the lowest grade of the Order, presented to him twenty years before when the Chevalier Guards entertained the King, then Swedish Crown Prince, at lunch in Petrograd.

Every door in Sweden was open to him; the ones that mattered were those of the British and French Embassies. The ambassadors were sympathetic, and consulted with their governments, but offered little encouragement. The Allied leaders were not interested in helping collaborators of the Germans. They were confident that the Whites would soon retake Russia and then Finland would revert to its former status. The ambassadors suggested that he go to London and Paris to convince them that a free Finland was to their advantage. His renown from the Finnish civil war would get him a hearing, and his facility with French and English would help. Mannerheim's cause suffered a body blow in October when—even as the German army in France was falling apart—the Finnish Senate voted to invite Prince Fredrick Charles of Hesse, Kaiser Wilhelm's brother-in-law, to become King of Finland. Mannerheim's only ray of hope was an authorization from Svinhufund to continue to talk with the Allies, so he travelled back to Finland for brief discussions with government leaders. The country was blockaded and close to starvation.

On his return journey to Stockholm, he travelled on the same ship as the Finnish delegation going to ask the German prince to accept the crown. He assured them that if they succeeded, the victorious Allies would punish Finland. He arrived in delirious London on 12 November. Three days later he had a long but discouraging talk with Lord Robert Cecil, the minister of blockade (and winner of the Nobel Peace Prize in 1937). Lord Robert did try to persuade the American member of the Blockade Commission to agree to lifting restrictions on supplying food to Finland, but warned that, "For the good of your country, you should not insist on the Prince." Mannerheim passed along Cecil's exact words to Svinhufund. He visited his elder daughter, now a nun in a Carmelite Convent in London; his younger daughter had returned to Finland. Article Twelve of the armistice obligated the Germans to keep troops in areas they now held that formerly had belonged to the Russians until the Allies instructed them to withdraw. It was a wise safeguard because on 13 November the Russian government announced that they were no longer bound by the Treaty of Brest-Litovsk. The Red Army would soon try to re-establish the former Russian frontiers, regardless of the wishes of the local residents.

On 14 November, Mannerheim received a telegram stating that the Bolsheviks were massing on the Finnish frontier and expressing the hope that if they invaded he would retake command of the Army. The staggering development came three days later as a cablegram, in which the Senate proposed to nominate him as the Regent of Finland—the German prince was out. He travelled to Paris a week later as prospective Regent, with his itinerary arranged by a suddenly accommodating British Government. The Finnish Diet voted for him unanimously. The final, popular election would take place within weeks. Ditching the German prince warmed French hearts. Now he must get his countrymen fed. Mannerheim had detailed, successful talks with Herbert Hoover—food would be sent. With the French on his side, he returned to London to educate the top men on the history of the Finnish Constitution to convince them that they had a competent, legal, operating government. He promised that the Finns would eject the Germans and request a French military mission to train the Finnish army. Mannerheim was officially designated Regent on 12 December. The Cabinet had six monarchists and six republicans—in time, the people would choose between a king and a president.

The Regent arrived in Finland on 22 December. The dock was jammed with honour guards and bands. At the fore was Senator Svinhufund, standing stiffly to attention in his uniform as a sergeant-major in the Army of Finland. He reported for duty. Mannerheim returned his salute and thanked him cordially—surely one of history's more gracious reconciliations. By happy coincidence, Hoover's first grain shipment arrived there on the same day.

IX

1919 and beyond

"War is a terrible teacher. Whether of good or ill we do not know yet."
Rudolph Binding, 1928

Herbert Hoover

Once in Paris, Hoover desperately needed a communications and intelligence network across Europe. Communications had broken down completely. The short-term solution was to station an American Navy vessel with a wireless in every major port. Then a telegraphic system was cobbled together with the pledge to host governments that all transmissions would be in the clear and would be available for inspection—hence much arcane American slang was transmitted on the telegraph wires. Only the French would not let their wires be used; they were bypassed by an American Army line running from France into Germany, from where the messages were rerouted onto the European net. In a few weeks Hoover was in telegraphic communication with his agents in every European country—most were American businessmen seconded from the Army. All governments except the British and French agreed to honour a passport signed by Hoover, which facilitated his agents' travel.

The problems of moving the supplies across the continent were complicated by the wear and tear of the war and by the establishment of new countries, each with new ministries and insisting on being addressed in their own language. Finally the Big Four—Wilson, Lloyd George, Clemenceau and Orlando—ordered each nation to turn over a specified consignment of railway rolling stock, barges and workers to Hoover's organization; he put them under the direction of experienced men from the American military. Soup kitchens for malnourished children were set up throughout Europe, staffed by local volunteers, supplied by Hoover's organization and paid for by the US taxpayers. They helped 14 to 16 million children and also fed un-repatriated war prisoners. A typhus epidemic started to spread westward across the continent. By early 1919 there were a million cases, and the death rate was about 25 per cent. Hoover set up a 'sanitary cordon' at the borders of the infected area. Only the deloused were permitted to cross the cordon, which was guarded by local police. The delousing supplies and equipment were gifts of the American, British and German Armies.

Hoover's thorniest problems were feeding the Bulgarians, the Turks, the Austrians and especially the Germans. The British representative at the signing of the armistice, Admiral Wemyss, had been taken aback by the Germans continually returning to the question of food; the British seemed quite unaware of the effectiveness of their blockade. The best the Germans could obtain was Article XXVI:

> The existing blockade conditions set up by the allied and associated powers are to remain unchanged, and all German merchant ships found at sea are to remain liable to capture. The Allies and United States contemplate the provisioning of Germany during the armistice as shall be found necessary.

After the Armistice was signed the British extended the blockade into the Baltic, and stopped German fishermen on all coasts from going to work, so the armistice made the food blockade more rigorous. When Hoover arrived in England in December 1918 he was cautioned not to inveigle against the food blockade "until the Germans learn a few things." When the Germans begged for permission to buy food the *Daily Mail* headline was: "Hun food snivel." The American press was also for further punishment. The French hated them most and naturally focused on the restoration of the devastated swath through their country, which they were determined the enemy should pay for. The Germans had $600 million in gold, now guarded by French soldiers. The French did not want to see any of this squandered on food. The Allies knew almost nothing about how things stood in Germany.

To get the facts, Hoover sent two of his collaborators in the CRB—Professors Alonzo Taylor (a nutritionist) and Vernon Kellogg (a biologist)—to Germany. Both had studied there and spoke the language. They reported that the 1918 grain and potato harvests were one-third that of 1914. One-third of the children were clinically malnourished and 800 people died every day in northern Germany from starvation and diseases caused by lack of nourishment. They met with the German physiologist Max Rubner, a great authority on human metabolism. He estimated that malnutrition had killed 750,000 Germans. With further data a few years later he dropped his estimate to 562,796. The new government could not stop the farmers from hoarding food and rationing was in tatters. The Bolsheviks used the continuing hunger to incite revolution. On 1 January 1919, Wilson endorsed a memo from Hoover calling for an end to the food blockade. Wilson's political muscle was already shrivelling—the blockade continued. Hoover went from one council to another and from one committee to the next—getting nowhere. He was accustomed to German foot-dragging and petty obstruction in Belgium; now he was banging against a stone wall on his own side.

Wilson forcefully presented the case against further starvation to the Big Four on 13 January, with Hoover sitting behind the President's chair. It was agreed that the Germans were to have food to be paid for with gold. Defying this instruction the Allied Blockade

Committee held firm; they refused to allow food in or gold out. On 1 February, the Big Four agreed to provide the Germans with 300,000 tons of grain and 70,000 tons of fat per month. Not an ounce entered Germany. Churchill, in the House of Commons, orated that letting them starve was "our means of coercion." The new German government was close to collapse. The peace conference officially opened on 18 January. The date was not chance—it was the forty-eighth anniversary of the formation of the Second Reich in the hall of mirrors in the palace at Versailles.

On 7 March, Hoover was requested to report immediately to Lloyd George's office. He found the prime minister with General Plumer, commander of the British occupation army in Germany. The general was in high dudgeon. His troops wanted to go home because they were anguished by watching "hordes of skinny and bloated children pawing over the offal from the British cantonments." Hoover added fuel by reminding them that Bolsheviks were now ruling Munich, Hamburg and Stettin. After Plumer left, Lloyd George wrathfully turned on Hoover—it was his job to provide food—why was there none there?—

> Thereupon, I turned on a torrent of expressions as to British and French officials that he ought to remember even in his grave.

When required, Hoover deployed an extensive vocabulary learned in mining camps. Hoover named the names of the "grasping and trickster … British minions." Lloyd George asked him if he would "deliver parts of that speech" to the Big Four. Hoover agreed and extracted the concession that Lord Robert Cecil, who had been Minister of Blockade and was now in the Foreign Office, would be empowered to represent Britain in all their economic interactions with the US. Cecil was humane, trustworthy and effective.

The crucial meeting was on 8 March. The Big Four sat on high-backed chairs on a podium, facing the national detachments of underlings. Wilson was away for the opening of the US Congress; Colonel House occupied his chair. Hoover introduced the topic and then Cecil read a detailed agreement that they had negotiated with the Germans. Marshal Foch urged them to keep the screws on the enemy. Lloyd George responded:

> The Allies were sowing hatred for the future; they were piling up agony, not for the Germans but for themselves.

French Finance Minister Klotz raised minor objections before coming to his bottom line. The French were willing to permit the Germans to be fed on a month-by-month basis, but only if someone would loan them the money. German gold was not to be touched. Lloyd George retorted that Klotz had made the same arguments a month before and been overruled. He appealed to Clemenceau to stop the obstruction, "otherwise Klotz would rank with Lenin and Trotsky among those who had spread Bolshevism in Europe." Some observers reported that he accompanied his words with gestures suggesting that Klotz was behaving like Shylock. Hoover found the prime minister's remarks dishonest, because his own compatriots obstructed as much as the French. But this did not mar the victory—the Big Four endorsed Hoover's proposal and ordered immediate action. Admiral Wemyss was appointed to lead a large delegation to formally present the terms to the Germans.

Wemyss's meeting was in Brussels. In the hotel lobby the old seadog said to Hoover:

Young man, I don't see why you want to feed these Germans.

Hoover records his reply as:

Old man, I don't understand why you British want to starve women and children when they are licked. We had no subsequent private conversations.

At the meeting, they came to terms with the Germans, who would surrender their entire merchant fleet and pay the remainder with gold. Wemyss permitted the Germans to fish in the Baltic, but would not let them into the North Sea. Hoover landed food in German ports before an ounce of gold had been transferred.

Naturally the German press published this news in large type, and it helped to prop up the struggling new government. A charity programme run by the Quakers promptly started to feed the children. Later in the month food was allowed into Turkey and Bulgaria. Hoover describes the continuation of the food blockade after the end of the fighting as "a crime in statesmanship against civilization as a whole." The Big Four had intelligence that the Bolsheviks would try to take over Vienna on May Day. Before the fateful day the walls of Vienna were plastered with proclamations, stating that any disorder would inevitably disrupt food supplies. It was signed Herbert Hoover. There was no uprising.

Russia was a continual problem for the peacemakers. In January Winston Churchill came to Paris to urge them to invade Russia immediately to rout the Reds. Hoover, who knew Russia firsthand, strongly opposed further military intervention—the French, British, Japanese and Americans already had troops there fruitlessly assisting the Whites. In this dispute Wilson still held the whip hand, because the US would have to pay for any escalation, and he held firm. Many Russians were starving. But Hoover knew that the Bolsheviks would never let his organization enter the country. He persuaded Fridtjof Nansen, a world-renowned Norwegian polar explorer, to head a new commission to sell food to Russia. The Big Four accepted the idea, with the proviso that all fighting within the country should be suspended while the food was brought in. Lenin welcomed the aid but could not stop the fighting single-handedly, so no food came. The Nansen organization was able to help many stateless persons in Eastern Europe (Nansen received the Nobel Peace Prize in 1922).

In late April, Hoover pressured Wilson to recognize independent Finland. The French were opposed, because they still hoped that the Bolshevik government in Russia would be overthrown. Wilson agreed that Hoover would present the case to the Big Four, but urged him to see Clemenceau first. He did so and Clemenceau endorsed immediate recognition but stipulated that no announcement would be made for a few days, when it would be formally announced as a joint decision. Both the British and French promptly passed the good news on to the Finns, each taking credit for the action.

The blockade on goods was still in force. Lord Cecil argued that trade would help the Germans to pay reparations. Neither the French nor the Big Four agreed. The goods blockade would be lifted only when a peace treaty was signed. On 7 May—the anniversary of the torpedoing of the *Lusitania*—the draft treaty was sent to the Germans for comment. Marshal Foch wanted to re-impose the food blockade until they signed. The Big Four knew Hoover would resign if they threatened to do so, so they decided that if pressure was required it would be by force of arms. Hoover was roused at 0400 on 7 May; a messenger had brought a document to be handed directly to him. It was the printed draft of the peace treaty. Hoover read the 75,000 words. Too agitated to go back to sleep, he went for a walk; within a few blocks he met General Smuts, the South African leader, and John Maynard Keynes, the British economist. There was no need to inquire why they were also out at dawn: they were deeply shaken. Each had seen parts of the treaty, but this was their first view of the entire misguided whole. Smuts had played a major role in Paris. He had written the outline for the Charter of the League of Nations, including League mandates for territories seized from the enemy, so that at least in theory there would be no new colonies.

Smut's presence in Paris was a tribute to the Treaty of Vereeniging, which ended the Boer War. Smuts had been a Boer general. He and his fellows negotiated face-to-face with the British; the settlement included a general amnesty, substantial British payments for reconstruction, a commitment to eventual self-government and agreement that the native population would not be permitted to enter the political process. Fourteen years after laying down arms General Smuts became the British Minister of Air. In contrast, although one of Wilson's points was "All parties in this war must join in the settlement of every issue anywhere involved in it," Germans were not allowed to meet with the peacemakers to discuss any issue; a few were permitted to respond to specific questions.

Smuts said they had hatched an "impossible peace." He was not sure that he could sign the treaty for South Africa. Keynes thought the treaty a recipe for economic catastrophe. Wilson's points lay in shatters. Hoover placed the blame on Wilson; he had not used his weapons skilfully:

> He could have stopped the huge American loans upon which many of the nations depended for their continued existence. He could even have cut off the daily bread which America could alone supply.

What Hoover did not appreciate was that Wilson was not negotiating a perfect peace; he was writing a peace palatable to the American voters.

The three men stood on the street corner, heads shaking, as they mourned for shattered ideals and contemplated a blueprint for another war. Their forebodings anticipated the 1930s, when Hitler rose to power excoriating the dictated peace of Versailles and British and French responses were muted by their leaders' guilty recognition that there was some truth in his position. Then they went into action. Hoover called in his principal associates for a breakfast meeting, planning how they might operate in political back rooms to change peacemakers' minds. Smuts brought over allies from London, who shifted Lloyd George on a few points. Keynes wrote memoranda about the economic consequences (and later wrote an influential book). Wilson was not interested in changes and objections irritated him. The Germans were given until 30 May to respond. If they did not agree to sign the armies would march into Germany on 19 June. Only minor alterations were made in response to written German objections. The treaty was signed in the Hall of Mirrors in the Palace of Versailles on 28 June, the anniversary of the murder of the Archduke. Marshal Foch refused to attend because he believed that the Germans had been let off far too lightly. Smuts signed for South Africa, and then held a press conference to state his reservations.

Many of Wilson's points had been ignored by the Allies. The treaty did establish the League of Nations, which his country rejected, and embodied his ideas regarding oppressed peoples—the Finns, Poles, Latvians, Estonians, Lithuanians, Czechs, Slovaks, Slovenes and Croats were liberated.

The cannon fire saluting the signing of the treaty with the Germans did not end the chaos or the problems facing the peacemakers still in Paris. For instance, in August the Hungarians had their fifth revolution in eight months. Power was now in the hands of a Habsburg, the Archduke Joseph, who had been installed by the machine guns of the occupying Romanian army. The Big Four telegraphed to the Archduke that his government would not be tolerated. It went via Hoover's lines and was delivered to the Archduke by the food representative there. He replied to Hoover:

Archie on the carpet at 7 p.m. Went through the hoop at 7:05 p.m.

Hoover showed this telegram to Clemenceau who, thanks to residing in the US for years, deciphered it effortlessly and retained the telegram for his book of memories. The Queen of Romania wrote Hoover a 1,200 word longhand letter, "the ink itself spluttered in her indignation." She let him know that he was a traitor to the Allied cause. Some writers state that Hoover was humourless. They should read his book and have a few chuckles.

It is diverting to see what the French and British leaders thought of Hoover. Clemenceau perceptively wrote:

And Mr Hoover, today President of the United States, who was conspicuous for the stiffness of the man whose nerves are at the end of their tether.

Lloyd George's evaluations:

> He had a surliness of mien and a peremptoriness of speech which evoked a negative answer to any request he made … Mr. Hoover has many great qualities, but tact is not one of them.

Hoover declined decorations and other honours, except for one order with only one holder: The Friend of Belgium and Honorary Citizen of Belgium. Funds remaining in the CRB treasury were donated to restore the Belgian Universities, including rebuilding the library in Louvain. He treasured the volumes sent to him with the signatures and drawings of millions of European children, thanking him for their meals. He returned to the US in September 1919. Lou and his oldest son shared his last few months in Paris.

The treaty was submitted to the US Senate in July. There were strong objections to parts of the covenant of the League, like Article X which authorized the council to "advise upon the means" by which an act of aggression would be met. This might challenge the constitutional responsibility of the Senate to declare war. Soon a list of reservations were prepared, with particular concern for the role of Congress in appointing representatives to the League and for Congress's right to withdraw from the League if they thought it necessary. The President suffered a stroke while on a trip west to sell the treaty to the voters. He was confined to bed and communications were through his wife, who maintained that he remained in complete control. Some of Wilson's advisers, including Hoover, wrote urging him to compromise with the senators, arguing that establishing the League was more important than fighting reservations. Hoover's letter was not acknowledged. Wilson, or whoever now spoke for him, would not budge. In November the treaty was seven votes short of the two thirds of the Senate needed for ratification. Manoeuvring continued for many months, but the treaty was dead.

Hoover ran unsuccessfully for election as senator from California in 1920. The following year he became secretary of commerce in the cabinet of President Harding. As Secretary, Hoover provided more than one million tons of food relief to Russians starving in the Volga basin and promoted public works, like the great dam that was later named for him, and the widening of the Saint Lawrence Seaway. He was thrust into the limelight again in 1927 when he successfully directed efforts to shelter the refugees from disastrous floods along the Mississippi River and to restore the levees, successes that added substantially to his political capital.

He was elected president in 1928. A year later the stock market crashed, heralding the great depression. Many blamed Hoover—his name again entered the language as shantytowns were called 'Hoovervilles.' In polls of historians rating the presidents he falls well down in the lower half. He was a wizard at directing great enterprises, using skills honed in the war, but inept as the leader of a democracy, because he was unable to rally a dispirited, fearful people. He lost in his bid for re-election in 1932. After World War II he led some of the American efforts to bring food to those starving in Europe. By the end of his long life—he died in 1964—his great humanitarian achievements had faded into the misty past. During the Great War he had been a beacon for decency, humanity and common sense.

Mustapha Kemal Atatürk

Everyone seemed to want a finger in the future of Turkey. Constantinople was under the guns of a British fleet and British control officers were stationed throughout Turkey to enforce the armistice terms. The Americans were considering accepting a mandate over Constantinople, the straits and parts of Anatolia. The Greeks wanted both the large concessions on the coast of Asia Minor they had been promised for entering the war and also a swath of territory on the southern coast of the Black Sea. Both regions had appreciable numbers of Greek inhabitants. Lloyd George saw the Greeks through the eyes of a classically trained schoolboy, and all of the Allied leaders were enchanted by Eleftherios Venizelos—the spirited, charming, and determined Greek premier. When peace negotiations began, it became obvious that the Italians and Greeks had been promised the same territory. The French were straining to take over Syria and Lebanon, so they were in no hurry for southern Turkey, but they did not want the Italians there and eventually helped Kemal with secret arms shipments.

The Sultan wanted above all to keep his throne and still hoped to preserve his Empire. Wilson's twelfth point was:

> The Turkish portion of the present Ottoman Empire should be assured a secure sovereignty, but the other nationalities which are now under Turkish rule should be assured an undoubted security of life and an absolutely unmolested opportunity of autonomous development, and the Dardanelles should be permanently opened as a free passage to the ships and commerce of all nations under international guarantees.

He envisioned a Kurdistan, an independent Armenia and perhaps Greek provinces in Thrace and Anatolia. Kemal and his associates—who are unfairly slighted in this brief account—wanted to create a westernized state in Thrace and Anatolia without separate enclaves for racial groups. To achieve anything like this would be an incredibly difficult and complicated political feat. What follows is a simplified summary of only the major events.

When the armistice was signed, the ruling triumvirate fled the country. Enver was killed in battle in 1922, fighting to establish Turkic rule in Central Asia. Talât and Djemal were both assassinated by 'Operation Nemesis'—Armenians taking revenge for the slaughter of their compatriots. Kemal was an unemployed general, whose rank had been reduced, living in a rented house in Constantinople, cheered only by a live-in lover, a divorced niece. He bought an interest in a newspaper and wrote anonymous articles promoting Turkish nationalism. The British instructed the Sultan to regain control of eastern Anatolia, which was prey to roving bands of brigands, by sending an energetic officer to restore order. His friends pushed Kemal for the post—arguing that he would create less political trouble from the hinterlands. His comrades on the General Staff drafted the appointment so that he would command all troops in the eastern part of the country and could issue orders to the provincial governors. Negligent civilian officials signed the appointment without scrutinizing the fine print. The Sultan's seal was applied on the last day of April 1919.

On 5 May, 20,000 Greek troops landed at Smyrna (now Izmir) on the Aegean Coast, with Lloyd George's permission. The Turkish garrison at Smyrna was ordered not to resist. Greek troops got out of hand and slaughtered several hundred Turks. The Italians landed troops in south Anatolia. On hearing the news 50,000 incensed citizens demonstrated in the square in front of the Sultan Ahmed mosque in Constantinople—the Sultan cried. Kemal and his staff sailed east twelve days later, with a few additional comrades as stowaways. When he landed on the south coast of the Black Sea he sent telegrams to the provincial governors requesting them to organize demonstrations to protest the seizure of Smyrna. He told his troops that their country's future was in their hands, encouraged the formation of local committees for the defence of rights, and reported to Constantinople every British violation of the armistice terms. When the people discovered that this slight, young, blue-eyed general was the legendary Kemal of Anafarta they cheered and waved as he drove by in his creaky open car. He soon moved inland to a thermal spring where his kidneys could be treated and there were no British control officers. His actions there illustrate his methods. He called together the local notables to tell them what was happening and then left them alone to debate what to do. Their response was a mass meeting at which all present swore to God to take arms to defend their country. Then they seized a shipment of 20,000 bolts from Turkish army rifles, which were on their way to the British to make the weapons unserviceable.

The Sultan's government wanted an American mandate, which many American politicians thought a fine idea—Hoover topped the list of possible proconsuls. Kemal wanted outside help, not outside rule. Kemal and three of his closest associates proclaimed that the people must save their country; their first step should be to form a National Congress. His advisers urged Kemal to resign from the army, so he could not be ordered back to Constantinople. He hesitated, but finally telegraphed his resignation. His telegram crossed with two from Constantinople: one dismissing him from his post and the second discharging him from the army. Suddenly he was powerless—an ordinary citizen; General Kiazim was appointed to replace him. The next morning Kiazim came to Kemal's head-quarters. He entered formally, came to attention and saluted. "I have brought your official carriage and cavalry escort. We are, all of us, at your orders, Pasha." Kemal kissed him on both cheeks. When the National Congress met two weeks later Kemal was elected president. He appeared in frock coat and fez. Orders to military officers were signed by Kiazim. In two weeks the Congress prepared a declaration based on Wilson's right of self-determination, claiming their entitlement to a Turkish state and specifying its boundaries.

At the peace conference in Paris, the grand vizier acknowledged Ottoman mistakes and crimes, but ludicrously demanded restoration of the pre-war Empire. The next National Congress meeting was held in September in central Turkey. Thirty-nine delegates met in a classroom where they sat at rough school desks; Kemal was in the chair. Many of the delegates favoured an American mandate; Kemal argued for assistance instead. They telegraphed the United States Senate, asking them to send a delegation to see the true state of the country and a British control officer arrived with a band of Kurds to arrest Kemal in the Sultan's name. They were shoved back to where they had come from. Turks were aghast to learn that their Sultan confederated with the British and Kurds to muzzle their war hero. Riding on a surge of popular support, the meeting wrote a prospectus for the country's future known as the National Pact.

With Pact in hand, Kemal telegraphed Constantinople, demanding that the interior minister come to the other end of the line. When he did so the Pact was telegraphed and Kemal demanded that it should be presented to the Sultan immediately. The minister refused. Telegrams flew back and forth; the minister and his colleagues thought they were dealing with Kemal personally, as if on a private line. Kemal knew that the telegraphers were nationalists; for weeks they had been secretly forwarding government messages to him. The telegraphers saw to it that the exchanges were distributed—almost in real time—throughout Turkey. Every major city in Anatolia listened in as the squabbling went on for days. The minister provided Kemal and his crew with a clear, if profane, picture of exactly how he regarded them. Kemal's stance was that the Sultan was above reproach but that behind his back the cabinet was giving away the country. The cabinet refused to forward the Pact to the Sultan, so the Congress demanded that the cabinet resign. The prime minister asked the British to help repress the Congress. The British, with a deft finger in the wind, declined, forbade any use of arms in the dispute and started to withdraw their control officers. The US Senate ruled out any mandates when they defeated the treaty establishing the League of Nations.

After long days in the telegraph office, calmly and with restraint dictating rejoinders to Constantinople along with a stream of moderate and precise messages to groups throughout Turkey, Kemal would go to his quarters, gather a group of his comrades, drink, bluster, bully and orate pompously until the early hours. They tolerated him because they knew the next day he would be as sage and prudent as ever. He issued draconian orders in the night and reversed them in the morning.

The Sultan felt the pressure, so he forced the prime minister to resign, appointed an interim cabinet of national conciliation and promised new elections. The new cabinet sent emissaries to talk with the nationalists. They agreed that only men trusted by both sides would be sent as delegates to the next peace conference with the Allies. In December Kemal moved to Angora (now Ankara), which he had selected, sight unseen, as the capital of the new Turkey. He drove to the city in his ancient Benz touring car, whose tyres he claimed were stuffed with old newspapers. At the city limits he was met by thousands of enthusiastic armed irregulars and the trade guilds. He led them in a tumultuous procession through the city. A majority of those elected to parliament were nationalists.

In June 1919, the Greeks expanded their bridgehead by seizing the sacred city of Bursa and also invaded Thrace. Kemal likened it to the invasion of Belgium. The Greeks advanced almost unopposed until the Italians and French persuaded the peace council to stop them in their tracks. The Turks and Russians signed a treaty in September, restoring their old 1914 borders.

Parliament met in January 1920 in Constantinople. Kemal ran for the presidency of the chamber. He lost, but the National Pact was adopted. The British landed more troops and their armoured cars patrolled the ancient city. Kemal had been warned by the French, so the top nationalists left before they could be captured. The British strictly censored the newspapers and arrested many deputies, some in the parliament chamber, before suspending parliament completely. Nationalists were outlawed—posters threatened death to those harbouring one. This heavy hand did not play well in world opinion. Kemal had the remaining British control officers in Anatolia arrested, declaring that the British had "destroyed the seven-centuries-old existence and sovereignty of the Ottoman Empire." He ordered the local authorities to protect Christian and other minorities—this was vital for the nationalist cause. The nationalists conducted an election in the countryside for a National Assembly to replace the defunct parliament.

To meet, the elected delegates had to sneak past Allied roadblocks and Greek irregulars armed by the British. The Sultan formed an Army of the Caliphate and issued a fetva ordering true Moslems to kill Kemal and other nationalists. A woman was one of those specifically condemned, the first to be so honoured in Ottoman history. Copies of the fetva were showered from British planes onto Turkish villages. The Assembly convened in April 1920. Kemal was elected as its president. The Sultan's army advanced into Anatolia to drive them from Angora. The nationalists were saved by Lloyd George and other Allied peacemakers. To break up the Empire they dictated the Treaty of Sèvres; all of the Arab lands were removed. The Greeks were to have the European part of the Empire in Thrace, the Turkish islands in the Aegean and Smyrna and its hinterlands. In the east there was to be an independent Armenia and a Kurdistan. The Italians would have the Dodecanese Islands, which they had been occupying since 1912, and the swath of Anatolia they had been promised. Another swath would go to the French. The straits would be internationalized; Turkey would be a small enclave in central Anatolia, policed by a Turkish gendarmerie officered by foreigners. The Ottomans were given a month to sign, the terms must be kept secret until then. The Greeks—who thought they were being short-changed—promptly published the proposed treaty. Now all Turks could see what was coming—it was just as Kemal had warned them. The people became overwhelmingly nationalist. The Army of the Caliphate stopped advancing toward Angora.

The next stroke of Turkish luck was delivered by a pet monkey. He bit his master, the young Greek King Alexander, who died within days. Venizelos, who had spent most of the past two years lobbying in the west, returned home and without testing the waters called a general election. The royalists campaigned to recall King Constantine, who had been exiled in 1917 for supporting the Germans. They won handsomely. Venizelos was out and the French and Italians stiffened their opposition to Greek ambitions in Turkey. The Allies proclaimed their neutrality in the Greek-Turkish conflict.

King Constantine was determined to have a good bite of Anatolia, so he personally led the next offensive, which pushed the nationalist army almost back to Angora. The terrified National Assembly made Kemal dictator for three months. He requisitioned animals, supplies, guns and ammunition. Each home was required to supply a pair of shoes, a bundle of clothing or a pair of socks. Women were mobilized to drive ox carts loaded with supplies across the mountain passes. For twenty-two days the Greeks thrust at the Turkish lines outside of Angora. Kemal directed the defence in a private's uniform—he did not hold military rank. The line bent but did not break. Finally the Greeks had to pull back because they could not supply their spearhead. The Assembly commissioned Kemal as a field marshal and commander-in-chief of the army and selected one of his old comrades as prime minister. Kemal slipped off secretly to the front. On 26 August he attacked the Greeks; they were completely surprised. The Greek lines were broken and they retreated to Smyrna. Ernest Hemingway vividly described these battles and the horrors of the retreat, which ended with the destruction of Smyrna, in *The Snows of Kilimanjaro*.

King Constantine was overthrown and exiled. The French agreed to what amounted to a separate peace, so only the British remained to be dealt with. Kemal moved part of the Turkish army north to face the major British position on the south shore of the straits, near ancient Troy. In a tense confrontation cool military heads on both sides kept the peace. They met in an oil-lamp lit room in a nearby hamlet and agreed that the Turks could reoccupy eastern Thrace, to the line drawn in the National Pact. In Britain, the outraged Conservatives withdrew from the coalition government and Lloyd George was out as prime minister. Kemal's most formidable enemy was gone.

The Allies were still in Constantinople; so was the Sultan. Step by step the nationalists took over the administration of the city. The British called yet another peace conference, this time at Lausanne. They invited both the Sultan and the nationalists to send delegates. The outraged Assembly voted unanimously to abolish the Sultanate. The British smuggled the former Sultan out of his palace in an ambulance and conveyed him into exile by battleship—but they would not fight the nationalists for him.

New elections were called. Kemal married a western-educated woman from a wealthy family of Smyrna. As he campaigned around the country she stood by his side, without a veil. The Treaty of Lausanne was signed on 24 July 1923, after weeks of negotiation and one bad-tempered gap. The Great War was finally over. All concessions were abolished and foreigners were subject to Turkish law. Ten weeks later the Allies withdrew from Constantinople. Kemal insisted that the capital remain in Angora, renaming it Ankara—Constantinople became Istanbul. He proclaimed a Turkish Republic and the new parliament elected him president. The president, in turn, selected the prime minister and the cabinet. Islam was no longer the state religion, religious schools became state schools and Islamic courts were abolished and replaced by a civil code based on the Swiss. In 1925 wearing the fez became a criminal offence. The resulting riots were harshly suppressed. Kemal promoted women's rights—but that did not stop him from divorcing his wife in the easy way provided by Islamic law shortly before the new legal code changed all of that.

The press was strictly censored. Kemal operated as a dictator within a façade of democratic institutions, believing it essential to retain the façade until the day when the new institutions were strong enough to work. No single act shows Kemal in clearer relief than his decision that the Turks should adopt a western-type alphabet. He set up a commission to devise it; they were given six weeks to do the job. Three months after the commission finished, the schools were required to use only the new alphabet and newspapers and publishers also had to conform. Somehow it all worked. In 1935, Turks were required to use the western calendar and to have a surname—parliament voted him the name Atatürk (father of the Turks). The next year he negotiated a revision of the treaty that allowed the Turks to remilitarize the straits. He fostered friendly relations with the British and the French, preparing Turkey for the neutrality that saw her safely through World War II. He died of cirrhosis of the liver in 1938—aware that his not having a son opened the way for Turkey to become a democracy. An opposition party won the elections in 1950.

Benito Mussolini

The Italians had paid an enormous price—689,000 dead; 1,000,000 seriously wounded; half of them permanently disabled. Crippled men were everywhere. The excess of civilian deaths produced by hunger and disease was about 600,000. They had spent 148 billion lire in three years—a meaningless number until you learn that it was twice the total of the Italian government's expenditures in all the years from unification until 1913. Most of the money was borrowed from abroad. The cost of everything soared and most people were impoverished. All they had were the promises that led them to go to war. Most of the promised cities on the Adriatic already flew the new Yugoslav flag. The only objective there that the Italians had in hand was Trieste, which had been one of the world's busiest seaports. They demanded the seaport of Fiume (now Rijeka, Croatia), because in Yugoslav hands it could be developed into a competitor to Trieste. The Italians owed so much money that they had no leverage at the peace conference. D'Annunzio and a small private army occupied Fiume, strongly supported by *Il Popolo*. Eventually they were forced out. For all they had sacrificed the Italians had little more than what the Austro-Hungarians would have ceded in 1915 in exchange for neutrality.

With victory Mussolini did not fade into the background; now he howled about inflation and the lack of jobs for demobilized soldiers. To his supporters he was an inspiring figure. Sarfatti described him:

> Mussolini, strong, robust, broad-shouldered, with the limbs of a fighter, his square Roman face and proud glance, the man of imperious strength and obstinate will.

Mussolini wrote: "they need a hero." *Il Popolo* changed its sub-banner from "The Socialist Daily" to the "Journal of the Fighters and Producers." He now defended capitalism:

> It is not simply and solely an accumulation of wealth, it is an elaboration, a selection, a coordination of values which is the work of centuries.

He denounced what he saw in Russia—the firing squads and the disdain for intellectuals and technicians; it was like watching savages ripping a fine watch to pieces. He fought the Italian Bolsheviks, many of whom were old socialist comrades. For relaxation he started to write a play and to learn how to fly. He began to use Nietzsche's motto as his own: "live dangerously."

With his sure political insight, on 23 March 1919 Mussolini spoke at the founding of the *Fasci di Combattimento*:

> We, we alone have the right to the succession, because we, we were the men who forced the country into the war, and into the victory.

The country should be governed by "the aristocracy of war." The *Fasci* ranks filled with unemployed *arditi*, still in their black shirts, fezzes and daggers. Better yet, veterans who had served in the line of supply could join and swagger about in *arditi*-like uniforms. They were organized into units, each with a name that honoured Italians at war, and each with a distinctive flag. They used the Roman salute, right arm extended. They were galvanized by the fiery oratory of their *Duce*, who with outthrust jaw and flashing eyes denounced the government, democracy, their Bolshevik opponents and the failure of the Italian leaders to obtain their due at the peace conferences. The *Fasci* did more than talk. They fought in the streets, pounding their opponents into submission and revelling in combat and comradeship. The fascist programme included the eight-hour day, a minimum wage, labour having a role in company management and lowering the retirement age to fifty-five. However, they did miserably in the elections. Mussolini received 4,637 votes; the socialists 160,000. Mussolini was not downcast, saying: "I prefer fifty thousand rifles to five million votes."

He was famous. When an Italian socialist delegation visited Moscow in 1920 Trotsky told them:

> You have lost your trump card; the only man who could carry through a revolution was Mussolini.

In 1921, he was elected to the Chamber of Deputies. The following year there was a general strike, which was broken by fascist violence. Next 20,000 fascists descended on the capital by train—the "March on Rome." Diaz and Badoglio notified the King that the military supported the Fascists; Mussolini became prime minister. In 1924 he made Diaz and Cadorna marshals of Italy. The black shirts became the Fascist Militia.—

> Obedience, in this Volunteer Militia, must be blind, absolute and full of respect towards ... the Supreme Chief.

Their strong-arm squads and the police ruthlessly dealt with political opposition; the remaining Bolsheviks were their special targets. They beat their enemies and dosed them with castor oil. In *Tender is the Night*, F. Scott Fitzgerald gives a graphic account of these thugs in action. Mussolini spoke grandly about the corporate state—which largely consisted of giving the industrialists free rein—and inaugurated massive public works. He was admired abroad for his constructions, for keeping the people quiet and for running trains on time. Churchill wrote:

> If I were Italian I would don the Fascist Black Shirt.

He made peace with the Pope by establishing the Papal State.

Then he set out to extend Italian rule—they invaded Ethiopia in 1935, with Badoglio in command. The League of Nations failed to restrain him. He was supported by his admirer Adolf Hitler—when they met they could converse in German and their bond was strengthened by recollections of the trenches. Both sent troops to help the Fascists overthrow the Spanish Republic, while the democracies stood on the sidelines. He arranged for Margherita Sarfatti to leave Italy when the anti-Jewish persecutions began. When Germany went to war in 1939, Italy prudently kept on the sidelines. Finally, when the Germans were overrunning France, the Italians invaded in the south, too late to gain much land or much credit from the Germans. They invaded Greece without telling the Germans, who eventually had to save them from defeat. After the Allies took Sicily and landed on the mainland, the Fascist Grand Council deposed and arrested Mussolini. Badoglio became prime minister and signed a separate peace. Hitler had his friend Mussolini rescued from a mountain hotel and made him ruler of northern Italy, which was occupied by the Germany army.

As the Allies drove north in 1945, Mussolini and his young mistress fled toward Switzerland. They were taken by partisans, executed, and their bodies hung upside-down at a filling station in Milan. He was ultimately buried in a tomb at his birthplace, which now has about 100,000 visitors every year.

Adolf Hitler

Hitler decided to remain in the army as long as they would have him. He was assigned to the 1st Reserve Battalion of the 2nd Infantry Regiment. He and his comrade Schmidt went to a POW camp at Traunstein in western Bavaria to guard Russian prisoners; later he claimed that they volunteered to distance themselves from the revolutionary furore in Munich. In February 1919, Hitler was back in the city, now in the 2nd Demobilization Company, waiting to be discharged, he was appointed as the *Vertrauensmann* (representative) of the company. On duty he was a guard at the principal railway station and he and Schmidt earned extra money testing old gas-masks. After the Communist Republic of Bavaria was proclaimed on 14 April Hitler was elected as the representative of his barracks. Munich was torn apart by armed struggle between the supporters of the Red government and the Bavarian *Freikorps*, who marched into Munich to put them down—the army ostensibly stood on the sidelines, while supplying the *Freikorps*. There was street fighting with armoured cars, artillery, flame-throwers and aeroplanes. Hitler claimed that he would have been arrested on 27 April had he not faced the three men who came for him with a rifle. The Whites prevailed by May 1919, with a final display of atrocities by both sides. Hitler was one of three men appointed to conduct an inquiry for the 2nd Infantry Division to determine whether any of its members had actively supported the Bolshevik government, which he describes as "my first incursion into the more or less political field." These duties allowed him to remain in the army.

Munich was now ruled by the military and was a haven for rightwing extremists from all of Germany. The army wanted to rid itself of Reds and to inculcate the troops with proper nationalist ideas. Hitler was recruited as an informant—a *V-Mann*—and was ordered to attend a course of army lectures at Munich University on "fundamental principals on which the soldier could base his political ideas." He was struck by a lecturer who explained that capital was the product both of labour and of speculation. Hitler concluded that by reining in stock-exchange capital, "it was possible to oppose the process of internationalization in German business." This was the basic idea of what he later called National Socialism. One day he joined in the discussion after the lecture, opposing a speaker who was defending the Jews, unleashing all of his vitriolic rhetorical fire. It must have made an impression because a few days later he was assigned to a regiment as what he terms "an instruction officer." In fact he was still a *V-Mann*, but lecturing was added to his duties. He was given a small private room in the barracks of Infantry Regiment 2. He spoke to large audiences, training his voice so that he could be understood in all parts of the hall. The men liked his fiery hyperbole: "He was a born popular speaker"—for Hitler it was "self discovery." His superiors were delighted at his success but ordered him to stop talking about hanging all of the Jews.

On 12 September, he was ordered to attend a meeting of the German Workers' Party at the Sternecker Brewery to report on its activities. Only a few dozen were there, mostly from the lower classes. As he listened to the lecture and gauged the audience he thought them just another ineffectual coterie. When the discussion began speakers rose to argue that Bavaria should leave Germany and form a union with the newly established German Austria. Hitler asked for the floor and proceeded to demolish their arguments. A week later he was surprised to receive a postcard announcing that he had been admitted to the Worker's Party and also had been appointed to their governing committee which would meet on the next Wednesday at the Alte Rosenbad tavern. He found the meeting "the worst kind of parish-pump clubbism." He had already decided to enter politics and thought of starting his own party—but how could he do this, unknown and with no educational qualifications? After days of what he described as internal debate he accepted membership in the Party and was issued—by his account—membership card number 7. In truth it was 555; he was number 7 on the committee. His commanding officer at the time testified later that he had ordered Hitler to join and supported his party work.

His entry into the Workers' Party epitomizes the behaviour pattern that caused him such difficulties in the past and that helped him so much in the future. He had been supremely confident that he would be admitted to the Art Academy and was crushed by rejection. Prompted to sidestep on the educational ladder to train as an architect, he would not even test the first rung, fearing that it too would splinter under his foot. Instead he waited at the bottom of society, secretly convinced that some day his artistic genius would be recognized and he would shoot to the top. In the army, he rejected opportunities to step onto the military ladder, as a higher NCO or as an officer candidate. When he decided to enter politics he did not join a major party to try to rise within it; instead he chose a tiny, obscure party, but he joined at the top and, as he anticipated, he was soon its leader. As he built up the party, he consistently refused to occupy any political office—where the rung might break—nothing would satisfy him except the leadership of the country. He succeeded—astonishingly, his first political office was as German chancellor.

As Hitler adapted to civilian life and prepared for a political career, his moustache continued its metamorphosis. When first in the army he sported an outspreading, western bad-man extravaganza, like the heroes of the novels of the American west that delighted his childhood. By 1918, it had become more restrained, perhaps trimmed back to fit under a gas mask. Now he progressed to the familiar toothbrush shape that we remember him by; someone had advised that the toothbrush disguised his broad nostrils. He built his party with gripping speeches—drawing on the resentments, fears and hates of his audience, his emotion and intensity building up step by step until it reached a frenzied, shrieking climax. He adjusted the pace and even the content of every speech by shrewdly evaluating his listeners' reactions; he was a master at reading a room. He was discharged from the army on 31 March 1920, but his feelings for it remained strong:

There is only one word to express what the German people owe to this army—everything!

He continued to receive financial help from the army, but increasingly depended on Munich businessmen to support his modest lifestyle and political activities. By September 1920 the Party had 2,000 members; Hitler's speeches pulled in the crowds. At a meeting on 1 August 1921 the members threw out the committee and elected Hitler as their leader with "dictatorial powers." They now had 3,300 members. The party soon became the National Socialist German Workers' Party—the Nazis—and he selected the swastika as its symbol. A cadre of uniformed members protected the meetings from disruption; they evolved into the SA (Storm Section). After Mussolini came to power in Italy, Hitler began to speak about a dictator for Germany.

On 1 September 1923, there was a huge rally in Nuremberg to commemorate the victory at Sedan in 1870. On the podium with such luminaries as General Ludendorff and Prince Ludwig Ferdinand of Bavaria, Hitler made the most effective speech of the day. He had plenty to talk about. The German currency was collapsing—a copy of the Nazi newspaper *Völkischer Beobachter* now cost 5,000 million marks. On 8 November 1923, Hitler and his henchmen began a putsch in Munich. At noon the next day 2,000 armed Nazis—Hitler and Ludendorff at their head—marched toward the *Odeonplatz* in the city centre. When they encountered a police cordon, firing broke out. Less than a minute later four policemen and fourteen Nazis were dead. Hitler went to jail and the party was banned.

Hitler was sentenced to five years imprisonment in Landsberg Prison, where he wrote *Mein Kampf*—a manipulated account of his life thus far and an exposition of his ideas. The basis of his political thought was the bad biology, obviously shared by many of his readers:

> At the beginning of the war, or even during the war, if twelve or fifteen thousand of these Jews
> who were corrupting the nation had been forced to submit to poison-gas, just as hundreds of
> thousands of our best German workers from every social stratum and from every trade and
> calling had to face it in the field, then the millions of sacrifices made at the front would not
> have been in vain.

In the drab uncertainty of post-war Germany, the Nazis provided simple ideas reiterated with certainty and using the rapidly-developing techniques of the advertising industry, including vivid colours and impressive spectacles. There were uniforms, armbands, songs, massed flags—the Nazi banner was designed personally by Hitler—parades, bands, mass rallies, torchlight processions, and the party salute and salutation. The uniforms revived the comradeship of the trenches. Hitler would not compromise; he struggled for power with fanatical determination. He lied whenever it suited and he became chancellor in 1933.

He began to rearm at once, with financing arranged by a talented banker. It primed the economy and lifted the country out of the great depression. When he took over, Germany had 6 million unemployed; two years later there were almost none. He guarded his political power from rivals by duplicating functions and institutions. In the party there was the SA and the SS; there was the Army and the Waffen SS; local government officials were paralleled by party members known as Gauleiters; the police worked side by side with the Gestapo. Political opponents were driven into exile, imprisoned or murdered.

He became the commander of all the armed forces and took a hand in the development of new weapons, personally insisting on tanks with longer, high-velocity guns. His first military adventure, the reoccupation of the Rhineland, was tolerated by the French and British. Then he took Austria and Czechoslovakia. His army conquered Poland and he began to think of himself as a military genius when he guided the campaign that snatched Norway from under the nose of the British Fleet. They invaded France with a thrust at the centre through the Ardennes, rather than the flanking envelopment favoured by most of his generals. France fell in weeks. He took a brief tour of his former battlefields in Northern France and Belgium, bringing along Max Amann, now director of publishing for the party, Ernst Schmidt and five other old comrades from the List. During World War II he never visited a military hospital and would have the shades on his private train lowered when it passed a hospital train.

Now supremely confident, he decided to take on the Russians; he would have the total victory that had eluded the Second Reich in the Great War. He compounded this error by declaring war on the United States after the Japanese attack on Pearl Harbour—the Japanese had declined to join in the attack on Russia. Step by step he led the Germans to total defeat, still guided by biological fantasies. His ideas were summed up by Albert Speer in a letter sent to Hitler on 29 March 1945, after a meeting in which Speer had requested instructions about making provisions for the civilians as the nation crumbled:

> In the evening you clearly and unambiguously explained to me, if I did not misunderstand you, that if the war is lost, then the people are also lost. This fate is inexorable. It is not necessary to consider fundamental things that a people needs to sustain its bare existence. On the contrary, it is better to destroy these things oneself. For the people would have proved itself to have been the weaker, and the future would belong exclusively to the stronger people of the East. Whoever survives the struggle would in any case be only the inferior, for the worthy would have fallen.

Hitler acted this claptrap out by having his beloved dog Blondi poisoned in the bunker in Berlin before his bride took her own dose and he shot himself.

Gustav Mannerheim

When the Finns voted in their plebiscite, they chose a republic, so the regency was abolished. Mannerheim travelled to Warsaw, where he found his furnishings safely in a warehouse. He moved his treasured settee to his house in Helsinki. In the 1920s he worked for the Finnish Red Cross, still directed by his sister Sophie, and for his own League for Child Welfare. He amused himself with travel and big game hunting. He was appointed head of the Defence Council in 1931 and two years later became field marshal. In late 1939, the Russians demanded Finnish land on the north side of the Gulf of Finland, so Russian coastal artillery could defend Leningrad (Petrograd at the time of the Great War) from sea attack. They offered to trade territory or to pay for it. The Finns refused and the USSR assaulted the Finnish fortifications, known as the Mannerheim line. The line held. Finnish ski troops cut the poorly led Russians to pieces in the snow and then disrupted Russian supply lines in what became known as the Winter War. With the spring thaw brute force prevailed, the Mannerheim line was breached and the Finns had to give up the land. When the Germans invaded Russia in 1941, the Finns joined in, fighting what they called the Continuation War. They recovered their lost territory and then held their frontiers. Hitler visited in 1942 to congratulate Mannerheim, who nonetheless managed to keep the Finns at arm's length from their German allies. They refused to join in the assault on Leningrad because they had promised the Russians in 1918 that they would never do so.

As the tide turned against the Germans, Mannerheim was appointed President of Finland. In 1944, he made a separate peace with the USSR and saw the German troops out of Finland. Finland was the only Axis country not occupied by the Allies at the end of World War II. He resigned as President because of failing health in 1946 and spent much of his remaining five years in Switzerland. He had played a major part in creating what has become one of the world's most successful nations.

Charles de Gaulle

After a few weeks leave, he was sent to a school that taught officers who had been imprisoned about how the army had changed—new weapons, new tactics and new organization. Meanwhile the Americans helped to build a Polish army in France. Poles from all over the world came to form six divisions, under command of Jósef Haller. Then the Haller army was transported to Poland, to defend the borders of the new state. De Gaulle applied to be seconded to the new Polish Army; he was eager for action and detested the Bolsheviks. He was assigned a Polish batman, who had served in the German Army opposite the 33rd Regiment in Champagne, perhaps shooting at his new master; they went to Warsaw, where de Gaulle instructed Polish officers. In his letters home he deprecated the Poles and the Jews, but by autumn he was writing that the work there had scraped away the crust of despair he had gathered in prison. He finally received his *Légion d'honneur*, was promoted to major and on closer acquaintance the Polish ladies proved to be quite charming. His students appreciated his lectures, which were laced with unanticipated flashes of wit.

In the spring of 1920, the Polish Army invaded the Ukraine and occupied Kiev. They were counter-attacked by a Soviet Army, in which Tukhachevsky—just as he had predicted—was a general and Stalin a political commissar. (Tukhachevsky became a Marshal of the Soviet Union. In the purge of the 1937, his signed confession was spotted with his blood; Stalin endorsed it so he was shot.) It was a mobile, horse army, which soon threatened Warsaw, and is portrayed vividly in Isaac Babel's *Red Cavalry*. The French instructors went to assist at the front; the Poles turned the Bolshevik left flank and put them to flight. De Gaulle left Poland at the end of the year, with highly favourable reports from his superiors.

Back in France, he married and became an instructor at Saint-Cyr. When his son was born the next year, Pétain, now a marshal, was godfather, but true to his convictions did not appear in the church. De Gaulle then attended the *École Supérieure de Guerre* for the two-year course. He graduated *Bien*, rather than *Tres bien*, dashing his ambition to become an instructor there. Pétain was unable to get his grade improved but assigned him to his personal staff. Then Pétain forced the École to invite de Gaulle to give three public lectures; Pétain personally took the chair, so all were obliged to attend. In 1927 de Gaulle became a battalion commander in the army occupying the Rhineland; two years later he was posted to the Middle East where he became a lieutenant colonel, once again doing staff work in Paris. By this time he was writing on the army of the future, advocating professionalism and mobility. His next post was commanding a tank regiment.

De Gaulle published *La France et son Armeé*, a philosophical work about the history of the army in 1938. The book started from an idea Pétain had in 1922; he set his staff officers to work on it, but before long, de Gaulle was doing most of the writing and Pétain was heavily editing the drafts. When de Gaulle moved on, he continued writing new chapters. In 1936 a publisher approached de Gaulle about a book. De Gaulle told him what he had in hand and then negotiated with Pétain. They agreed that de Gaulle's name would be on the cover, and that a dedication would state the marshal's contributions. De Gaulle wrote the dedication, and submitted it to Pétain, who revised it. The book appeared without his revision, and relations between the two were never the same thereafter. By May 1940 de Gaulle was a temporary brigadier commanding an armoured division. It was his highest military rank. Early in June, he became Under-Secretary of War.

The rest of his story is well known. When the Germans were overwhelming France, General Spears, the head of British liaison, brought de Gaulle to England—selected because he was the highest-ranking French official who would agree to come. De Gaulle declared himself the Leader of the French—an act of almost unparalleled presumption. He succeeded by force of personality and political skill—despite antagonizing almost every non-Frenchman he dealt with. After the war de Gaulle wrote his memoirs while criticising bitterly each successive government, especially voluble if he detected communist influences. In 1958, with the crisis in Algeria, he entered the government and soon was president, under a new constitution reflecting his political ideas. He put down an insurrection by elements of the army in Algiers and the French withdrew from North Africa. He changed the constitution by referendum, so that the president was elected by universal suffrage, and won a second term. In 1968, shaken by the student uprisings and the savage police response, he submitted a referendum to the people to reform local government. He was beginning to find his role trying:

How can you govern a country that has 246 varieties of cheese?

As usual, his position was that if the referendum failed he would resign. This time his political antennae were malfunctioning. It was rejected by a narrow margin—he resigned in 1969 and died a year later.

In French public opinion polls today, de Gaulle usually comes first in the list of greatest Frenchmen.

Harold Macmillan

When the war ended, the warriors were thunderstruck by how rapidly the civilians put it all behind them and returned to normal life. As Robert Graves put it:

> What life to lead and where to go
> After the War, after the War?

Macmillan was at ease with former soldiers but awkward with and suspicious of those who had sat on the sidelines. Now he had to decide what to do next; returning to Oxford was just too painful. Eight other young men had come up to Balliol in his year with scholarships—two were still alive. The cloisters were haunted by ghosts. He was not ready for a desk in the publishing house.

Early in 1919, he returned to limited duty with the Reserve Battalion at the Barracks. Discipline in the army was cracking due to a logical but fatally flawed demobilization plan, which permitted those with a job waiting to be released first, regardless of length of service. The government did not want a swarm of unemployed men who would be rife for Red propaganda. In February 1919, almost 3,000 soldiers were in Victoria Station to board leave trains to take them back to France or Germany. They were pushed about by the hated military police, things got out of hand and the men refused to board their trains; instead they marched down to the Horse Guards to demonstrate. The Household Cavalry was called out and was reinforced by companies of the Grenadier Guards. Macmillan's company was in reserve in Green Park. Happily the mutineers were dealt with sensibly. They were encircled without violence and shepherded to the Wellington Barracks, near to Buckingham Palace, where they were fed a good breakfast before marching to the station and the trains. When Churchill became Secretary of War he altered the demobilization scheme to take in account length of service and wounds sustained, and the problem faded away.

Macmillan was invited by the newly appointed Governor of Bombay, an acquaintance from Oxford, to become his aide-de-camp, but he did not pass the medical board for tropical service. Then he heard through his mother that the Duke of Devonshire, the Governor-General of Canada, was looking for staff officers to replace those who wanted to be demobilized. The Duke was a great grandee, reputed to be richer than the King. Happily, Nellie Macmillan knew the Duke's mother. Macmillan arrived in Ottawa at the end of March 1919; he was in Canada for ten months. He met many prominent Canadians when they visited Government House. The province was dry, but Government House was extraterritorially wet, so its entertainments were highly popular. He toured the country and studied Canadian politics. Handsome, wearing three wound strips, limping and with sad eyes, he was irresistible—he became engaged to the Duke's daughter Dorothy, who was nineteen.

Retrospectively Macmillan was sure that the army had been good for him. In his earlier life he had relished evading his mother's authority; in the Guards he found high standards of discipline and drill a pleasure. He had willed himself through fear and insecurity and had shown himself to be a man. His view of society had changed, learning that fellow officers without intellectual interests still had ideas and skills worth knowing and coming to know and to empathize with men from the poorer classes.

He returned to England in 1920, married Dorothy Cavendish and joined the family publishing business. In 1924 he was elected to Parliament as a Conservative. He remained an MP, except for a few short breaks when he lost an election, until 1963. But his recovery from the war went slowly; in 1931 he spent two months in a German clinic, suffering from his old wounds and "a form of neurasthenia." He studied and wrote about the deprivations and malnutrition in the working class. During the 1930s he was on the outside with his party's leadership because he opposed appeasement. He and a small group of MPs, which included General Spears, supported Churchill. In World War II he served in minor cabinet posts and as a minister in North Africa. When Churchill returned to power in 1951 he became minister of housing and in the next three years more public housing was built than in any other period in British history. He then served as minister of defence, foreign secretary and Chancellor of the Exchequer.

In 1957, Anthony Eden was forced to resign after the Suez invasion and Macmillan became prime minister. He gradually took on the public persona of a charming relic of an earlier age. He reunited his party and led them to an election victory in 1959. His foreign policy stressed the "special relationship" with the US, so he cultivated President Kennedy, and the need for peaceful coexistence with the USSR, so he also cultivated Nikita Khrushchev. He tried to bring Britain into the European Economic Community, but was blocked by de Gaulle. He speeded the withdrawal from what remained of the British Empire, which he regarded as a detrimental vestige of the past. He was elected Chancellor of Oxford University. By 1963 he was having difficulties with economic policies—the Conservatives were losing popularity with the voters and he was pilloried when his war secretary was revealed to be sexually intimate with a woman who also shared her favours with an official from the Russian Embassy. He resigned.

He then wrote four volumes of thoughtful and evocative memoirs. When Margaret Thatcher became Prime Minister she started by consulting him, but stopped when he criticized her handling of a miners' strike and for selling off state-owned industries. In 1984, he was made an Earl. To the end of his long life he spoke movingly in the House of Lords, attacking measures that he thought inimical to the common good. He died in 1986 and is remembered as one of the better prime ministers.

Acknowledgements

I am grateful to Judy Samarel, Teresa M. C. Van der Kloot and Peter A. Van der Kloot for help with the manuscript; and to Professor Bernard Semmel for thoughtful advice. I thank the staff of the London Library, the British Library, the Bodleian Library, the Imperial War Museum and the Melville Library of the State University of New York at Stony Book for expert help.

Selected Bibliography

Audoin-Rouzeau, Stéphane, and Jean-Jacques Becker, eds., *Encyclopédie de la Grande Guerre 1914–1918*. Paris: Bayard, 2004.

Barton, Peter, *The Battlefields of the First World War*. London: Constable, 2005.

Bean, C.E.W., *The Official History of Australia in the War of 1914–18*. Sydney: Angus and Robertson, 1921–1943.

Binding, Rudolf, *A Fatalist at War*. Translated by I. F. D. Morrow. Boston: Houghton Mifflin, 1929.

Cecil, Hugh, and Peter Liddle, eds., *Facing Armageddon. The First World War Experienced*. London: Leo Cooper, 1996.

Clark, Alan, *The Eastern Front*. Gloucestershire: Windrush Press, 1999.

Edmonds, Brigadier General J.E., *Official History: Military Operations, France and Belgium*. 14 vols. London: HMSO, 1926–1947.

Ferro, Marc, *The Great War 1914–1918*. Translated by N. Stone. London: Routledge & Kegan Paul, 1973.

Gilbert, Martin, *The First World War. A Complete History*. New York: Henry Holt, 1994.

Gray, Randal, and Christopher Argyle, *Chronicle of the First World War*. 2 vols. New York: Oxford, 1990–91.

Hardach, Gerd, *The First World War 1914–1918*. Translated by P. B. Ross. London: Allen Lane, 1977.

Hart, B.H. Liddell, *History of the First World War*. London: Book Club Associates, 1973.

Haythornthwaite, Philip J., *The World War One Source Book*. London: Arms and Armour Press, 1992.

Herwig, Holger L., *The First World War, Germany and Austria-Hungary 1914–1918*. London: Arnold, 1997.

Hindenburg, Marshal von, *Out of My Life*. Translated by F. A. Holt. 2 vols. New York: Harper and Brothers, 1921.

Ludendorff, Erich von, *Ludendorff's Own Story*. 2 vols. New York: Harper and Brothers, 1919.

Reichsarchiv, *Der Weltkrieg 1914 bis 1918*. 14 vols. Berlin, 1925–1956.

Simpkins, Peter, *Chronicles of the Great War. The Western Front 1914–1918*. Godalming: Bramley Books, 1998.

Strachan, Hew, ed., *World War I. A History*. Oxford: Oxford University Press, 1998.

Strachan, Hew, *The First World War. Volume I. To Arms*. Oxford: Oxford University Press, 2001.

Travers, Tim, *How the War was Won. Command and Technology in the British Army on the Western Front, 1917–1918*. London: Routledge, 1992.

Tucker, Spencer C., ed., *The European Powers in the First World War. An Encyclopedia.* London: Garland Publishing, 1996.

Woodward, Sir Llewellyn, *Great Britain and the War of 1914–1918.* London: Methuen, 1967.

De Gaulle

Ashcroft, Edward, *De Gaulle.* London: Oldhams Press, 1962.

Babel, Isaak, *Red Cavalry.* Translated by J. Harland. London: A.A. Knopf, 1929.

Bolton, G., *Pétain.* London: George Allen and Unwin, 1969.

Bouffe, René, *Tragèdie Bouffe. A Frenchman in the First World War.* Translated by J. B. Donne. London: Sidgwick & Jackson, 1966.

Cook, Don, *Charles de Gaulle.* London: Secker & Warburg, 1984.

Crawley, A, *De Gaulle.* London: Collins, 1969.

Crozier, Brian, *De Gaulle.* New York: Charles Scribner Sons, 1973.

Desagneaux, Henri, *A French Soldier's War Diary. 1914–1918.* Translated by G. J. Adams. Morley, Yorkshire: Elmfield Press, 1975.

Evans, A.J., *The Escaping Club.* Harmondsworth: Penguin, 1939.

Gaulle, Charles de, *Mémoires.* Paris: Gallimard, 2000.

Gaulle, Charles de, *The Enemy's House Divided.* Translated by R. Eden. Chapel Hill: University of North Carolina Press, 2002.

Lacouture, Jean. *De Gaulle. The Rebel 1890–1944.* Translated by P. O'Brian. New York: W.W. Norton, 1990.

Pétain, Henri Phillippe, *Verdun.* Translated by M. M. Veagh. New York: Dial Press, 1930.

Renoir, Jean, *Grand Illusion.* France, 1937.

Ryan, Stephen, *Pétain the Soldier.* New York: A.S. Barnes, 1969.

Schoenbrun, David, *The Three Lives of Charles de Gaulle.* New York: Atheneum, 1968.

Spears, Sir Edward, *Two Men who saved France. Pétain and de Gaulle,* 1966.

Spears., E.L., *Liaison, 1914.* Garden City, New York: Doubleday, Doran & Co., 1931.

Tournoux, Jean-Raymond, *Sons of France. Pétain and De Gaulle.* Translated by O. Coburn. New York: Viking Press, 1964.

Williams, Charles, *The Last Great Frenchman.* London: Little Brown, 1993.

Hitler

Barnett, Correlli, ed., *Hitler's Generals.* London: Weidenfeld and Nicolson, 1989.

Crown Prince William of Germany, *My War Experiences.* London: Hurst and Blackett, 1926.

Heiden, Konrad, *Hitler. A Biography.* London: Constable and Co., 1938.

Heinz, H.A., *Germany's Hitler*. London: Hurst and Blackett, 1934.

Hitler, Adolf, *Mein Kampf*. New York: Reynal & Hitchcock, 1939.

Jetzinger, Franz, *Hitler's Youth*. Translated by L. Wilson. London: Hutchinson, 1958.

Joachimsthaler, A., *Korrektur einer Biographie: Adolf Hitler 1908–1920*. München: Herbig, 1989.

Jünger, Ernst, *Storm of Steel*. Translated by M. Hoffmann. London: Allen Lane, 2003.

Kershaw, Ian, *Hitler. 1889–1936: Hubris*. London: W.W. Norton, 1998.

Koch-Hillebrecht, Manfred, *Hitler. Ein Sohn des Krieges. Fronterlebnis und Weltbild*. Munich: Herbig, 2003.

Maser, Werner, *Hitler's Letters and Notes*. Translated by A. Pomerans. London: Heinemann, 1973.

Meyer, Adolf, *Mit Adolf Hitler im Bayr. R.I.R. 16 List*. Neustat-Aisch: Georg Apperle, 1934.

Remarque, Erich Maria, *All Quiet on the Western Front*. Translated by A. W. Wheen. Boston: Little, Brown, 1996.

Schramm, Percy Ernst, *Hitler. The Man and the Military Leader*. Translated by D. S. Detweiler. London: Allen Lane , 1972.

Schreiner, George Abel, *The Iron Ration*. London: John Murray, 1918.

Solleder, Fridolin, *Vier Jahre Westfront. Geschichte des Regiments List R.J.R. 16*. Munich: Verlag Mar Schief, 1932.

Speer, Albert, *Inside the Third Reich*. Translated by R. & C. Winston. New York: Macmillan, 1970.

Toland, John, *Adolf Hitler*. New York: Anchor Books, 1992.

Witkop, Philipp, ed., *Kreigsbriefe gefallener Studenten*. Munich: A. Langer/G. Muller, 1928.

Hoover

Bodleian Library, *H.H. Asquith's letters to Venetia Stanley MSS. Eng. c. 7091–8*

Brock, Michael & Elenor, *H.H. Asquith. Letters to Venetia Stanley*. Oxford: Oxford University Press, 1982.

Clemenceau, Georges, *Grandeur and Misery of Victory*. London: George G. Harrap, 1930.

George, David Lloyd, *Memoirs of the Peace Conference*. New Haven: Yale University Press, 1939.

Hoover, Herbert, *Memoirs of Herbert Hoover 1874–1920*. London: Hollis and Carter, 1952.

Hoover, Herbert, *The Ordeal of Woodrow Wilson*. New York: McGraw-Hill, 1958.

Kellogg, Vernon, *Fighting Starvation in Belgium*. Garden City NY: Doubleday, Page & Company, 1918.

Knox, John, *The Great Mistake*. Washington DC: National Foundation Press, 1931.

Nash, George H., *The Life of Herbert Hoover. The Engineer 1874–1914. Vol. 1*. New York: W.W. Norton, 1983.

Kemal Atatürk

Aspinall-Oglander, C.F., *Military Operations Gallipoli*. London: William Heinemann. 2 vols, 1932.

Atatürk, K. *Memories of the Anafarta Battles* (ed. U. Igdemar). Imperial War Museum document collection.

Erickson, Edward J., *Ordered to Die: A History of the Ottoman Army in the First World War*. Westport, CT: Greenwood Press, 2001.

Hamilton, Ian, *Gallipoli Diary*. London: Edward Arnold, 1920.

Hemingway, Ernest, *The Snows of Kilimanjaro*. In *The First Forty-nine Stories*. London: Jonathan Cape, 1944.

Igdemir, Ulug, Enver Ziya Karal, Salih Omurtak, Enver Sökmen, Ihsan Sungu, Raik Resit Unat, and Hasan-Ali Yücel, *Atatürk*. Translated by A. J. Mungo. London: Ankara University Press, 1963.

James, Robert Rhodes, *Gallipoli*. London: Pan Books, 1974.

Kinross, Lord, *Ataturk*. New York: William Morrow, 1965.

Liman von Sanders, General, *Five Years in Turkey*. New York: Williams and Wilkins, 1928.

MacMunn, G.F., and C.B. Falls, *Military Operations, Egypt and Palestine*. London: HMSO, 1928–1930.

Mango, Andrew, *Atatürk*. London: John Murray, 1999.

Moorehead, Allan, *Gallipoli*. Ware: Wordsworth Editions, 1977.

Orga, Irfan, and Margarete Orga, *Atatürk*. London: Michael Joseph, 1962.

Volkan, Vamik D., and Norman Itzkowitx, *The Immortal Atatürk*. Chicago: The University of Chicago Press, 1984.

Wavell, General Sir Archibald, *Allenby. A Study in Greatness*. London: George G. Harrap & Co., 1941.

Weir, Peter, *Gallipoli*, 1981.

Weir, Peter, *The Lighthorsemen*, 1987.

Macmillan

Ball, Simon, *The Guardsmen*. London: Harper Perennial, 2005.

Brown, Malcolm, *The Imperial War Museum Book of the Somme*. London: Sidgwick & Jackson, 1996.

Fisher, Nigel, *Harold Macmillan, a biography*. London: Weidenfeld and Nicolson, 1982.

Gibbs, Phillip, *Realities of War*. London: William Heinemann, 1920.

George, David Lloyd, *War Memoirs: 2 vols. Vol. 1*. London: Oldmans Press, 1938.

Graves, Robert, *Goodbye to All That*. London: Doubleday Anchor, 1957.

Hart, B.H. Liddell, *The Tanks. Volume One 1914–1939*. New York: Frederick A. Praeger, 1959.

Horne, Alistair, *Macmillan: The Official Biography*. London: Macmillan, 1989.

Macmillan, Harold, *Winds of Change*. New York: Harper & Row, 1966.

Maze, Paul, *A Frenchman in Khaki*. London: William Heinemann, Ltd., 1934.

Ponsonby, Frederick, *The Grenadier Guards in the Great War of 1914–1918*. London: Macmillan, 1920.

Richards, Frank, *Old Soldiers Never Die*. London: Faber & Faber, 1933.

Sampson, Anthony, *Macmillan: a Study in Ambiguity*. London: Allan Lane, 1967.

Turner, John, *Macmillan*. London: Longman, 1994.

Mannerheim

Brussilov, A.A., *A Soldier's Note-book. 1914–1918*. London: Macmillan, 1930.

Cornish, Nik, *The Russian Army and the First World War*. Stroud: Spellmount, 2006.

Liddell, R. Scotland, *On the Russian Front*. London: Hamilton, Kent & Co, 1916.

Mannerheim, *The Memoirs of Marshal Mannerheim*. Translated by C. E. Lewenhaupt. New York: E.P Dutton, 1954.

Mannerheim, C.G., *Across Asia from West to East*. Translated by E. Birse. Helsinki: Soumalis-Ugrilainen Seura, 1940.

Rodzianko, Paul, *Mannerheim. An Intimate Portrait of a Great Soldier and Statesman*. London: Jarrolds, 1940.

Sandberg, Peter, ed., *C.G. Mannerheim's Fotografier Fraon Asienresan 1906–1908*. Helsingfors: Schilts, 1990.

Screen, J.E.O., *Mannerheim: The years of preparation*. London: C. Hurst & Co., 1970.

Sergeyev-Tsensky, S., *Brusilov's Break-through*. Translated by H. Altschuler. London: Hutchinson & Co., 1945.

Stone, Norman, *The Eastern Front 1914–1917*. London: Penguin, 1998.

Tillotson, H.M., *Finland at Peace and War 1918–1993*. London: Michael Russell, 1993.

Warner, Oliver, *Marshal Mannerheim and the Finns*. London: Weidenfield & Nicholson, 1967.

Mussolini

Bosworth, R.J.B., *Mussolini*. London: Arnold, 2000.

Cross, J.A., *Sir Samuel Hoare, a Political Biography*. London: Jonathan Cape, 1977.

Dalton, Hugh, *With the British Guns in Italy*. London: Methuen & Co., 1919.

Falls, Cyril, *Caporetto 1917*. London: Weidenfeld & Nicholson, 1966.

Fitzgerald, F. Scott, *Tender is the Night*. London: Grey Walls Press, 1948.

Mussolini, Benito, *My Autobiography*. Translated by R.W. Child. London: Hutchinson & Co.

Mussolini, Benito, *My Diary 1915–17*. Translated by R. Wellman. Boston: Small, Maynard and Company, 1925.

Mussolini, Rachele, and Michael Chinigo, *My Life with Mussolini*. London: Robert Hale Limited, 1959.

Sarfatti, Margherita G., *The Life of Benito Mussolini*. Translated by F. Whyte. London: Thornton Butterworth, 1925.

Schindler, John R., *Isonzo. The Forgotten Sacrifice of the Great War*. Westport, CT: Praeger, 2001.

Templewood, Viscount (Sir Samuel Hoare), *Nine Troubled Years*. London: Collins, 1954.

Index